MEASUREMENT AND MEANINGS

MEASUREMENT AND MEANINGS:
Techniques and Methods of Studying Occupational Cognition

Anthony P.M. Coxon
and
Charles L. Jones

ST.MARTIN'S PRESS NEW YORK

Library of Congress Cataloguing in Publication Data

Coxon, Anthony Peter Macmillan.
 Measurements and meanings, techniques and
methods of studying occupational cognition.

 Bibliography: p.
 1. Occupational prestige — Methodology. I. Jones,
Charles L., joint author. II. Title.
HT675.C69   301.44'4'018   78-26705
ISBN 0-312-52418-8

Contents

List of Figures

Preface

This book describes a number of methods for the collection and analysis of sociological data. We think that these methods are likely to be useful to research workers in sociology, psychology, marketing and government. The material is presented as a series of technical appendixes to the empirical chapters in two previous books: *The Images of Occupational Prestige* and *Class and Hierarchy* (both published by Macmillan). There may possibly be one or two readers who are sufficiently interested in methodology for its own sake that they will feel able to read this book by itself. However, most people will find it easier to read it in conjunction with the relevant chapters in the other two books.

The methods of data analysis that we discuss are mostly new to sociology. They include (*a*) multidimensional scaling in a number of forms; (*b*) statistical analysis of directional data; and (*c*) computer-aided content analysis. This book can be regarded as a 'How to do it' guide for these methods. Our data collection methods also have novel features. Perhaps our use of free and constrained sorting methods will be of most interest to sociologists.

ACKNOWLEDGEMENTS

The research reported in this volume was made possible by two grants from the (British) Social Science Research Council, over the period from May 1972 to December 1975 (HR/1883/1 and HR/1883/2). We gratefully acknowledge this support. We are also grateful to our various universities for providing computer time.

We again thank our research staff who bore the brunt of most of the exacting interviewing and of much of the data analysis work. A large number of people have had to cope with the often illegible and complicated written versions of this volume, and turn it into reasonable typescript. We are particularly grateful to May Fraser in Edinburgh, who stayed with us as secretary throughout the Project. Our thanks are also due to Vijaya Bharatha, Chris Downey, Shirley McGill and Jackie Tucker in Hamilton, and Jacquie Markie, Myrtle Robins and Margaret Simpson in Cardiff, for secretarial help.

Grateful acknowledgements are also due to Mike Anderson, Frank Bechhofer, Bob Blackburn, Scott Boorman, Tom Burns, Mike Burton, Lillian Brudner, Aaron Cicourel, Peter Davies, Tom Fararo, Moshe Hartman, Eddie Laumann, Ken Macdonald, Noel Parry, Peter Pineo, Ken Prandy,

Mike Prentice, Michael Stephens, Sandy Stewart, Phil Stone, Doug White, Harrison White, and (not least) John Winckler. Their critical comments have been appreciated, though not always heeded.

Throughout the Project, Doug Carroll of Bell Laboratories, Jim Lingoes of the University of Michigan and Eddie Roskam of the Catholic University of Nijmegen have given freely of their expertise in the scaling area; we owe them an especial debt of thanks.

Finally, our special thanks to Monnie Coxon who provided support, advice and sustenance throughout the project.

As in *The Images of Occupational Prestige* and *Class and Hierarchy*, the authorship of the book is truly joint; and, as always in our publications, we have adhered to the rule that 'Gentlemen publish in alphabetical order'. However, there has been some specialisation. Coxon was responsible for the appendixes concerned with the analysis of similarities data, the analysis of free grouping data, the analysis of hierarchies data, and content analysis with the General Inquirer. Jones was responsible for the appendixes concerned with the analysis of rankings and ratings data, and the analysis of sentence frames data. The descriptions of the fieldwork are based on technical reports produced by our research staff, and particularly by Mrs Francoise Rutherford.

Cardiff, Wales
and Hamilton, Ontario

A.P.M.C.
C.L.J.

1 Measurement, Meanings and Social Research Based on Interviews

We believe that empirical sociology can usefully be divided into three areas: — variable-centred, structure- or network-centred, and meaning-centred. Variable-centred research is the study of individuals and organisations, treating each one as an isolated unit, which has scores on a number of characteristics (variables). A powerful armoury of modern statistical techniques is available to aid the investigator, but the fiction that each unit of analysis is quite separate from any other unit is sometimes difficult to maintain belief in. Structure- or network-centred analysis is the study of systematic aspects of the relationships between individual persons, or between organisations. Thirdly, there is meaning-centred analysis, where interest is focused upon the varying interpretations people make of their social situations, and on how these interpretations relate to social action.

This book is about meaning-centred analysis, and in particular it is about the methods of studying social cognition and evaluation. As such, it addresses a central issue in contemporary sociology — the place of actors' meanings in the sociologist's accounts of their behaviour. At one extreme, there are some sociologists who would argue that the study of such meanings and interpretations is the essential nature of the discipline. At another extreme, it can be argued that they are merely epiphenomena, and unreliable ones at that.

The trends in social research over the years since about 1950 have been such as to facilitate a separation between the very easily quantifiable aspects of social reality and the less easily quantifiable ones. This has resulted in the development of sociological sub-specialities concerned entirely with the analysis of unstructured interview material (typically in the form of audio-tape recordings) by relatively informal techniques of a literary or a journalistic kind. When well done, this can be an effective research tool. What has been neglected however is any linkage between what each respondent says, and his (or her) scores on quantifiable attributes. A similar criticism could be made of other sociological sub-specialities, which have concentrated entirely upon data analysis using the techniques of conventional applied statistics, and which leave subjective meanings entirely out of account.

In adopting a structural and systematic approach to the study of individual

1

cognition and evaluation, we follow the work of Osgood and his colleagues (Osgood and Luria 1954), personal construct theorists (Bannister and Mair 1968; Slater 1976), and some modern anthropologists who consider themselves 'social ethnographers', (Berlin, Breedlove and Raven 1968). However, we differ and hopefully progress from the work of these authors in that our work is more firmly based in scaling and measurement theory (and particularly in the individual-differences scaling procedures devised by J.D. Carroll at Bell Laboratories). Our work also reports new techniques in data analysis and data collection, for example the use of free and constrained sorting tasks, the use of computer-aided content analysis, and the mapping out of logical implications implicit in belief systems.

This book contains the methodological details for two of our previous books: *The Images of Occupational Prestige* (hereafter referred to as *Images*) and *Class and Hierarchy*. Taken together, the three books are the results of a research project which continued over three-and-a-half years, from 1972 to 1975, at the University of Edinburgh. Our aim has been to make the first two books as readable as possible by segregating material which is of essentially technical interest into this third volume.

Throughout our work, but particularly in *Images*, we have used the metaphor of idiosyncratic cognitive or evaluative 'maps', as part of our attempt to capture the notion that individuals may have varying interpretations of the 'same' social situation. Our first task was to find a social situation that might be differentially interpreted by people with different experiences of the social structure. We chose the domain of occupational titles, for reasons that we discuss rather fully in the first two chapters of *Images*. Our second task was to select a sample of people to interview. A nationally representative sample would have been prohibitively expensive, and in any case our main research objective was to produce counter-examples to some rather general propositions made by such sociologists as Treiman (1977). We chose to study men from the Edinburgh area, and to arrange the sampling procedures in such a way as to maximise the range of variation on two dimensions: people-orientation, and educational qualifications. Our third task was to select a manageable number of occupational titles to be judged by our interviewees. Issues of proper sampling procedure arise here also, and we devote the second chapter in this book to a description of our methods of resolving them. Chapter 2 also describes our standard interviewing procedures, and the methods we used for collecting data on life-histories, pairwise and triadic judgements of overall similarity between occupations, rankings and ratings of occupations on five criteria of judgement, and unconstrained sortings of occupations on the basis of overall similarity. These comprise the methods used in *Images*. The somewhat different sampling procedures and the different techniques of interviewing which were used in *Class and Hierarchy* are described in Chapter 5, which contains parallel material to Chapter 2. A word of explanation may be due here. The sub-headings for the various technical appendixes which make up the nine chapters following this one are identified by numerical symbols, each preceded by the letter T or U; for example the section on 'Statistics for directional data' is section T.4.7, and the section on 'Tag specification for the Harvard IV-3 (Edinburgh) dictionary' (for Content Analysis) is U.4.3. The letters T or U serve to indicate which book the appendix refers to — T indicating *Images,* and U indicating *Class and Hierarchy,* as the case may be), and the next number (if any) serves to distinguish one appendix from another in the same chapter. The notation may be clumsy, but it should serve to point the reader backwards and forwards between the appendixes in this book, and the relevant chapters in *Images* or *Class and Hierarchy.*

Chapter 3 (T.3) is concerned with the technical aspects of detecting individual and group-level 'cognitive maps' from judgements of overall similarity. Both metric and non-metric methods of multidimensional scaling are used, and the chapter also contains a discussion of a hierarchical clustering method. We have made much use of J.D. Carroll's individual differences scaling procedure (INDSCAL), and a full description of the method is given here. The chapter also contains the first published description of a non-metric method for scaling similarities data derived from triadic judgements (M.J. Prentice's TRISOSCAL, which is a generalisation of E. Roskam's MINI-TRIEX). All multidimensional scaling procedures, both metric and non-metric, are subject to the possibility that there may exist a better solution than the one found in a particular analysis. A number of cross-method comparisons are made in Chapter 3, and we are confident that the group level 'cognitive map' derived from INDSCAL is indeed an accurate representation. We also include (as T.3.21) a small example of the intermeshing of quantitative analysis with the qualitative judgements made by individual respondents.

Chapter 4 (T.4) is to a large extent built upon conclusions established in the preceding chapter (T.3). In particular, we used the group level 'cognitive map' that was derived in Chapter 3 as an *a priori* structure into which we mapped data in the form of rankings and ratings. The seven appendixes in Chapter 4 explore the adequacy of this mapping procedure, and examine a number of alternative procedures. Since one of the virtues of the methods used in *Images* was that they made economical summary of a large amount of data, our exploration of alternatives inevitably generates a considerable proliferation of statistical tables. The first appendix in Chapter 4 shows a conventional analysis of ratings and rankings data, using means and standard deviations. The method used derives from Tukey's recent work in 'exploratory data analysis'. Chapter 4 goes on to examine the effects of analysing rankings and ratings of occupations by an 'internal' scaling analysis (where an evaluative map is generated from the rankings and ratings data themselves). In this appendix, we introduce the reader to a balanced sub-set of data from 48 respondents. This set of data is used in a number of expository scaling analyses.

Throughout this book, but particularly in Chapter 4, we have been very concerned about the degree of 'goodness of fit' between data and their summary-values. Sociological methodologists have written much about the importance of correct measurement. However, our study is the first that we know of (in sociology) where alternative measurement models are tested (for each respondent) before proceeding to the more conventional kinds of statistical analysis. This approach of considering the measurement model first, and the statistical analysis afterwards, led us to the view that rank orders and ratings of sets of occupational titles could best be represented as vectors (directions) over a cognitive or evaluative map, and this in turn led us to the use of specialist techniques for the analysis of directional data (see T.4.7).

In Chapter 5, we move to the set of appendixes for our second book, *Class and Hierarchy*. Chapter 5 itself (U.1) describes how we selected a number of different sets of occupational titles, and also a set of occupational descriptions. It also describes a type of 'combing procedure' that we used as a means to obtain a sampling frame from which to select potential interviewees. Finally, it contains detailed descriptions of the three tasks we used in interviews; free sorting, constrained sorting (the hierarchies task), and the sentence-frame substitution task. As with Chapter 2, this material is provided in order to document what we did, but we hope that it will serve to guide research workers in other areas.

One or two sociologists have begun to use free-sorting as a data-collection method (see Kraus, Schild and Hodge 1978). However, their methods of data analysis have been comparatively crude. Chapter 6 (U.2) shows that sortings data can be an invaluable tool for investigating differential cognition and evaluation. First, the method serves to stimulate commentary and discussion from the respondent. These verbalisations can be recorded for use in later analysis. Second, the data from several sortings can be put together in such a way as to generate an aggregated 'cognitive map' of the occupational stimuli that were being sorted. Thirdly, it is possible to measure how similar one person's sorting is to another person's sorting of the same set of stimuli, and therefore the data collection method makes it possible to proceed to variable-centred analysis, as a second stage. This last application is new to sociology, and promises to be of great usefulness in further studies of attitudes.

All the data collection methods that we used served to stimulate comments from our interviewees, though some were more effective at this than others. All the same, there was a tendency for many of these comments to be highly specific in nature, referring only to localised attributes of occupations. We were particularly surprised by the low frequency of mention for 'social class' terminology. It seemed that we were failing to detect any higher order generalising types of concept that might exist. Accordingly, we devised a type of constrained sorting task which we call 'hierarchies' (see U.1.4 for details). An important feature of this task is that the interviewee can be questioned about his thought-processes at all levels of generality in the judgemental process. Furthermore, a type of distance measure is defined between all pairs of stimuli, and is generated for each subject. Finally, it is again possible to measure how similar one person's sorting is to another person's, and so similar strategies of data analysis to those used with free sortings data can be followed. The hierarchies task yields such rich data of both quantitative and qualitative varieties that it merits serious consideration as a standard inter-viewing tool.

The large number of interviews that we carried out generated a considerable number of comments from respondents. We have used many of these in order to flesh out our discussions in this book and the two earlier ones. However, we also carried out more formal attempts at content analysis. These are discussed in Chapter 4 of *Class and Hierarchy,* and in the related appendixes (U.4 in Chapter 8), as well as in appendixes U.3.12 to U.3.15. Our use of computer-aided content analysis grows from the basic work done by P. J. Stone and his colleagues. While Stone's *General Inquirer* computer programme has been available (in several versions) for more than a decade, hardly any sociologists have taken it up. This can be ascribed firstly to technical difficulties with earlier (large and expensive) versions of the computer pro-gramme, and secondly to a paucity of examples of its use in sociologically interesting problems. The technical difficulties have now been overcome, and the detailed examples given in Chapter 8 of this book should provide guidance to other researchers. This chapter not only contains the Harvard IV-3 (Edinburgh) Dictionary specification, and an identification between Bernstein's grammatical elements and Inquirer tags. It also contains baseline material on the frequencies of tags in our occupational data, and in two other quite separate data sources.

The final set of appendixes describes our attempts to relate occupational titles and descriptive phrases involving occupations into belief systems based upon logical interrelationships. A comparatively simple 'sentence-frames' substitution task served to generate a variety of 'cognitive map' representa-tions, some in a continuous geometrical space and some not. As is indicated in Chapter 5 of *Class and Hierarchy,* the belief systems that have a non-spatial representation (i.e. those produced by the logical implications method) appear to be more useful for the purpose of understanding how people think about occupations than two- or three-dimensional configurations of occupa-tional titles, as produced by multidimensional scaling programs. This does not mean that the scaling enterprise is a blind alley; merely that it would be naive to suppose that thought-processes operate in a similar manner to (say) Carroll's INDSCAL model. While such scaling procedures may have features which suggest that one thought-process is more likely to be operating than another (see Arnold 1971), they are essentially data reduction devices. For this reason, we have felt safe in leaving out of this book any re-analyses of our data using the techniques recently developed by Carroll (1976) and by Ramsay (1977). The material in these three books should be a sufficient basis for approaches such as simulation modelling to be fruitful.

To summarise, this book describes the 'nuts and bolts' of applying sophisticated tools for data collection and analysis in the traditional sociological interview situation. This goes against the recent trends in 'sociological methodology', which have emphasised the adaptation of statistical techniques imported into sociology from econometrics and agricultural statistics. We hope that our concern with adequate measurement and the retention of meaning will be something of a corrective to these trends.

2 Design and Methods of Research in *The Images of Occupational Prestige*

INTRODUCTION

The methods we have used in the first stage of this research are based on the following five propositions which we have discussed in *Images*.

1. The information we seek of how people construct and construe the nature of their occupational world cannot be obtained directly; it must be inferred from their behaviour and speech.

2. Two main sorts of enquiry are often used in such circumstances — the naturalistic and the formal. We have deliberately chosen a mixture of these styles, using systematic methods of data collection (taking the form of cognitive puzzles or tasks) but paying especial attention to what subjects actually say whilst performing the task.

3. Occupational discourse is inherently indexical: it is therefore important to look at, rather than through, the taken-for-granted features of our subjects' verbalisations.

4. The often-invoked distinction between objective and subjective aspects of social position is neither very useful nor particularly apposite. In any event, we have no intention of claiming that our (or any other social scientists') version or account is generically distinct from that of the subject.

5. It is methodologically dubious, as well as sociologically ill-advised, to proceed directly to aggregating data before examining the extent of variation and the social bases of individual differences.

Such a set of assumptions puts strong limits on the type of investigation we make. Reduced to essentials, the fundamental research procedure we employ is that of occupational judgement:

We ask
(i)   a set of *subjects* (each having a particular occupation)
(ii)   to judge a particular set of *occupational titles*
(iii) in terms of a variety of *different methods* and/or criteria and
(iv)   to *report verbally* on their judgements.

7

In this chapter, we discuss each of these components in turn, and explain how we varied them in order to examine the general bases, rather than the particular features, of occupational judgement.

The methods we report have represented those chosen after a period of experimenting with various alternative approaches. Our earliest work began by using a number of procedures for eliciting glossaries or lists of occupational titles by a variety of ethnographic methods developed in cognitive anthropology (Black 1963, Sturtevant 1964) and by using a number of psychometric techniques for gaining information about the relational organisation of (occupational) concepts — in particular, free listing (Bousfield 1958) and Kiss' (1966, 1971) recursive concept analysis. These methods were abandoned at a fairly early stage for a variety of reasons, most important of which was the fact that they yielded data that were either too complex or unsuited to comparative study. Following this, a number of other strategies were used, including sampling occupational titles from the *Classification of Occupations 1970* (Office of Population, Censuses and Surveys) and from the *Dictionary of Occupational Titles* (Department of Employment).

Readers interested in a more detailed description of the development of the Project are referred to the Final Report (Coxon and Jones 1976). We proceed now to examine the reasoning underlying the choice of occupational titles, subjects and methods of data collection.

T.2.1 Selecting Occupational Titles

In contrast to the meticulous care which has been taken to select a sample of persons to judge the status of occupational titles, the sampling of the occupational titles themselves has usually been a rather ill-specified compromise between:

  (i)　　the desire to keep compatibility with titles used in census classifications and by previous sociologists; and

  (ii)　　the desire to limit the size of the list in some way.

In an earlier paper (Coxon and Jones 1974b) we have documented the way in which both the NORC tradition in the United States (stemming from Smith's classic 1943 paper) and the British tradition (originating with Hall and Jones' 1950 paper) have inherited and idiosyncratically modified a 'classic' list of occupations which were originally selected on no very explicit or rigorous grounds. On the other hand, the strategy adopted by the Chicago school of Hodge, Siegel and Rossi (1964) — and see Hodge and Siegel 1966, 1968, and Siegel 1971 — namely to sample directly from existing lists of census categories and occupational titles — has one critical assumption which for a study such as ours is crucial. It treats these census categories as having some form of real existence *independent* of and external to the ideas of social actors using them, whereas such categories are merely constructions made by civil servants.

By contrast, we begin with the notion of a population of occupational titles considered as cultural and cognitive objects. Unfortunately there are a number of reasons why such a population, if not infinite, is not denumerable. First, different cultures (and subcultures within a culture) recognise different titles and most individuals only recognise a restricted range of occupations. Secondly, the 'same' occupation is frequently referred to by titles which may have quite different connotations. For example 'parish priest' and 'minister' are both legitimate titles for an Anglican incumbent but they carry quite different meanings, and differ from the terms 'rector', 'parson' and 'clergy-man'. Thirdly, titles differ considerably in the extent to which they are qualified in terms of such things as skill, seniority and authority (consider the prefixes: foreman, superintendent, assistant, head, jobbing, principal, administrative, graduate, ganger). Yet just these qualifiers modify occupational titles in on-the-job situations, and are usually dropped in moving from one sociologist's list to his successor's (cf. Coxon and Jones 1974b, 373-4), and their absence produces the 'rag bag' or 'n.e.c.' (not elsewhere classified) census categories which vitiate the attempt to maintain comparability and equivalence of meaning. The problem of sampling from such a population of cognitive objects is not, of course, unique to occupational studies; it is common to a wide range of areas. Since there is no obvious solution to the problem, we have adopted a three-fold strategy:

(1)   to vary the set of 'objects' (occupations) to be judged, within the limits of comparability, operational feasibility and representative-ness (see Coxon and Jones 1974b);

(2)   to use a common set of titles for selecting both 'subjects' (respondents) and 'objects' (occupations) in order to test the hypothesis that those within a given occupation judge it differently from those outside it; and

(3)   to widen the notion of 'occupation' to refer not only occupational titles (names) but also to include descriptions of the kinds of people who typically exercise an occupation.

This last strategy is not used until the analyses reported in *Class and Hierarchy*.

We are primarily interested in investigating the extent to which differences exist in the perception of occupational structure. Because such differences are widely believed to stem from differences in social experience, it made sense to begin by considering three factors which are regularly cited in the literature:

(a)   socio-economic status (and/or the formal educational requirements of an occupation);

(b)   people-orientation;

(c)   stage in the life-cycle.

The first factor is too obvious to require much elaboration. Suffice it to say that even in studies where the highest degree of consensus in occupational judgements has been claimed, systematic differences are still discernible (see, for instance, Alexander 1972).

The second factor is concerned with the extent to which a job requires its incumbents to work *directly with people,* as opposed to being required to work with 'things' (data or machines). This factor is less salient in sociological thinking, but it forms one of the major distinguishing characteristics of job-families used in the US Department of Labor's definitive *Dictionary of Occupational Titles* (see also Fine and Heinz 1958). Furthermore the Michigan Survey Research Center workers, summarising the literature on occupational typologies and measurement, have concluded: 'We have found that one of the most fruitful of the frequently used distinctions in this volume is the distinction between working with data, with people and with things.' (Robinson 1969: 402.)

The third factor, contrasting the 'mature' and the 'novice' worker differentiates incumbents of the same job, and is therefore irrelevant in selecting occupational titles.

If the first two factors are dichotomised and combined, they yield the fourfold typology of occupations shown in Table T.2.1.1, which is used extensively in this research.

TABLE T.2.1.1   The fourfold typology of occupations

	FACTOR II	
	JOB REQUIREMENTS: Work predominantly with	
FACTOR I	*People*	*Data and machines*
EDUCATIONAL REQUIREMENTS	**QUADRANT A**	**QUADRANT B**
Relatively high	e.g. Clergyman School Teacher Social Worker Doctor	e.g. Qualified Actuary Chartered Accountant Civil Engineer Geologist
Relatively low	**QUADRANT C** e.g. Ambulance Driver Policeman Nurse Postman	**QUADRANT D** e.g. Building Site Labourer Machine Tool Operator Barman Garage Mechanic

Quadrant A: Occupations which require a high degree of formal education, and involve work directly with other people.

Quadrant B: Occupations which require a high degree of formal education, and involve work predominantly with data or machines.

Quadrant C: Occupations which require relatively little formal education and involve work directly with other people.

Quadrant D: Occupations which require relatively little formal education and involve work predominantly with data or machines.

(This typology is not meant to be interpreted as an experimental design in any strict statistical sense. We are not primarily concerned with classical experimental inference but rather with exploring models for representing sociological aspects of processes involved in making judgements about occupations.)

Lacking a systematic rationale for selection, we first listed a number of occupational titles as instances of each of these quadrants. From each list we then chose the two occupations which we thought would prove easiest to gain access to, or with whom we already had research contacts. These 'core occupations' then formed the basis for selecting both occupational titles and groups of subjects.

Quadrant A: Church of Scotland Minister
                 Comprehensive School Teacher
Quadrant B: Qualified Actuary
                 Chartered Accountant
Quadrant C: Male Psychiatric Nurse
                 Ambulance Driver
Quadrant D: Building Site Labourer
                 Machine Tool Operator

THE MAIN SETS OF OCCUPATIONAL TITLES

A. The Basic Set: Label Set 06

In order to attain a measure of comparability with other occupational studies, one-half of the occupational titles in the basic set were drawn from the set of 30 used by Hall and Jones (1950) in their classic British study. (At the time we were not aware of the curious history of inaccurate transcription to which these titles were subject, which came to light in our later investigations: see Coxon and Jones (1974b: 373-5).)

The maximum number of titles which are feasible using the pair-judgement task turned out to be 16, so a further eight titles were added (two from each quadrant). Since it is clearly relevant to examine the effects of differential familiarity upon their judgements about occupations, and since we wished to ensure that a range of occupations from each of the subject quadrants was represented among the stimuli, the occupations of the subjects we intended to investigate provided the basis for these additions. The full set of 16 titles came to be a standard set, common to several tasks used in the Project. This set is defined in Table T.2.1.2, together with the abbreviations for the titles which are adopted throughout this work.

TABLE T.2.1.2   The basic set of 16 occupational titles (Label set 06)

A:Project Self-referent set:	(Abbrevia- tions)	NORC* 1950	Hall- Jones 1950	Goldthorpe- Hope 1974
		Grading scores in other studies		
1. *Church of Scotland Minister*	(MIN)	52	6.3	62.33
2. *Comprehensive School Teacher*	(CST)	72	10.4	61.14
3. *Qualified Actuary*	(QA)	(78)	–	82.05
4. *Chartered Accountant*	(CA)	78	3.6	76.29
5. *Male Psychiatric Nurse*	(MPN)	46 or 22	–	61.14
6. *Ambulance Driver*	(AD)	24 or 26	–	28.35
7. Building Site Labourer	(BSL)	7	–	18.36
8. Machine Tool Operator	(MTO)	22 or 28	–	35.55
B: Hall-Jones markers:				
9. Country Solicitor	(SOL)	93	2.8	82.05
10. Civil Servant (Executive)	(CSE)	84	5.9	61.14
11. Commercial Traveller	(CT)	39 or 66	12.6	39.85
12. *Policeman*	(PM)	40	15.5	64.30
13. *Carpenter*	(C)	19	17.4	37.72
14. Lorry Driver†	(LD)	15	26.2	27.23
15. Rail Porter	(RP)	4 or 25	24.8	18.36
16. Barman	(BM)	19	26.2	22.95

*Reiss (1961, App B). It is not possible to match these titles exactly, and there is therefore some ambiguity in citing appropriate socio-economic index scores.
†Changed from archaic title 'Carter'.

Notes: 1. Occupations from which subjects are also drawn are italicised.
         2. Several of the Self-referent set also appear in similar form in the original Hall-Jones set, viz: Nonconformist Minister and Elementary School Teacher.

B. The Reduced Basic Set: Label Set 10
A smaller subset of 13 titles, which includes the entire Self-referent Set, was defined for efficient use in the method of triadic similarities. This task was only made feasible at all by the use of a balanced incomplete block design for selecting the triads of occupational titles to be presented (see T.3.1). In order to obtain information sufficient to map the data of single individuals, two replications of each pair of occupations are necessary, and with 16 occupational titles this would have necessitated the presentation of 80 triads, which was excessive. Thirteen titles involved the presentation of 52 triads, which turned out to be close to the limit of respondent tolerance.

TABLE T.2.1.3   The reduced set of 13 occupational titles (Label set 10)

	Abbreviation
1. *Church of Scotland Minister	MIN
2. *Comprehensive School Teacher	CST
3. *Qualified Actuary	QA
4. *Chartered Accountant	CA
5. *Male Psychiatric Nurse	MPN
6. *Ambulance Driver	AD
7. *Building Site Labourer	BSL
8. *Machine Tool Operator	MTO
9. Commercial Traveller	CT
10. Policeman	PM
11. Carpenter	C
12. Lorry Driver	LD
13. Barman	BM

*Self-referent Set

C. The Extended Set: Label Set 08

The set of 32 occupational titles used in the Free Sorting task (see Table T.2.1.4 below) has its origin in a meeting in June 1973 between the Edinburgh Project and members of a University of California at Irvine research group (Drs L. Brudner, M. Burton, and D. White) planning a cross-cultural comparative study of occupational cognition using the free-sorting method. The main purpose was to investigate contextual differences in sortings, and in particular the processes involved when sortings on the basis of 'local', known and experienced, occupational titles are augmented by widely-known cosmopolitan or symbolic ones. (Thus, a Mexican villager sees and knows referents of the title 'potter', 'teacher', 'bus driver' etc., but whilst he may have some idea of the meaning of such titles as 'airline pilot', 'scientist', he is unlikely to encounter them.)

The design for the study consisted of a type of 'cluster selection' round the four project occupational types:

1. *Quadrant A:* Social Worker, Minister of Religion, Primary School Teacher, Photographer, Actor, Sales Manager, Journalist.
2. *Quadrant B:* Statistician, Computer Programmer, Bank Clerk, Civil Engineer, Airline Pilot, Geologist, Eye Surgeon.
3. *Quadrant C:* Ambulance Driver, Male Psychiatric Nurse, Policeman, Restaurant Cook, Taxi Driver, Postman, Bus Conductor.
4. *Quadrant D:* Carpenter, Plumber, Unskilled Machine Operator in a factory assembly line, Building Site Labourer, Railway Engine Driver, Trawler Deckhand, Laboratory Technician.

TABLE T.2.1.4   The extended set of 32 occupational titles (Label set 08)

	Abbreviation
1. *Chartered Accountant	CA
2. *Secondary School Teacher	SST
3. *Garage Mechanic	GM
4. *Barman	BM
5. Statistician	ST
6. Social Worker	SW
7. Carpenter	C
8. Ambulance Driver	AD
9. Computer Programmer	CPR
10. Minister of Religion	MOR
11. Plumber	PL
12. Male Psychiatric Nurse	MPN
13. Bank Clerk	BCK
14. Primary School Teacher	PST
15. Unskilled Machine Operator in a factory assembly line	UMO
16. Policeman	PM
17. Civil Engineer	CE
18. Photographer	PHT
19. Building Site Labourer	BSL
20. Restaurant Cook	RCK
21. Airline Pilot	AP
22. Actor	A
23. Railway Engine Driver	RED
24. Postman	PO
25. Geologist	GEO
26. Sales Manager	SMG
27. Trawler Deckhand	TDH
28. Taxi Driver	TDR
29. Eye Surgeon	ESG
30. Journalist	JN
31. Laboratory Technician	LT
32. Bus Conductor	BCR

*Basic project markers

T.2.2 Selecting and Sampling Subjects

In the study of occupational cognition the names of occupations serve to denote both the subject and the object of occupational judgement.

As objects, these names serve as labels for the symbolic social entity denoted by the occupational title ('I admire *nurses*', '*Accountants* are obsessively precise'). Moreover, the fact that the speaker belongs to a particular occupation is often used intentionally to legitimate his judgements. (Consider sentences like those beginning 'One of my patients . . .', which often serve as a deliberate disclosure of occupational allegiance (Williams 1976: 38).)

Initially we were simply concerned to demonstrate the existence of the differential perception of the occupational structure, in the sense outlined above, and since we believed that differential perceptions arise out of different social experience, we attempted to 'cluster' our selection of respondents according to their occupational histories or their occupational intentions. In order to achieve this, and to incorporate the basic duality we have referred to, it was necessary to have at least some occupation names which served both as occupational titles for the judgemental tasks *and* as a source of subjects. The occupational typology provided the most obvious way of doing this — two 'core' occupations were chosen to represent each quadrant, and subjects were then obtained from these groups. Then the 'core occupations' were supplemented by other, similar occupations.

Since the study was an exploratory one, there was no point in sampling randomly from any nationally-based frame. Indeed, the very topic of this investigation was 'experimental' rather than 'descriptive'; the purpose of the design was rather to show what could be the case about occupational cognition under particular specified condition, not to estimate parameters in the sense that a census statistician might wish. In any event, financial constraints restricted our concern to the city of Edinburgh, and there is no doubt that this fact affects our results to some extent: the considerable respect traditionally accorded in the Scottish culture to the Minister and the 'Dominie' (schoolmaster), for example, is clearly reflected in our studies.

The logic of our approach dictated that we adopt a form of quota sampling. Having specified the core occupation to represent each of the quadrants, the intention was to sample a fixed number of subjects from each of the occupations, and then allocate them to tasks on a random basis.

Where, as in the case of publicly-accessible professional registers, it was possible to obtain a random sample, we did so. In other cases we had hoped to adopt a form of 'place of work sampling' — selecting work sites, and then sampling subjects randomly on the spot. In the event, there were considerable practical difficulties, but we came close to achieving our aim in the selection of policemen and ambulance crews (see below). The subjects from the 'supplementary occupations' consisted of people taking day-release and vocationally-specific courses in Edinburgh colleges, and in large part they served as subjects in the pilot stages of the project.

The occupational composition of the respondents' 'sample' is given in Table T.2.1 and details of subject group selection are given in Table T.2.2.2. Since the number of subjects differs according to the particular task done, this information is presented in the relevant chapter. (In the second part of the Project, quite different sampling procedures were used, and these are described in full in Chapter 2 of *Class and Hierarchy*.)

TABLE T.2.2.1   The occupational composition of the respondent sample

FACTOR II

JOB REQUIREMENTS: Work Predominantly with

FACTOR I

EDUCATIONAL
REQUIREMENTS:

	People	Data and machines
Relatively high	**QUADRANT A** *Core:* Clergymen Teachers *Supplementary:* Education students Theological students Journalists	**QUADRANT B** *Core:* Qualified actuaries Chartered accountants *Supplementary:* Chemical engineering students, Electrical engineering students
Relatively low	**QUADRANT C** *Core:* Ambulance drivers Policemen *Supplementary:* Nurses	**QUADRANT D** *Core:* Engineers Joiners-Fitters *Supplementary:* Builders and related trades, Printers

Core and Supplementary subjects   (264)
Additional Supplementary groups: Law students
        Business Administration students   23

$N = 287$

Notes: 1. 'Clergymen' covers Church of Scotland ministers and Scottish
            Episcopalian priests.
         2. All the subjects in Quadrant D, with the exception of printers,
            are day-release apprentices.

TABLE T.2.2.2   Selection of subject groups

QUADRANT A SUBJECTS

CORE OCCUPATIONS

Clergymen were drawn from two denominations — the (established) Church of Scotland (Presbyterian) and the Episcopal Church in Scotland (Anglican). In each case the sample was restricted to practising parochial clergy, and to the Edinburgh addresses in the Presbytery or Diocesan list. The sampling frame was provided by *The Church of Scotland Yearbook 1972*, and by *The Scottish Episcopal Church Yearbook, 1972*.

Teachers: It was not possible to obtain access to a professional list. The subjects consisted of practising teachers studying on a part-time basis for the M.Ed. degree of the University of Edinburgh.

SUPPLEMENTARY GROUPS

Education students: final year students attending the Primary teaching qualification course at Moray House College of Education.

Theological students: third year students reading the B.D. course at New College, University of Edinburgh (they included, but did not consist only of, ordinands).

QUADRANT B SUBJECTS

CORE OCCUPATIONS

Qualified actuaries: The sampling frame was *The Faculty of Actuaries Yearbook, 1971*, restricted to Edinburgh addresses, and consists in large part of Fellows of the Faculty.

Chartered accountants sampled from *List of Scottish Chartered Accountants 1971*, and restricted to Edinburgh addresses.

SUPPLEMENTARY GROUPS

Chemical engineering students: Final year and postgraduate students of the department of Chemical Engineering, Heriot-Watt University, Edinburgh.

Electrical engineering students: Final year students of the department of Electrical Engineering, University of Edinburgh.

QUADRANT C SUBJECTS

CORE OCCUPATIONS

Ambulance drivers: Consisted of operational crews (ambulance driver and attendant) on duty at the St. Andrew's Scottish Ambulance Service Depot at the City Hospital, Edinburgh. Crews were made available for interview by the operational controller.

Police: A group consisting of officers, sergeants, experienced constables and recruits of the Peebles and Lothian Police, made available by the Chief Constable.

SUPPLEMENTARY SUBJECTS

Nurses: Trained nurses attending the full-time Tutor (Nursing Education) Certificate Course in the Department of Nursing Studies, University of Edinburgh.

QUADRANT D SUBJECTS

The core occupational groups consisted of Engineers and Joiner-Fitter apprentices attending day release courses at Telford and Esk Valley Colleges of Further Education. The supplementary subjects consisted of pre-apprentice students attending courses in the Department of Building, Esk Valley College, and a number of printers.

Other unallocated groups: Third year Law Students studying for the LL.B. and postgraduate students taking the Diploma in Business Studies at the University of Edinburgh.

T.2.3 Interviewing and the Interview

The demands on interviewers in all tasks used in the Project were very heavy, which meant that they needed to be thoroughly trained. Interviews were first conducted by us and later by research assistants. Since most interviews were tape-recorded, it was possible to check that no distortions were introduced by interviewers during the administration of the tasks.

Before an interview, subjects were usually in possession of one or two short texts, one describing the purpose of the project, the other a brief description of what being interviewed would entail.

The interviewing techniques were unusual in that they combined the administration of complex structured tasks with instructions to encourage verbalisation at all stages. A summary of the instructions received by interviewers included the following points:

(i) *Introduction*
'After introducing himself or herself as a project worker, the interviewer should check whether the subject has received and read the publicity documents. More copies can be given at that point and a brief résumé of the project's purpose and sponsorship can be given to revive the subject's motivation to be interviewed. It is important to pitch the description at a

level of complexity which is comprehensible but justifies relatively lengthy questioning and this varies with each interview. Specific questions from the subject regarding respondent selection, possible usefulness of the research findings etc. should be answered honestly and briefly taking care not to bias the following interview by mentioning such catch words as status, mobility, skill, etc. Some less confident subjects need to be assured that their own views are exactly what we are interested in, that their knowledge of some and guesses about other occupations are all of interest. Before starting to administer a task, the subject must also be asked if he objects to the interview being tape-recorded, explaining that this is most useful to you when reporting on the interview, to be able to use the exact same words that he has used. The tapes are not to be used for any other purpose and will be destroyed after the end of the project. The tape-recorder should be placed in a position as little conspicuous as possible. At that time record the tape position on the tape counter and the time.'

(ii) *Administering structured tasks*

'As many of the tasks are relatively complex, it is very important to read out the instructions as worded and check that the subject has understood them. This may mean repeating some important criterion included in the instructions. It is particularly important to establish an 'equivalence of meaning' with the interviewee and written comments should be provided if there is any indication that this was not achieved. Interviewers should check carefully that the subject is not departing from the standard procedure.'

(iii) *Encouraging verbalisation*

'This is the most difficult but also the most challenging and rewarding part of the interviews. As the project is concerned with "sociolinguistic" aspects of occupations, interviewers must take care to collect the precise phraseology used by subjects when making judgements about occupations. These judgements should not be suggested in any way by the probing of the interviewer, whose purpose here is to encourage the articulation of thoughts about occupations as they occur during the administration of the task. Ideally, the subject should decide when a thought is worth expressing, clarifying, expanding, relating to other judgements and situations. It is also very often a matter of requesting clarification and elaboration on a snigger, a mumble or a short comment. This is done by many standard methods, the pregnant pause, the encouraging grunt, "uh uh, yes, I see, that's interesting", repeating part of the comment, asking "how so?", "why?", "what do you mean by?", "tell me more about . . .". It is also important not to reword or interpret the comment, thereby possibly shutting the door to other aspects of the subject's thought.'

(iv) *Keeping control of pace and maintaining rapport*

'As in any type of interview, it is essential for the interviewer to be sensitive to a respondent's impatience, boredom or frustration, which can greatly impair the quality of the data collected. As the interviews are usually very long (commonly over two hours), time should be reserved for short chatty breaks between tasks. The life-history task is often very useful in the middle of an interview as most subjects enjoy talking about themselves. An interview can be speeded up by doing relatively less probing for a while or simply by pointing out how much more is left to be done. Slowing someone down is usually more difficult as the subject gets a sense of achievement from completing a structured task fast and finds it difficult to get interested in the analysis of his own thinking. The interviewer must then decide whether little more verbalisation can be reasonably expected or whether there is a mysterious way in which the subject could be motivated to contribute more comments. Words of reassurance about the worthiness of subjects' comments are sometimes called for, in addition to positive probing, but care should be taken not to encourage a biased response by appearing to agree.'

The Interview

An interview consists of a number of 'tasks'. Each task is self-contained, and refers to a particular method of data-collection. The actual tasks done and the sequence in which they have been used underwent a good deal of experimentation during the course of the Project.

A typical interview lasted between two and three hours and consisted of the following type of sequence:

1. Collection of *background information* and 'face sheet' variables — name, address, date of birth, present job, or last full-time job of the father of the interviewee, type of secondary school, age of terminal education for self, father and mother, length of service in present job, length of service in type of job.
2. Obtaining a detailed *job life-history* from the year the subject leaves school.
3. The interviewer then administered the *pairwise similarities ratings* task and/or the *triadic similarities comparison* task (these and the next two tasks are described in the following section).
4. Most subjects then went on to make a series of *rankings or ratings* of occupational titles according to a set of five different criteria.
5. In some cases reported in this volume, the subject made a *free-sorting* of a different set of occupational titles.

The actual number of tasks done by a subject depended upon the speed at which a subject worked and, to a lesser extent, on the interviewer's judgement as to when 'enough was enough'. Interviewers were also given the freedom to decide the point at which the life-history was taken.

Context of the interview and quality of the data

Interview data were obtained in three ways:

(1)　by individual interview, either at the subject's home or in the Project interviewing room;

(2)   by individual interview in a place-of-work setting; or
(3)   by group administration.

The majority of subjects were interviewed in the first manner, and although conditions were not always perfect (television in the background, interruption from families etc.), the data obtained in this manner are of the highest quality.

Ambulance drivers and attendants and policemen were interviewed at their place of work. The ambulance staff interviews were all carried out on Sunday mornings (when emergency calls were least likely). Although they were all separately interviewed, it happened from time to time that the interview was interrupted by an emergency call. It was sometimes possible to continue such an interrupted task either later that day, or on a subsequent visit. Despite this ever-present possibility of interruption, the quality of data was generally very good indeed.

The group-interview situation took the form of administering the schedules to a classroom of subjects. Interviewing staff explained the tasks, and walked around answering questions and supervising the data collection, but it was not possible to exercise the same direct control as in the other conditions. Data were collected in this way from:

full-time	theological students
	education students
	chemical, electrical and mechanical engineering students
practising	school-teachers studying part-time for their postgraduate degree of Master of Education
practising	nurse tutors attending a full-time nursing course.

T.2.4 Specification of Methods of Data Collection

(A full description of these methods of data collection (and of others subsequently abandoned) is contained in: *Methods of data collection used in the Project on Occupational Cognition: a handbook for interviewers* (RM2, 1973) a copy of which is part of the supporting documentation to the Project files, and is available at cost from the SSRC Survey Archive. Each method is also discussed at greater length in the relevant chapters.)

The data described and analysed differ in three main ways:

1. in the *size and composition* of the set of occupational titles (*object set*);
2. in the *design and procedure* for selecting the particular (sub)set of titles between which the subject is asked to make a judgement (*judgemental design*);
3. in the *method of data collection,* or mode and criterion of judgement which is used (*method*).

The *object sets* used are:
    LABL06 (the basic set of 16 occupational titles);
    LABL10 (the subset of LABL06, consisting of 13 titles);
    LABL08 (the 32 titles designed for cross-national use).

The *judgemental designs* used are:
    a balanced incomplete block design (BIBD) for triadic judgements;
    the complete set of pairs;
    the complete set of single titles.

The *methods* used are:
    (complete) ranking;
    (complete) rating;
    picking 2 out of 3 objects;
    partitioning into an unspecified number of groups.

The main criterion of judgement is similarity, but the rankings and ratings data (see below) are distinguished in terms of criteria used.

TABLE T.2.4.1   Summary of data collection methods used in *The Images of Occupational Prestige*

Brief name	Project abbreviation	Object set	Judgemental design	Method
Pairwise Similarities	PB	16 Occupational titles (basic set)	Complete randomised set of 120 pairs	Rate the similarity of each pair
Triadic Similarities	TB	13 Occupational titles (reduced set)	BIBD set of 52 triads	Pick the least similar pair and pick the most similar pair in each triad
Rankings and Ratings	RA RB	16 Occupational titles (basic set)	Complete randomised set of single titles	RA3: Rank/ General standing RA4: Rank/ Prestige 'ought' RB6: Rate/Social usefulness RB7: Rate/ Estimated income RB8: Rate/ Knowledge
Free Sorting	FA	32 Occupational titles (extended set)	Complete randomised set of single titles	Partition into unspecified number of groups

Each of these types of data, and the occupational life-history, is described in detail below.

The occupational life-history

An example of a life-history schedule is given in Table T.2.4.2. The schedule was adapted, with permission, from one used by the Johns Hopkins University social researchers (Blum *et al.* 1969).

Life-history information was recorded for every subject. It includes full details of career patterns from the year when the respondent left full-time education and it describes job moves, promotions and geographical moves, reasons for leaving a job, whether a new job was lined up, how the new job or further qualifications were obtained, together with such marking events (e.g. marriage, father's death) as the subject mentioned. This job history also included information regarding name, address, date of birth, father's last occupation, type of secondary school, school-leaving age for self and parents, years in last job, years in same type of job.

Interviewers were advised to record job descriptions in sufficient detail to permit coding according to the Office of Population and Censuses *Classification of Occupations.*

Most subjects enjoyed telling their occupational life-history, some with flourishing details, whilst others gave a simple bare-bone *curriculum vitae.* Giving the life-history often provided reassurance and relief in the middle of long interviews.

Pairwise similarities task (PB data) (Thurstone 1927, Guildford 1928, Gulliksen 1946, David 1963)

The subject was presented with the full set of 120 pairs of the 16 occupational titles. In each schedule the order in which the pairs appeared, and the order of the titles within each pair, were randomised.

The initial instructions to the subject were as follows:

Below you will find pairs of names of occupations, separated by nine numbers. We would like you to judge how similar in your opinion each of these pairs of occupations is. Will you please do this by circling the number which best expresses the amount of similarity you think there is — a 9 means totally similar, and a 1 means totally dissimilar. I realise that this is sometimes a difficult task, and you may find it hard to decide in some cases. Please make a judgment nonetheless, but mark that pair with an 'x'.

CHURCH OF SCOTLAND MINISTER   *AND*   CHARTERED ACCOUNTANT
    Totally similar   9. 8. 7. 6. 5. 4. 3. 2. 1   Totally dissimilar

BUILDING SITE LABOURER   *AND*   MALE PSYCHIATRIC NURSE
    Totally similar   9. 8. 7. 6. 5. 4. 3. 2. 1.   Totally dissimilar

(etc.)

CONFIDENTIAL

Type 2ndary school

11 junior secondary school
12 secondary modern school
13 technical high school
14 non-fee-paying senior 2ndary
15 fee-paying Corporation senior 2ndary
16 fee-paying grant aided senior 2ndary
17 grant-aided (English direct grant)
18 grammar school of English 11-plus sort
19 wholly independent school ("Public" school)
21 comprehensive school
22 other   (specify)
91 no information, not know, etc.

NAME CARD

1	2	3	4	5	6	7	8	9	10	11	12	13	14	15	16	17	18	19	20	21	22	23	24	25	26	27	28	29	30	31	32	33	34	35	36	37	38	39	40
1	1	8	M	5	5						M	S	J	C			M	A	C	L	E	A	N																

Title M-Miss Mrs   Initials   Surname

ADDRESS CARD

1	2	3	4	5	6	7	8	9	10	11	12	13	14	15	16	17	18	19	20	21	22	23	24	25	26	27	28	29	30	31	32	33	34	35	36	37	38	39	40
2	1	8	M	5	5			2	4		S	T	A	T	I	O	N		R	O	A	D		I	N	V	E	R	L	E	I	T	H						

41	42	43	44	45	46	47	48	49	50	51	52	53	54	55	56	57	58	59	60	61	62	63	64	65	66	67	68	69	70	71	72	73	74	75	76	77	78	79	80

OTHER DATA CARD

1	2	3	4	5	6	7	8	9	10	11	12	13	14
3	1	8	M	5	5			2	0	3	1	9	4

Day | Month | Year of Birth

telephone no. (not punch)

15	16	17	18	19	20

R-G 1970
Present job of interviewee. Describe very fully with employer's business or industry and any special rank or grade held, and qualifications too. *Management Consultant*

R-G 1970
Present job or last full-time job held by father of interviewee Describe fully as before. *Production line paint sprayer, BMC.*

21	22
1	9

23	24	25	26	27	28	29	30	31	32
1	8	1	6	1	6	0	5	0	5

self | father | mother

age at end of full-time education

code in years   don't know is 91

how many years since entered present specific job
code in years

how many years since entered present general type of job
code in years

CONFIDENTIAL
Dept. Sociology
Univ. of Edinburgh
A. Coxon C. Jones
POOC project.

PROJECT ON OCCUPATIONAL COGNITION   (Form based on NORC Survey 4068 and C.S.S.O.S, JHU, with acknowledgements)   APMC.

YEAR	AGE	FULL-TIME EMPLOYMENT OR UNEMPLOYMENT						COMMENT
(from this june 00)		Month	Occupation /Grade	Firm, Industry, Institution	Left Job: Own decision Not —	At present After my old Changed job	Has job been Broken down Eliminated etc	
1955	16	SEPT	CLERK.	Insurance Co			ADS	
1956	17							
1957	18							
1958	19							
1959	20	AUG	PRIVATE	PayCorps				NAT SERVICE
1960	21	JUNE / AUG	LANCE CORPORAL / CORPORAL					
1961	22	AUG	CLERK					SAME JOB.
1962	23							
1963	24							
1964	25							
1965	26							
1966	27	JAN / DEC	CLERK / TRAINEE MENTAL WELFARE OFFICER	YEB / W.R.C.C.	O	N. * H	AD. APPLIED	Vocational Guidance
1967	28	JUNE	MENTAL WELFARE OFFICER		Own.	Neither.		
1968	29	JULY	STUDENT	CSW COURSE				Seconded.
1969	30							
1970	31	JULY	Snr Mental Welfare Officer.				Other.	Job Kept Open
1971	32	APRIL	Social Worker *					Reorganization *
1972	33	DEC	Senior Social Worker	SCCS *	O	H	AD	
1973	34							
1974	35							

I.D. No.

Date of Interview			
TASK	DONE? (TYPE)	EMAS ?	
RA3			
RA4			
RB6			
RB7			
RB8			
PB			
TB			
FA			
FB	*139 CARDS* X		
HA16	X	X	
MA			
Other:			

Interviewers were instructed not to treat the similarities task as a self-completion questionnaire — partly to overcome reading difficulties and chance omissions, but mostly to encourage verbalisation. Subjects were asked to give their own opinion of the degree of similarity and the basis for judgement was not specified by the task or suggested by the interviewer. Since the bases of general similarity were to be inferred from subjects' responses, all verbalised bases of judgement, constructs, sequences in problem-solving, etc., were recorded by the interviewer when they arose. The subject was also asked to 'say something' about the preceding judgement after the last line on each page, and after the task was completed more verbalisation was again encouraged, in order to see what 'strategies of similarity judgement' were being used.

It was not uncommon for a subject to assign the rating (1) — totally dissimilar — to a large proportion of the pairs of occupations. Without biasing the answers of those who really held such a view, interviewers found that a second look at the meaning of the task would sometimes lead to more subtle judgements and they were asked to point out that a 'totally dissimilar' score would be taken to mean that there is no attribute or characteristic *at all* which is common to both occupations.

The data thus obtained were punched directly from the interview schedules. As in the case of other data, the information was first checked for consistency and correct subject identification, permissible values, correctly placed case separators, etc. Once a case was in acceptable form, the randomly ordered similarities judgements of that individual were re-ordered and output to the clean data file (DPB106AD) in the form of a lower-half matrix of similarities between the 16 occupations. This, and other cleaned data files, have been deposited at the SSRC Survey Archive at the University of Essex.

Triadic judgements of similarity (TB data) (Richardson 1938, Torgerson 1958, Roskam 1970, Burton and Nerlove 1971)

In the method of triads, subjects are requested to make *relative* similarity judgements. They were presented repeatedly with sets of three occupational titles and asked to choose (1) which two titles were most alike and (2) which two titles were least alike. They were also asked to explain their decision and if possible, suggest a basis for their judgement. This exercise amounts to getting the subject to order two of the three possible pairs of stimuli in the triad, and then state the criterion (or criteria) for his ordering.

A major difficulty in using this method is the large number of possible triads derived from a relatively small stimulus set. The 13 stimuli used here can be combined into 286 distinct (unordered) triads.

To make data collection feasible, the method of balanced incomplete block designs was therefore used (see T.3.1). By this technique, it is possible to ensure that each pair of stimuli appears a given number of times (in this case twice) on each subject's schedule. In this way we reduced the number of triads considered by any one subject to 52. In the schedule, the order of appearance of the triads and the order in which the three titles appeared were randomised separately for each subject.

An example of a triad, together with the instructions read by the interviewer, is given here:

Please suggest some important way in which two of the three occupations below are alike — and at the same time different in the same way from — the third. Use a sentence or two to do this.

13 Barman
10 Policeman
01 Church of Scotland minister
— Which pair of the three occupations is the most similar one, i.e. which two are the most alike?
— Which pair of the three occupations is the least similar one, i.e. which two are least alike?

In those cases where subjects were asked to give the bases of their similarities judgements, this verbal information was typed up separately. At a later stage the file of verbal constructs was merged, triad by triad, with the raw similarities data file. From this merged file a relatively simple utility program was able to pick out all the comments made when a particular pair of occupations had been judged as most (or least) similar. This was most useful in identifying semantic space in which the occupations were embedded.

Despite the fact that the triads task involves making fewer judgements than pairwise similarities, the subjects often experienced it as a difficult and unrewarding task, as this interviewer's report indicates:

> Some difficulty with this task, principally because, though he started out well enough, after a time he confused 'least alike' with 'next most likely pair'. This became obvious, was cleared up once, then again, and the third time I changed 'least alike' to 'not alike' . . . At one time I thought we'd never finish; I felt the need to nurse him along the whole time. He needed water after 37 [of the triads] . . .

Although the methodological advantages of (incomplete) triadic data-collection are considerable and should yield contextually specific judgements, these advantages were outweighed in our experience by the toll on the subject's concentration and on his goodwill.

After cleaning, the data were output in the form of individual lower-half dissimilarity matrices, and are filed as DTB110AD at the SSRC Archive.

Ranking and Rating tasks (RA and RB data) (*Ranking:* Barrett 1914; Thurstone 1931, *Rating:* Richardson and Kuder 1933, Guildford 1954, Dawes 1972)

Ranking and rating tasks have been routine and standard methods of investigating subjective occupational structure in sociology for a long time. In this investigation subjects were asked to *rank-order* the 16 occupational titles for two of the criteria: according to their 'degree of general standing in the community' (a descriptive criterion) and according to the 'prestige or rewards which the job-holders ought to receive' (a normative criterion). (They were allowed to 'tie' two occupations to the same rank, if they so desired.)

In the *rating* task, subjects are told to consider each stimulus and award them a 'score' on some specified attribute. The implication is that each stimulus is to be judged in relation to other stimuli in the presented set but is also to be given a rating with reference to some absolute standard. Three rating tasks were employed in this investigation. The first used a normative criterion: subjects were asked to rate the 16 occupations by marking them out of 100 in terms of their 'usefulness to society'. The second was descriptive: subjects were required to 'estimate the average income received' in an average week by a job-holder aged 30 who had been working in the same occupation for about five years. The final rating task used as an index of cognitive distance the criterion of 'how much you know about what is involved in the job', and subjects were again asked to mark each occupation out of 100.

Each set of occupational titles (in randomised order) was headed by the following instructions:

(RA3) Please rank order the following 16 occupations in terms of your own personal opinion of their general standing in the community. Assign a rank of one (1) to the occupation which has the most excellent general standing, and a rank order of sixteen (16) to the occupation which has the poorest general standing. You may 'tie' two occupations with the same rank if you like. By the way, please try not to judge any occupation according to your opinion of some person you know who has such an occupation.

(RA4) Please rank order the following 16 occupations in terms of your own personal opinion of the prestige and rewards they ought to receive. Assign a rank of one (1) to the occupation which you think ought to have the highest prestige and rewards, and a rank of sixteen (16) to the occupation which you would give the lowest prestige and the poorest rewards to. You may 'tie' two occupations with the same rank if you like.

(RB6) Please rate each of the following 16 occupations in terms of their usefulness to society.
    Give each of them a 'percentage' mark out of 100, just as if you were marking an examination paper.
    Give high marks to any occupation which you think of as being extreme ly useful to society, and low marks to any occupation which you think of as being not at all useful to scoiety.

(RB7) Please make as accurate a guess as you can about the average income that people working in the 16 occupations below would be likely to receive. We want to know what you think such people actually receive. (We do not want to know what you think they ought to get.) To make the task more specified, please answer for each occupation in terms of the total income likely to be received in an average week by a man aged about 30, who had been working in the same occupation for about five years. Guess at his average expected weekly income before tax deductions, and including any other sources of income (e.g. overtime, dividends, etc.).

(RB8) Please rate each of the following 16 occupations in terms of how much you know about what is involved in the job. Give each of them a 'percentage' mark out of 100, just as if you were marking an examination paper. Give high marks to any occupation which you know a very great deal about — for example one which you have worked in for a fair period of time — and low marks to any occupation which you know very little about.

Interviewers were asked to read the task instructions aloud and ensure that the important distinguishing criterion had been correctly understood. They were also made aware of the normative/descriptive distinction in order to make certain that tasks RA4 and RB6 reflected the subject's notions of what ought to be, in contrast to tasks RA3 and RB7 where the subject's ideas of what actually pertains were required. (This was especially important in RA3, where the potential ambiguity involved in asking the subject to give his opinions of other people's opinions had to be avoided.)

The ratings of average income (RB7) were accepted in weekly, monthly or yearly amounts, as the subject preferred, but the responses were edited to give the equivalent monthly salary to the nearest £1. As usual, verbalisations — 'mumbles', hesitations, etc. — were noted down or transcribed from tape in order to provide insight into both the problems encountered during the tasks and the subjects' solutions to them.

A good deal of support had to be given to some respondents at each step of the rating or ranking. Some had to be encouraged to complete (or even to start) the tasks by probes such as 'Which occupation had the most excellent general standing?', 'Which has the next best general standing?', and so on. Others, understandably, wished to differentiate between 'prestige' and 'rewards' in RA4, and if they insisted on doing so they were allowed to form two rank-orders instead of one. Some respondents felt that they knew too little, and were disturbed by the realisation that they would have to guess. On the other hand, one or two subjects found the rating of income task complicated by the fact that they knew too much.

The interviewee was concerned about average pay for lorry drivers: 'Pay goes in tonnage from about £22 basic for up to 3 tons to £40 basic for 10 tons and over, and more for long distance.' Also he brought up the fact that one must remember that policemen get rent allowances, free travel on public transport when in uniform, etc. [extract from interview report].

Raw data were cleaned and output in a standard row format as files DRA (3,4,6,7,8)06AD (as ranked data) and DRB(6,7,8)06AD (as ratings data). These are available from the SSRC Archive.

Free-sorting data (FA data) (Sherif and Hovland 1953, Miller 1969, Imai and Garner 1968, Burton 1972)

The purpose of the free-sorting task is to discover some elementary properties of the ways in which people differentiate their occupational world and categorise their experience of it.

The subjects were given the standard set of 32 randomly-ordered cards and asked to sort them into as many or as few groups as they wished, in any way which seemed 'natural' to them. The titles were each printed on a separate punched card and the subjects were encouraged to rearrange, break and remake clusters until they reached a partition which was satisfactory to them. (This was intended to provide insight into the rules according to which subjects were working and to ensure that the final rearranged partition was more reliable in the sense that a replication of the task would provide a highly similar sorting.)

Subjects were asked to verbalise throughout the process of sorting, since the rules of classification they used and the group descriptions they gave are important for the interpretation of results. At the end of the task, the subject was asked whether or not the groups were in any particular 'arrangement' (which might, or might not, be an ordering).

The instructions used were as follows:

I have here 32 cards, each with the name of an occupation on it. We should like you to group them in any way that seems natural to you. There can be as many or as few piles as you want, and if you make sure that you can see the titles as you are doing the task you can easily change them around if you want to. Please do talk about the task as you are doing it, because any comment you make is very relevant to us. The numbers on the cards are for office use only and you may disregard them.

Verbalisation was encouraged throughout the task; subjects were told that we were not only interested in the rules of classification which gave rise to their final grouping, but also in the strategy they followed in arriving there: in systematic assignment of each card to a pile, tentative groupings, partial or complete changes of forms for each group, evidence of hierarchies, etc. When the subject had arrived at a final grouping, the interviewer placed a blank card on the top of each group and asked him to give a short descriptive summary of the group. Finally, note was taken on any arrangement which the subject perceived in the groups; if they were ordered, the groups were collected together in the appropriate sequence, and it is in fact only these subjects' data which are analysed in *Images*. Comments were recorded at all three stages of the task — initial sorting, summary descriptions, and final arrangement. Interview reports also included remarks made before and after the task, and descriptions of the subjects' procedures and strategies.

Free-sorting was generally found to be an enjoyable task by most subjects. Interestingly, several of them expressed the intention of using certain rules of classification at the very outset, which were not in fact always followed during the sorting. Spoken comments were usually difficult to obtain whilst the cards were actually being sorted.

Less articulate respondents tended to describe individual occupations rather than groups and found it difficult to give general descriptions which applied to all titles in one group. This often made it a very demanding task for the interviewer, who had to refrain from assuming that the rules of classification he perceived were actually present in the subject's thinking.

The data were transformed into individual co-occurrence matrices, available as file DFA108AD at the SSRC Archive.

3 The Analysis of Similarities Judgements: Appendices to Chapter 3 of *The Images of Occupational Prestige*

T.3.1 Balanced incomplete block designs and effect of context in triadic judgements

In his study of the properties of various methods of systematic data collection, Coombs (1964, Chapter 2) uses the method of pair comparisons as his base for assessing the relative power (channel capacity) and the capability of checking for inconsistency (redundancy) of other more complex methods. The method which is best adapted to examine cognitive mapping is the 'pair of pair' method, having the form 'Which pair is more similar – (A,B) or (C,D)?', but it is entirely unfeasible for anything but a trivially small number of objects.

A method often used as an approximation to the 'pair of pair' is the method of triads, in which one element is common to both pairs. The method of triads is also much more efficient, and less time-consuming per bit of information obtained than the method of pair comparisons – in fact, a gain of about 80 per cent efficiency over pair-comparisons is reported by Coombs (1964: 41).

Yet the number of triads involved in a full presentation increases rapidly, and also becomes rapidly unfeasible. A task involving a very large number of judgements would test the patience of any subject, and a procedure was therefore sought which would maximise the information gained from the subject yet minimise the number of triads presented.

Balanced Incomplete Block Designs (BIBDs) provide such a procedure, and were exploited for the collection of triadic data (see T.2.4 above). An extensive study of such designs for the method of triads had been made by Burton and Nerlove (1971), and their results were used to define the design used here. The design chosen involved $n=13$ stimuli (a subset of the 16 – see Table T.3.1), $p=3$ stimuli in each presentation, $r=12$ replications of each single stimulus, $\lambda = 2$ replications of each pair of stimuli, producing

b=52 presentations (or blocks), satisfying the necessary conditions:

$$\lambda = r(p - 1 / (n - 1)$$
$$\text{and } m = \text{bp}.$$

When triadic data are scaled, it is common practice to turn the ordered triple (the datum) into a 'vote count', counting the frequency with which a particular pair is judged more similar that another. Roskam (1970: 406) has shown that such a procedure badly misrepresents the order information in the data, and yields ill-fitting and distorted scaling representations. Moreover, the vote-count procedure destroys information which is unique to the method of triads, namely whether the similarity between two objects is the same when the third element changes. The third element provides a varying context for judgement, and the vote-count method cannot, as it were, carry this information through to the final configuration. Roskam (1970) also explores the deficiencies of the vote count method by directly scaling triadic similarities data, and this approach was generalised in the TRISOSCAL algorithm developed by M.J. Prentice (see T.3.11), where a partial order of the pairwise similarities is constructed on the basis of triadic judgements, and the attempt is made to transfer contextual information directly to the final configuration.

Context effects are only discernible if there are two or more replications of each pair of stimuli. In $\lambda = 1$ designs, each pair is presented once only, and there is thus no possibility of constructing a partial order of similarities, since each implicit pairwise similarity can only be compared to the other two in the same triad. Direct scaling of data from such a design often leads to an indeterminate solution, since there are not sufficient constraints to determine a solution. By contrast, $\lambda = 2$ designs do allow a partial order to be constructed between triads, and this design is well suited to the scaling of individual configurations by the TRISOSCAL algorithm.

T.3.2 Distribution of similarity ratings (portrayed in Figure T.3.1, p. 00)

Rating value	Frequency	Percentage
0 (Missing data)	122	0.35
1 (Totally dissimilar)	11491	33.37
2	5364	15.57
3	4549	13.21
4	3320	9.64
5	2869	8.33
6	2386	6.93
7	2306	6.70
8	1424	4.13
9 (Totally similar)	609	1.77
Total	34440	100.00

T.3.3 Percentages of 'totally dissimilar' judgements given by different subject groups

QUADRANT A: 29%	QUADRANT B: 30%
Clergymen 31% Teachers 25% (Education students (29%), Theological students (25%), Journalists (30%))	Qualified actuaries 34% Chartered accountants 29% (Chemical engineering students (32%) Electrical engineering students (25%))
QUADRANT C: 40%	QUADRANT D: 44%
Ambulance drivers 53% Policemen 51% (Nurses 21%))	Joiners and fitters 55% Engineers 37% (Building and related trades (44%), Printers (50%))

(Law students (29%), Business administration students (22%))
Overall percentage: 33

T.3.4 Pairwise similarity ratings distributions

Pair	(MD)	1	2	3	4	5	6	7	8	9
				Similarity rating distribution						
2 1:	0	28	9	19	25	49	34	70	33	20
3 1:	2	63	34	34	35	30	34	26	23	6
3 2:	3	40	23	43	37	42	38	38	16	7
4 1:	1	56	28	41	38	35	44	27	10	7
4 2:	3	40	23	45	37	30	47	33	24	5
4 3:	2	8	7	11	10	27	16	55	94	57
5 1:	2	47	22	28	38	44	49	35	18	4
5 2:	1	37	26	30	44	48	38	37	19	7
5 3:	1	102	40	51	26	30	22	10	1	4
5 4:	1	111	49	38	38	24	19	7	0	0
6 1:	0	79	52	50	36	24	17	17	8	4
6 2:	1	88	68	43	36	26	16	7	1	1
6 3:	1	145	54	37	33	9	4	1	1	2
6 4:	2	139	66	45	21	5	6	3	0	0
6 5:	1	14	23	38	32	51	36	52	29	11
7 1:	0	190	58	24	4	6	0	1	0	4
7 2:	0	174	65	30	9	3	2	2	2	0
7 3:	1	212	47	14	5	4	1	2	0	1

| | | | | | | *Similarity rating distribution* | | | | |
Pair		*(MD)*	*1*	*2*	*3*	*4*	*5*	*6*	*7*	*8*	*9*
7	4:	1	205	51	17	5	3	2	1	1	1
7	5:	3	135	58	40	21	12	7	6	5	0
7	6:	0	90	55	44	33	24	19	14	4	4
8	1:	1	156	60	38	12	12	3	4	1	0
8	2:	0	104	60	60	24	16	8	12	1	2
8	3:	0	140	69	32	22	9	9	4	1	1
8	4:	0	134	70	42	12	15	8	2	2	2
8	5:	1	112	52	41	29	16	17	13	6	0
8	6:	1	85	44	42	34	28	24	23	5	1
8	7:	1	47	33	39	34	38	35	40	16	4
9	1:	2	35	21	23	30	37	40	55	31	13
9	2:	1	35	24	34	35	48	47	36	18	9
9	3:	2	13	8	25	25	35	45	64	53	17
9	4:	1	8	5	13	27	36	42	58	73	24
9	5:	1	80	41	49	49	30	20	13	4	0
9	6:	0	119	52	61	31	13	7	2	1	1
9	7:	0	195	58	18	5	3	3	2	3	0
9	8:	0	157	49	42	20	10	5	2	0	2
10	1:	1	45	30	28	32	44	42	45	16	4
10	2:	2	32	17	30	33	45	50	50	21	7
10	3:	1	7	11	20	20	34	50	71	49	24
10	4:	2	12	10	14	20	34	36	66	64	29
10	5:	2	86	44	57	28	24	24	16	5	1
10	6:	0	120	58	48	31	16	9	4	1	0
10	7:	1	210	43	21	6	2	2	1	1	0
10	8:	2	151	53	36	23	8	12	2	0	0
10	9:	1	13	12	31	24	33	42	72	45	14
11	1:	1	86	54	50	39	31	14	5	5	2
11	2:	0	73	47	59	47	26	23	7	4	1
11	3:	1	79	62	51	30	28	23	9	2	2
11	4:	1	61	42	70	55	17	20	12	7	2
11	5:	0	104	46	49	33	22	18	7	7	1
11	6:	1	44	39	50	47	39	32	22	8	5
11	7:	1	118	54	42	29	21	14	5	3	0
11	8:	2	96	53	39	38	27	18	12	2	0
11	9:	2	68	54	63	46	23	18	12	1	0
11	10:	0	74	47	66	41	24	22	8	4	1
12	1:	1	46	32	33	43	37	37	38	14	6
12	2:	0	39	26	46	40	48	39	33	13	3
12	3:	2	96	52	46	32	30	21	7	0	1
12	4:	2	85	60	45	37	30	14	8	5	1
12	5:	1	42	22	22	45	37	45	41	27	5

Pair	(MD)	1	2	3	4	5	6	7	8	9
				Similarity rating distribution						
12 6:	2	22	16	31	38	40	48	50	24	16
12 7:	1	113	62	46	25	22	10	5	1	2
12 8:	0	106	51	40	34	26	13	10	6	1
12 9:	1	32	44	39	38	55	39	21	12	6
12 10:	0	53	42	42	52	44	25	17	10	2
12 11:	1	80	42	48	43	28	18	15	9	3
13 1:	2	131	50	51	21	19	8	2	1	2
13 2:	1	99	59	51	37	19	11	7	3	0
13 3:	1	138	59	44	21	15	6	2	1	0
13 4:	1	118	77	43	20	16	6	2	3	1
13 5:	2	114	45	41	22	32	15	12	2	2
13 6:	1	90	45	32	38	29	30	15	5	2
13 7:	2	31	14	33	36	47	35	42	31	16
13 8:	2	11	8	16	30	45	39	54	53	29
13 9:	1	140	64	35	16	15	6	5	3	2
13 10:	0	144	59	41	15	14	8	2	2	2
13 11:	0	101	41	51	34	29	12	12	4	3
13 12:	1	107	37	38	29	28	25	19	2	1
14 1:	1	168	73	22	12	6	1	1	1	2
14 2:	1	155	63	41	19	6	2	0	0	0
14 3:	1	179	66	19	11	3	3	1	1	3
14 4:	0	177	70	29	2	4	1	2	2	0
14 5:	2	128	58	38	31	12	7	8	2	1
14 6:	0	9	9	16	21	42	40	58	68	24
14 7:	1	17	22	35	28	26	41	61	45	11
14 8:	1	55	26	41	28	38	33	43	14	8
14 9:	1	167	69	28	10	6	1	2	2	1
14 10:	0	179	55	32	14	3	3	0	1	0
14 11:	1	27	23	29	47	47	35	40	23	15
14 12:	1	84	46	54	38	27	25	10	1	1
14 13:	1	68	43	36	37	29	22	35	11	5
15 1:	1	157	64	34	16	5	2	3	2	3
15 2:	0	150	73	42	11	5	2	4	0	0
15 3:	2	205	51	17	5	4	1	1	0	1
15 4:	2	189	61	22	5	3	3	0	1	1
15 5:	0	126	57	43	34	11	9	5	2	0
15 6:	1	45	48	44	24	42	39	26	12	6
15 7:	0	15	19	27	26	25	22	58	55	40
15 8:	0	75	42	42	23	42	23	31	8	1
15 9:	0	180	65	30	5	5	1	1	0	0
15 10:	0	163	70	36	6	7	2	0	2	1
15 11:	1	86	51	49	36	32	19	7	3	3

Pair	(MD)	1	2	3	4	5	6	7	8	9
				Similarity rating distribution						
15 12:	0	66	54	59	47	25	21	9	4	2
15 13:	2	84	40	38	39	35	27	11	10	1
15 14:	1	14	28	34	36	35	33	48	45	13
16 1:	3	157	54	29	19	9	6	3	4	3
16 2:	0	138	61	44	24	7	6	4	3	0
16 3:	2	174	58	32	10	5	3	1	0	2
16 4:	1	162	52	42	16	4	7	2	0	1
16 5:	1	112	51	46	25	15	19	11	6	1
16 6:	1	103	51	36	35	22	16	16	3	4
16 7:	1	73	33	46	28	26	18	30	23	9
16 8:	1	87	53	37	37	18	24	23	4	3
16 9:	1	153	62	37	16	11	0	2	4	1
16 10:	2	157	65	40	12	4	3	1	3	0
16 11:	1	64	24	47	35	42	26	29	16	3
16 12:	1	86	52	49	43	19	21	11	3	2
16 13:	1	88	47	43	31	21	22	24	8	2
16 14:	2	79	30	34	31	31	28	23	22	7
16 15:	0	50	38	31	27	35	26	42	30	8

T.3.5 Spatial models

The Distance Model

The distance model assumes that a subject's judgement of similarity between
two objects i and j is a decreasing function of the distance between the
location of the points representing object i and object j in his cognitive space:

$$s_{ij} = F(d_{ij})$$

The generalised distance function is given by:

$$d_{ij} = (\sum_a |x_{ia} - x_{ja}|^r)^{1/r}$$

where x_{ka} gives the location of object k on dimension a, and the exponent r
defines the type of metric. The most commonly used exponents are $r = 1$
(so-called City-block metric), $r = 2$ (Euclidean metric) and $r = \infty$ (Dominance
metric). See Attneave (1950), Shepard (1960), Cross (1965).

When interpreted strictly as a substantive theory of human information-
processing, the distance function defining the model makes extremely strong
assumptions about how information is combined into a similarity judgement.
It implies that the subject has compared each pair of objects or stimuli in
terms of how they differ on each dimension, and has then combined this
information into a final overall measure by a complex summative rule. In

particular (see Beals *et al.* 1968: 133-5) it asserts (by reference to the general distance function above)

(i)   the absolute differences on each dimension (*a*)
(ii)   which are transformed by the same power function (*r*)
(iii) combine in an additive manner
(iv)   to produce the overall distance measure between a pair of points.

In effect, these four propositions form a theory of *how* subjects combine information into overall impressions or judgements, which is very akin to impression-formation theory in social psychology. However, the propositions advanced there are much weaker than those of the distance model, and tend to be restricted to straightforward additive and difference models (Anderson 1962, 1968). Almost no empirical evidence exists at present on how judgements about occupations are in fact made, and what theory exists is almost entirely borrowed from impression-formation and cognitive-consistency theories.

A further proposition assumed (at least by default) in most analyses of occupational judgements is that the distance function is Euclidean. Besides its greater familiarity, the robustness of the Euclidean metric (Shepard 1964, 1969; Hyman and Well 1967) probably accounts for its popularity in analysis of occupational judgemental data.

On the other hand, Arnold (1971) has shown that the simpler dominance metric provides a better account of data collected by means of procedures which impose severe information-processing constraints on the subject. Whilst the grounds for this conclusion have been questioned (Carroll and Wish 1975) the point he makes is both important and valid. It is interesting that the data-collection process itself should be pinpointed as the source of these characteristics, for it suggests that methods which are more attuned to the analytic rather than the synthesising aspects of information-processing will differentiate and break up the apparently refractory nature of sociological concepts such as 'prestige'.

It should not be thought that the argument is being made that occupational judgements are always complex; people may well use a more convenient and fast procedure in socially significant encounters. The point is, rather, that to *ask* subjects to make very general assessments is to trade upon one of man's most notable deficiencies — namely to synthesise and combine multifaceted information into overall assessments (Yntema and Torgerson 1961).

T.3.6 Hierarchical clustering schemes

Cormack (1971: 337) defines a hierarchical stratified system as a tree, $T = (R,N,F)$, consisting of a root R (covering all objects), a finite set N of nodes, C (clusters of objects) together with a mapping F of N into itself, such that, for all $k \geqslant 1$, $F^k C = C$ iff $C = N$, and a real valued function s on N

such that $s(C) \leqslant s(C')$ if there exists a $k \geqslant 0$ such that $F^k C' = C$. Both Hartigan (1967) and Johnson (1967) pointed out that a (dis)similarity measure, d conforming to such a structure will satisfy the *ultrametric inequality*:

$$d(i,j) \leqslant \max (d(i,k), d(j,k))$$

whilst the (Euclidean) metric makes the weaker requirement of the *triangular inequality*:

$$d(i,j) \leqslant d(i,k) + d(j,k)$$

Holman (1972) shows that a set of *errorless* data will never satisfy both the Euclidean distance model and the hierarchical model completely, but will always satisfy one of the models to some extent, and proves that a (dis)-similarity measure on n objects will be strictly monotonically related *either* to the ultrametric distances of the hierarchical model *or* to the distances in a Euclidean space of less than $(n-1)$ dimensions, but never to both. With real (errorful) data the position is unfortunately not so clear-cut. One can attempt to detect systematic deviation, which should occur from one model, but not from both.

In the case of errorful data, two bases for clustering are suggested by Johnson (1967: 247-9), which will give rise to identical hierarchical clustering in the case of data which satisfy the ultrametric inequality. They are:

(i) the minimum ('connectedness' or 'single-link') method:

$$d([x,y],z) = \min [d(x,z),d(y,z)]$$

where $[x,y]$ is an existing cluster, and z is a third point

(ii) the maximum ('diameter' or 'complete link') method:

$$d([x,y],z) = \max [d(x,z),d(y,z)]$$

The first method tends to produce 'chaining' (i.e. the repeated addition of single points to a cluster) and often produces less interpretable solutions than the second method.

Other methods have been proposed which are compromises between the minimum and maximum methods (see Jardine and Sibson 1971: 53), but the solutions obtained are not unique under monotone transformations of the data.

T.3.7 Testing Euclidean distance and hierarchical model assumptions

The similarity ratings data of each subject were tested to investigate the extent to which they conformed to the triangle and ultrametric inequality assumptions of the (Euclidean) distance and hierarchical clustering models respectively.

The 560 triplets of the occupational similarity judgements of each subject were examined to detect infractions of the triangle inequality, and of the ultrametric inequality. In the case of the triangle inequality, only 3.6 per cent of triplets violated this condition. Individual percentages lay between zero and 18, and average (subject group) values varied only between two and five per cent and in no systematic fashion.

In the case of the ultrametric inequality, percentages were considerably higher, due, of course, to the greater stringency of this condition. The overall percentage was 39.23, individual values were between 6 and 63 per cent, but aggregate group differences were once more fairly trivial and unsystematic.

These results should be treated with considerable caution. Straight-forward tests of this sort, which operate directly on ratings, will generally display artificially high conformity to the inequality tests because the range of variation values is so highly restricted. Moreover, where judgements of *1* predominate, as is often the case in these data, the inequality conditions will be trivially satisfied in many triplets of points. None the less, there would seem to be an unacceptably high number of infractions of the ultra-metric inequality and any HCS analysis based on these data is therefore treated with considerable caution.

T.3.8 Aggregate pairwise summary statistics

Note on the use of the root mean square
When using the metric distance model to analyse these data, the assumption is made that the (dis)similarities are a linear function of distances in cognitive space. If this assumption is true, then it is better to use an average such as the RMS $(= \sum_i X_i^2 / N)^{1/2})$ which is based upon the squared rating values, since distances are not additive whereas squared distances are (see Young, 1975: 127). The arithmetic mean and the RMS are monotonically related, as can readily be seen (see Tables T.3.8.1 and 3.8.2).

T.3.9 Distance model: aggregate scaling analysis

The distance model asserts that the data (dissimilarities δ_{ij}) are a function of the distances (d_{ij}) separating the occupations in the cognitive space:

$$\delta_{ij} = F(d_{ij})$$
$$\text{where} \quad d_{ij} = (\sum_k |x_{ij} - x_{jk}|^r)^{1r}$$

The metric model assumes that the function F is linear and the non-metric model that it is only (weakly) monotonic.

In this analysis, a number of different algorithms and options were employed in order to test the stability of the eventual solution, but were

TABLE T.3.8.1   Similarity ratings data (DPB106AD): average ratings
(Upper figure: arithmetic mean
Lower figure: root mean square)

	MIN (1)	CST (2)	QA (3)	CA (4)	MPN (5)	AD (6)	BSL (7)	MTO (8)	SOL (9)	CSE (10)	CT (11)	PM (12)	C (13)	LD (14)	RP (15)	BM (16)
1. (MIN)	—															
2. CST	5.53 (2.35)	—														
3. QA	4.02 (2.01)	4.43 (2.10)	—													
4. CA	4.05 (2.01)	4.47 (2.11)	6.93 (2.63)	—												
5. MPN	4.44 (2.11)	4.53 (2.13)	2.92 (1.71)	2.65 (1.63)	—											
6. AD	3.20 (1.79)	2.76 (1.66)	2.09 (1.45)	2.01 (1.42)	5.13 (2.27)	—										
7. BSL	1.63 (1.28)	1.70 (1.30)	1.46 (1.21)	1.50 (1.22)	2.25 (1.50)	3.01 (1.74)	—									
8. MTO	1.93 (1.39)	2.57 (1.60)	2.11 (1.45)	2.16 (1.47)	2.71 (1.65)	3.25 (1.80)	4.23 (2.06)	—								
9. SOL	5.06 (2.25)	4.63 (2.15)	5.87 (2.42)	6.30 (2.51)	3.14 (1.77)	2.33 (1.53)	1.59 (1.26)	2.00 (1.41)	—							
10. CSE	4.43 (2.11)	4.89 (2.21)	6.10 (2.47)	6.23 (2.50)	3.09 (1.76)	2.35 (1.53)	1.47 (1.21)	2.05 (1.43)	5.71 (2.39)	—						
11. CT	2.91 (1.71)	3.10 (1.76)	2.98 (1.72)	3.28 (1.81)	2.81 (1.68)	3.88 (1.97)	2.50 (1.58)	2.86 (1.69)	3.03 (1.74)	3.06 (1.75)	—					
12. PM	4.27 (2.07)	4.27 (2.07)	2.81 (1.68)	2.90 (1.70)	4.67 (2.16)	5.17 (2.27)	2.47 (1.57)	2.78 (1.67)	4.18 (2.04)	3.69 (1.92)	3.26 (1.81)	—				
13. C	2.28 (1.51)	2.63 (1.62)	2.12 (1.45)	2.25 (1.50)	2.75 (1.66)	3.20 (1.79)	5.03 (2.24)	6.02 (2.45)	2.19 (1.48)	2.13 (1.46)	2.90 (1.70)	3.00 (1.73)	—			
14. LD	1.74 (1.32)	1.83 (1.35)	1.70 (1.30)	1.63 (1.28)	2.33 (1.53)	6.18 (2.49)	5.38 (2.32)	4.25 (2.06)	1.76 (1.33)	1.68 (1.30)	4.87 (2.21)	3.01 (1.74)	3.72 (1.93)	—		
15. RP	1.93 (1.39)	1.85 (1.36)	1.47 (1.25)	1.57 (1.25)	2.32 (1.52)	4.00 (2.00)	5.93 (2.43)	3.54 (1.88)	1.60 (1.26)	1.77 (1.33)	2.98 (1.73)	3.15 (1.77)	3.29 (1.81)	5.25 (2.29)	—	
16. BM	2.07 (1.44)	2.13 (1.46)	1.73 (1.32)	1.89 (1.38)	2.71 (1.65)	2.91 (1.70)	3.85 (1.96)	3.17 (1.78)	1.97 (1.40)	1.84 (1.36)	3.91 (1.98)	2.97 (1.72)	3.22 (1.80)	3.82 (1.95)	4.40 (2.10)	—

TABLE T.3.8.2 Similarity ratings data (DPB106AD): standard deviations

(Upper figure: standard deviation
Lower figure: number of cases)

	MIN (1)	CST (2)	QA (3)	CA (4)	MPN (5)	AD (6)	BSL (7)	MTO (8)	SOL (9)	CSE (10)	CT (11)	PM (12)	C (13)	LD (14)	RP (15)	BM (16)
1. (MIN)	–															
2. CST	2.28 (287)	–														
3. QA	2.41 (285)	2.23 (284)	–													
4. CA	2.25 (286)	2.27 (284)	2.03 (285)	–												
5. MPN	2.24 (285)	2.21 (286)	1.98 (286)	1.75 (286)	–											
6. AD	2.10 (287)	1.74 (286)	1.47 (286)	1.31 (286)	2.13 (286)	–										
7. BSL	1.28 (287)	1.17 (287)	1.05 (286)	1.09 (286)	1.67 (284)	2.03 (287)	–									
8. MTO	1.37 (286)	1.75 (287)	1.53 (286)	1.56 (287)	1.95 (286)	2.10 (286)	2.27 (286)	–								
9. SOL	2.39 (285)	2.22 (286)	2.09 (285)	1.95 (287)	1.88 (286)	1.49 (287)	1.21 (287)	1.44 (287)	–							
10. CSE	2.27 (286)	2.19 (285)	1.99 (286)	2.11 (285)	2.01 (285)	1.54 (287)	1.00 (286)	1.44 (285)	2.12 (286)	–						
11. CT	1.84 (286)	1.81 (287)	1.87 (286)	1.88 (286)	1.92 (287)	2.07 (286)	1.73 (286)	1.86 (285)	1.72 (285)	1.81 (187)	–					
12. PM	2.26 (286)	2.10 (287)	1.79 (286)	1.85 (286)	2.30 (286)	2.20 (285)	1.69 (286)	1.93 (285)	2.08 (286)	2.02 (287)	2.08 (286)	–				
13. C	1.60 (286)	1.69 (287)	1.43 (185)	1.53 (285)	1.95 (285)	2.10 (286)	2.32 (286)	2.09 (285)	1.67 (286)	1.58 (287)	1.96 (287)	2.07 (286)	–			
14. LD	1.25 (285)	1.11 (286)	1.32 (286)	1.10 (286)	1.68 (285)	2.03 (286)	2.26 (286)	2.37 (286)	1.27 (286)	1.10 (287)	2.25 (286)	1.85 (286)	2.32 (286)	–		
15. RP	1.48 (286)	1.19 (286)	1.01 (287)	1.09 (287)	1.58 (287)	2.23 (287)	2.43 (286)	2.20 (287)	0.97 (287)	1.22 (287)	1.90 (286)	1.84 (287)	2.09 (285)	2.27 (286)	–	
16. BM	1.68 (284)	1.50 (287)	1.25 (285)	1.34 (286)	1.96 (286)	2.05 (286)	2.51 (287)	2.13 (286)	1.45 (287)	1.27 (285)	2.26 (286)	1.90 (286)	2.18 (286)	2.47 (285)	2.50 (287)	–

found to give virtually identical results. The solutions reported were obtained from Young's Polynomial Conjoint Analysis (POLYCON) program. The input data in each case were the RMS average ratings.

A. Metric analysis

The solution was obtained in 5 to 1 dimensions, by means of the classic Young-Torgerson metric procedure (Torgerson 1958) and Roskam's (1968) MRSCAL procedure. The main analysis was in terms of the Euclidean metric, since tests in·city-block ($r=1$) and dominance ($r=32$) metrics produced considerably higher overall badness-of-fit measures.

For purposes of comparison with the non-metric analysis, the stress values are as shown in Table T.3.9.1.

TABLE T.3.9.1.   Metric distance model solution to aggregate occupational similarities data

Dimension	$Stress_1$	$Stress_2$
5	.099	.342
4	.121	.387
3	.145	.426
2	.199	.501
1	.291	.584

	Two-dimensional solution (rotated to principal components)	
	Dimension	
Occupational title	I	II
MIN	643	−416
CST	611	−099
QA	557	352
CA	824	459
MPN	170	−564
AD	−356	−609
BSL	−1000	213
MTO	−536	462
SOL	790	087
CSE	803	101
CT	−078	138
PM	094	−460
C	−472	421
LD	−862	007
RP	−884	−154
BM	−604	064
	(coordinate values x 1000)	

(In Figure T.3.2 this configuration has been rotated to maximum conformity with the INDSCAL solution presented in T.3.14.)

B. Non-metric analysis

The solution was obtained in 5 to 1 dimensions, by means of Roskam's MINISSA-1 (Lingoes and Roskam 1973) and POLYCON. In the latter case, various minimisation options were employed, but none produced significant improvement on the Young-Torgerson quasi-nonmetric initial configuration, followed by the Young-Torgerson linear gradients method, using Kruskal's (1964a) least squares transformation, minimising $stress_2$, and adopting the secondary approach to ties. Badness-of-fit values were as shown in Table T.3.9.2.

TABLE T.3.9.2.   Nonmetric distance model solution to aggregate occupational similarities data

Dimension	$Stress_1$	$Stress_2$
5	.024	.051
4	.030	.094
3	.043	.117
2	.066	.158
1	.100	.201

The two-dimensional configuration (rotated to principal components) is:

Occupational Title	Dimension I	Dimension II
MIN	605	−350
CST	604	−224
QA	824	215
CA	777	303
MPN	223	−515
AD	−340	−320
BSL	−1000	013
MTO	−520	450
SOL	745	140
CSE	770	067
CT	024	201
PM	104	−158
C	−519	355
DD	−774	−126
RP	−838	−169
BM	−684	−119

(In Figure T.3.2 this configuration has been rotated to maximum conformity with the INDSCAL solution presented in T.3.14.)

The Shepard diagram, relating the distances in this solution to the original data, is presented in Figure T.3.1.

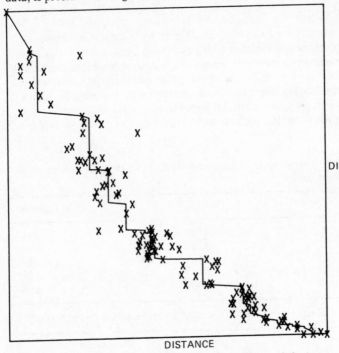

Fig. T.3.1 Shepard diagram: 2D non-metric PB data dolution

T.3.10 Determination of underlying dimensionality

The methods used to determine appropriate dimensionality typically proceed as follows:

(i)   Define a 'true' configuration of n points in r dimensions
(ii) Introduce random error in differing amounts (usually sampled from a normal distribution, although there are differences in how the variance is defined (see Isaac and Poor 1974), and add to each coordinate.
(iii) The distances between the points of this 'error-perturbed configuration' are then scaled in a range of dimensions.

The method and program (M-SPACE) developed by Spence and Graef (1974) assumes that the user has obtained a set of five $stress_1$ values from scaling his empirical proximity matrix in 5 through 1 dimensions, and these values are compared to those obtained by scaling configurations involving the same number of points of known dimensionality and having known amounts of error, derived from the simulation studies.

(To date, simulation data exist only for stress$_1$ values for non-metric Euclidean distance model analyses of square symmetric proximity matrices.)

For the averaged similarity data, the results of comparing the five stress$_1$ values with the simulation studies values are as follows:

A. Non-metric solution (16 points)

Scaling of Aggregate Occupational Similarities data Stress$_1$ values		Simulation data (M-SPACE) Stress$_1$ values corresponding to scaling 16 point configurations with 'True' Dimensionality of:			
		1	2	3	4
1-D:	.100	.088	.297	.288	.306
2-D:	.066	.068	.013	.126	.139
3-D:	.043	.049	.010	0	.044
4-D:	.030	.039	.007	0	0
5-D:	.024	.032	.006	0	0
At error level		18%	3%	0%	0%
Fit index:		8.3	93.2	97.9	99.2
		best fit			

(corresponding to 'true' dimensionality of 1)

*B. Metric solution**

Scaling of Aggregate Occupational Similarities data Stress$_1$		M-SPACE *simulation data corresponding to 'True' Dimensionality of:*			
		1	2	3	4
1-D:	.291	.305	.372	.372	.398
2-D:	.199	.196	.187	.192	.198
3-D:	.145	.136	.128	.116	.115
4-D:	.121	.097	.091	.082	.077
5-D:	.099	.072	.068	.061	.057
At error level		66%	53%	46%	37%
Fit Index		17.9	41.9	45.8	56.7
		best fit			

*These values are presented for illustrative purposes only. M-SPACE values assume a *non-metric* distance model.

T.3.11 Triadic similarities scaling

Scaling solutions for triadic similarities data were obtained by using a version of Roskam's MINI-TRI program (see Roskam 1969, 1970), generalised by M.J. Prentice to accommodate both 'global' and 'local' stress (see below) and implemented in the MDS (X) series as the TRISOSCAL program.

A. Algorithms

The scaling solution to the aggregate data (obtained by combining all the triads of all the subjects) was obtained using the same procedure as Roskam's, but individual sets of data were scaled separately under the option STRESS-TYPE = 1 of TRISOSCAL, which imposes stronger constraints on the data. The main differences between the procedures can be illustrated as follows:

Consider a situation involving the two triads (ABC) and (BCD):

(i)   Suppose that in *ABC* the pair *AB* are judged most similar and the pair *BC* least similar. This implies the following rank order of similarities $AB > AC > BC$

(ii) Suppose that in *BCD*, *BC* are judged most similar and *BD* least similar. This implies $BC > CD > BD$

Taken together, (i) and (ii) imply the overall, or 'global' rank order: $AB > AC > BC > CD > BD$.

The difference between the two approaches hinges upon whether the attempt is made to fit the full ('global') implied rank order, or only the separate ('local') rank orders.

(I) *Roskam's 'local stress' approach* (used for the aggregated data)
In Roskam's procedure, the purpose of scaling triadic data is to fit the rank order of similarities, but only *within* each triad. No attempt is made to invoke transitivity of order relations between triads and fit a 'global' rank order.

The basic raw loss-function (stress) which is minimised in non-metric scaling has the form:

$$L = \sum_{ij} (d_{ij} - d_{ij}^O)^2$$

where d_{ij} is the distance between the point x_i and x_j in the solution space, and d_{ij}^O is a fitting value which is order-isomorphic with the data, that is, satisfies the constraints implied by the rank order of pairs of stimuli. In Roskam's approach there are as many d_{ij}^O values as there are occurrences of the pair (i,j) in the data, each satisfying the constraints of a different triad rank order. (In the example above, there will be *two* fitting values representing the pair *BC*). In order to reconcile these different values, Roskam suggests that L should be minimised for the *average* fitting-value, $\bar{d}_{ij}^O$, and the loss function then becomes:

$$L = \sum_{ij} n_{ij} (d_{ij} - \bar{d}_{ij}^O)^2$$

where n_{ij} is the number of times that the pair (ij) occurs in the set of triads to be analysed.

Such an averaging procedure imposes rather weak constraints on the consistency of the data, and since it does not require transitivity between triads a 'good' (i.e. low-stress) solution can be obtained even with highly inconsistent data. This is in fact an advantage when the data consist of a very large amount of similarities data, or are drawn from a number of individuals. In such a case, it is quite likely that inconsistent triadic similarity judgements (e.g. both $AB > AC > BD$ and $BD > AC > AB$) will occur. An averaging procedure is a reasonable way of dealing with what would be a large number of inconsistent data if separate fitting values for each triad were not allowed. Indeed, when the aggregate data were required to satisfy *global* consistency, stress$_1$ values in excess of 0.95 were frequently encountered.

(II) *Prentice's 'global stress' approach* (used for individual's data)
For the individual solutions presented in Section 3.21 the 'global stress' approach was employed, which *does* require transitivity between triads (requiring for instance that the rank order $AB > AC > BC > CD > BD$ in the example be fitted by a sequence of values in the same order).

Where a large number of inconsistencies occur in the data, the weak monotonicity criterion can often impose a single fitting value on a high proportion of pairs involved. For example, given the four triadic data $\{ABC\}$, $\{BCD\}$, $\{CDA\}$, $\{DAB\}$, (where $\{ABC\}$ means AB is judged most similar followed by BC, and AC is judged least similar), the program imposes the following constraint on the fitting values:

$$AB \leqslant BC, BC \leqslant AC, BC \leqslant CD, CD \leqslant BD, CD \leqslant AD, AD \leqslant AC,$$
$$AD \leqslant AB, AB \leqslant BD$$

which can only be satisfied by: $AB \geqslant AB = BC = CD = AD \geqslant BD$.

Thus analyses of data sets with a large number of intransitivities between triads lead to the degeneracies in the form of fitting values which assume only a small number of values. If all the pairs are involved in intransitivities, *all* the fitting values assume the same value. This actually happened when all the available triadic data were scaled under the global stress option.

The main advantage of the TRISOSCAL algorithm is that for the price of its intolerance of intransitivity, it imposes much stronger constraints on a small set of data (e.g. a $\lambda = 2$ balanced design), thus generating a more stable and rigidly defined configuration.

B. Definitions of local and global stress

Global stress
Roskam (1970, p. 414-15) shows that, under the assumptions of 'local' constraints, the 'total' stress$_1$ value may be partitioned into 'between' stress$_1$ (the deviation of the configuration distances from the averaged fitting

values) and 'within' stress$_1$ (deviation of the average fitting values from the actual triadic fitting values). Roskam's 'total' stress$_1$, it should be emphasised, represents only the deviation from *within-triads* rank orders, and must be interpreted as such.

In the case of 'global' constraints, there is only one fitting value for each pair, and 'global' stress$_1$ may be expressed as:

$$\text{Global stress (1)} = GS_1 = \left(\frac{\sum\limits_{i,j} n_{ij}(d_{ij} - d_{ij}^O)^2}{\sum\limits_{i,j} n_{ij} d_{ij}^2} \right)^{1/2}$$

where n_{ij} is the frequency of pair (ij).

Roskam's 'local' stress$_1$ must be interpreted differently from Kruskal's since it is based on an 'unconnected' set of short rank-orders, but 'global' stress$_1$ is based on what is probably an 'overconnected' partial order, in the sense that the transitivity constraints are probably too demanding.

In the limiting case, no matter how many times in a data set each pair occurs, if one occurrence of each pair is involved in an intransitivity, global stress will reach its limiting value of one since all the d_{ij}^O will take on the same value, $\bar{d}_{ij}$. In general, if one occurrence of a particular pair is involved in an intransitivity, the d^O for that pair will be merged with the others involved.

C. Stress values for TRISOSCAL scaling of aggregated triadic data sets

(1) *All Triads* ($n = 1866$)

	Roskam Local Stress		
Solution in	*'Within'*	*'Between'*	*'Total'*
5 Dimensions	0.0550	0.0226	0.0594
4 Dimensions	0.0642	0.0248	0.0688
3 Dimensions	0.0808	0.0326	0.0871
2 Dimensions	0.1028	0.0466	0.1129
1 Dimension	0.1715	0.1055	0.2013

(2) *'Construct' Triads* ($n = 1032$)

	Roskam Local Stress		
Solution in	*'Within'*	*'Between'*	*'Total'*
5 Dimensions	0.0484	0.0192	0.0520
4 Dimensions	0.0560	0.0230	0.0606
3 Dimensions	0.0762	0.0351	0.0839
2 Dimensions	0.0947	0.0433	0.1041
1 Dimension	0.1634	0.1062	0.1948

T.3.12 The INDSCAL model

A.Basic model

According to the INDSCAL model, the main source of individual differences in perception and cognition is the differential relative importance (salience, sensitivity, attention, or weight) ascribed by subjects to the dimensions of their perceptual world (see Tucker 1960; Jackson and Messick 1963). Like the ordinary MDS model, INDSCAL assumes that every subject *i* has the freedom to rescale or weight each dimension of the common Group Space differently, thus producing a 'private space', **Y**, consisting of the Group Space, **X**, rescaled in his own subjective metric:

$$y_{ja}^{(i)} = w_{ia}^{\frac{1}{2}} x_{ja} \tag{1}$$

Within the subject's private space, the conventional MDS distance model holds:

$$\delta_{jk}^{(i)} = F(d_{jk}^{(i)})$$

with the Euclidean distance defined in the usual way:

$$d_{jk}^{(i)} = \{ \sum_a (y_{ja}^{(i)} - y_{ka}^{(i)})^2 \}^{\frac{1}{2}} \tag{2}$$

If (1) is substituted into (2) then this yields a more general, weighted, Euclidean distance model, referred to as a common Group Stimulus Space **X**:

$$d_{jk}^{(i)} = \{ \sum_a w_{ia} (x_{ja} - x_{ka})^2 \}^{\frac{1}{2}}$$

The weights, w_{ia}, thus represent a type of differential sensitivity of individual *i* to dimension *a*, for if it is small, then changes along dimension *a* will contribute relatively little to the distances in his private space. Thus, individual differences are parameterised by individual sets of 'importance weights' for the dimensions of a common space.

B. Estimation procedures

The (metric) INDSCAL estimation methods proceed as follows (see Carroll and Chang 1970 and Carroll and Wish 1974a):
(i) input (dis)similarities are converted to estimated absolute Euclidean distances, by addition of the smallest constant, *c,* ensuring maximal satisfaction of the triangle inequality:

$$d_{jk}^{(i)} = \delta_{jk}^{(i)} + c^{(i)}$$

where $\qquad\qquad c^{(i)} = \max_{(j,k,l)} \; (\delta_{jl} - \delta_{jk} - \delta_{kl})$

(ii) distances are converted into scalar products by double centring the squared distance matrix, whose entries in terms of coordinate values are:

$$b_{jk} = \sum_a x_{ja} x_{ka}$$

For each subject i, therefore

$$b_{jk}^{(i)} = \sum_a y_{ja}^{(i)} y_{ka}^{(i)} \qquad\qquad (4)$$

and substituting the definition of the $y^{(i)}$ values given in (1) above into (4) yields the weighted inner product form of INDSCAL:

$$b_{jk}^{(i)} = \sum_a w_{ij} x_{ka} + e_{ijk}$$

(iii) The estimation of the subject weights (**W**) and coordinate values (**X**) proceeds by minimising $\sum_i \sum_j \sum_k e_{ijk}^2$ over the free parameters w_{ia} and x_{ja} by means of a Non-linear Iterative Least Squares procedure described in Carroll and Chang (1970). Subsequently Schönemann (1972) has provided an exact algebraic solution to subjective metric models, including INDSCAL, which is unique for error-free data satisfying the representational conditions he devises. More recent developments include Carroll and Chang's (1974) development of a fully non-metric version, De Leeuw's (1974) suggestions for improving the minimisation process and extending it to non-metric data, and Bloxom's (1974) exploitation of Jöreskog's generalised covariance method (ACOVS) to improve convergence.
(iv) An important property claimed for INDSCAL is its rotational invariance, or dimensional uniqueness, meaning that the solution is unique up to a permutation of axes, followed by a diagonal transformation. Because of the normalising conventions employed (origin of the space at the centroid of the stimulus space configuration, and unit scaling of the squared projections on each dimension), permissible transformations are restricted to permutation of axes and reflection of dimensions for all but a very limited set of conditions (see Carroll and Wish 1974a, p. 92).

The uniqueness may be interpreted geometrically or statistically. It can be shown that each angle of rotation of the INDSCAL axes produces set of distances which are different in each case, and any rotation leads to a solution where less variance in the data will be accounted for (Carroll and Wish 1974a, p. 63). Whilst Schönemann (1972, p. 443) has rightly questioned the implications that rotationally invariant dimensions will be psychologically meaningful, it is usually found that INDSCAL dimensions are readily interpretable.

T.3.13 Selection of balanced set of data for initial analysis by INDSCAL

Similarities data exist for 287 cases. Of these, 38 have one missing datum, 13 have between two and seven missing data, and one case has 44 missing data (due to his turning over two pages of the schedule at once). This last case was excluded entirely from further analysis.

In 29 cases two-thirds or more judgements consisted of 1s (totally dissimilar), and in 18 cases the proportion was three-quarters or more.

A. *'Population' Definition*

In constructing a frame for producing the balanced set sample, it was decided to exclude from consideration:
(i)   Subjects from 'supplementary' occupations (see *Images*, Table 3.2)
(ii)   Cases having *more than* one missing datum
(iii)   Cases having *more than* three-quarters of the judgements in the '1' category
(these are not mutually exclusive conditions).
This produces the 'population' frame of 108 cases shown in Table T.3.13.1 (e.g. Table 3.2 of *Images* (p. 69)).

TABLE 3.13.1   Population of subjects for INDSCAL analysis

QUADRANT A (N = 36)	**QUADRANT B** (N = 27)
Clergymen (19) Teachers (17)	Qualified actuaries (17) Chartered accountants (10)
QUADRANT C (N = 20)	**QUADRANT D** (N = 25)
Male nurses (3) Ambulance drivers (11) Policemen (6)	Engineers (15) Joiners-Fitters (10)

(N = 108)

B. *Sampling*

Sample size was set at 17 in each quadrant, and subjects were sampled (without replacement) by means of pseudo-random numbers drawn from a rectangular distribution.

C. *Data modification*

Eight cases had one missing datum. The modal judgement value was substituted in each case.

T.3.14 INDSCAL solutions to the balanced set of similarities data

The INDSCAL program requires a random number to act as 'seed' in generating the initial configuration. Previous experience had indicated that although the overall measures of goodness of fit (between input data and fitted values) seemed independent of the initial configuration, the orientation of axes, and extent of their correlation sometimes differed quite substantially from run to run. Indeed, the configuration presented in Coxon and Jones (1974a) was subsequently found to be suboptimal and different orientations of the axes occurred in later runs.

In order to ensure greater stability, a large number of runs were made under a range of options, to check the consistency of the configuration finally accepted.

In all initial runs, option parameters were set as follows:

ITERATIONS	(maximum number of iterations permitted) = 15
CRITERION	(threshold in improvement in fit to terminate iterative computation) = .001
SET MATRICES = 1	(ensuring equivalence of stimulus coordinates, i.e. INDSCAL analysis)
SOLUTIONS = 0	(simultaneous solution of all dimensions)

The sequence of INDSCAL runs (with different random number starters) was as follows:

(i) 6 runs were made in 5 to 3 dimensions (goodness-of-fit values for the 5-dimensional solutions lay between .810 and .815)
4 runs in 4 to 2 dimensions (.787 to .794)
4 runs in 3 and 2 dimensions (.761 to .764)

Whilst there were no very major differences between Group Space configurations, the orientation of axes and relative positioning of several points changed from solution to solution, although the goodness-of-fit values (overall correlation between data and fitted values) varied very little.

The 4-dimensional solution which had a goodness-of-fit value considerably better than others and a configuration most similar to the other solutions was selected as the optimal solution.

(ii) This solution was then run in 3 and 2 dimensions, with a higher number of iterations and a lower cut-off criterion (ITERATIONS = 25 and CRITERION = .0005) to produce an improved fit. The resulting 3-dimension solution was accepted as the final configuration, and is given in T.3.15.

(iii) A solution was obtained with SOLUTIONS = 1. This produces an INDSC analysis where the dimensions are estimated *successively* in a way which ensures that the Group space coordinates are as close to being uncorrelated as possible, although it is somewhat less general than the simultaneous solution. The Group Space configuration turned out to be very similar to the simultaneous solution. It differs only in locating Carpenter and Machine Tool Operator close to Building Site Labourer on the second dimension, reflecting the unstable location of these two points noted in the aggregate analysis.

It is also worth noting that the one-dimensional solution has an overall goodness-of-fit correlation of .648, with .722, .762, .790 and .812 as the successive values for 2 to 5 dimensional solutions.

T.3.15 Individual differences scaling of occupational similarities data: stimulus space configurations

Occupational title	Dimension I	II	III	Dimension I	II
MIN	0.22135	0.28210	0.07400	0.21956	0.26282
CST	0.21557	0.22575	−0.05887	0.21418	0.13723
QA	0.34556	−0.20751	0.02325	0.34622	−0.13856
CA	0.35344	−0.23087	−0.02437	0.35481	−0.19245
MPN	0.00215	0.47642	0.14783	0.00082	0.43871
AD	−0.23386	0.30599	0.31064	−0.23284	0.39423
BSL	−0.30355	−0.32675	−0.24138	−0.30494	−0.36192
MTO	−0.17601	0.03456	−0.55049	−0.17601	−0.30853
SOL	0.32113	−0.05273	0.07830	0.32143	0.00758
CSE	0.32355	−0.09872	0.06026	0.32369	−0.03411
CT	−0.05049	−0.14512	0.22699	−0.04825	0.01362
PM	−0.02250	0.37103	0.19691	−0.02261	0.38020
C	−0.14018	0.06021	−0.60381	−0.14041	−0.32160
LD	−0.32963	−0.17228	0.14487	−0.32768	−0.05369
RP	−0.31123	−0.30402	0.08210	−0.31183	−0.15945
BM	−0.21529	−0.21806	0.13377	−0.21614	−0.06407

Three-dimensional INDSCAL *solution* *Two-dimensional* INDSCAL *solution*

Summary of overall INDSCAL *measures of goodness of fit, and correlation between axes – simultaneous solution of 'balanced set'*

	3-dimensional solution	2-dimensional solution
A. Goodness of fit measures		
1. Correlation between data and fitted (predicted) similarities	0.765	0.722

T.3.15 *continued*

	3-dimensional solution	2-dimensional solution
2. Percentage of variance accounted for by INDSCAL solution	58.45%	52.09%
3. Average subject correlation	0.758	0.714

B. *Correlations between dimensions*

3D: 1 1.000
    2 0.120 1.000
    3 0.112 0.148 1.000

2D: 1 1.000
    2 0.153 1.000

The two-dimensional MINISSA solution, rotated into maximum conformity with the first two dimensions of the INDSCAL solution is presented in Figure T.3.3.

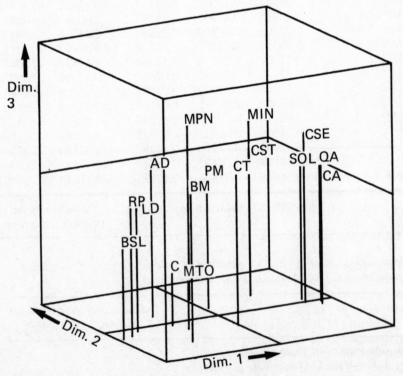

Fig. T.3.2 Three-dimensional INDSCAL solution

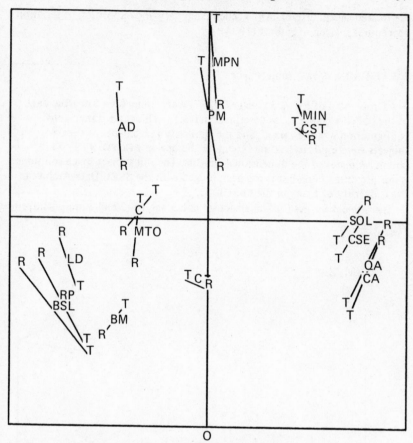

Fig. T.3.3 First two dimensions of the non-metric solution rotated into maximum conformity with the INDSCAL solution

(T = Target (INDSCAL) location; R = MINISSA rotated location)

T.3.16 Seriation and metrics

The occurrence of essentially one-dimensional, but non-linear, configurations embedded in higher-space non-metric MDS solutions has also been commented on by van de Geer (1971, pp. 239-42) and at some length by Shepard (1974, pp. 385 *et seq.*).

Kendall (1972, p. 225) points out that the type of similarities which produce systematic distortions of linear sequences tend to include a large number of very low similarities, and conform to the so-called 'bounded metric'. Such a (Lie-group) metric is topologically equivalent to the Euclidean metric when two objects are sufficiently close, but *all* distances beyond a certain level are treated as equidistant. An excellent summary and exposition of seriation procedures is given in Hubert (1974).

T.3.17 The INDSCAL subject space

The Group Map of Fig. 3.3 (*Images,* p. 77) was obtained by using the data of the 68 'core' subjects, as described in T.3.13. This three-dimensional configuration was then fixed, and the similarity judgements of the 286 subjects were input to INDSCAL (under the option FIX POINTS =1) to obtain estimates of the dimensional weights. The full subject space solutions is not presented here, but it has been lodged with the SSRC Data Archive at the University of Essex in file PBSUBDC.

The Subject Spaces for Dimensions 1 and 3 and for 2 and 3 are portrayed below.

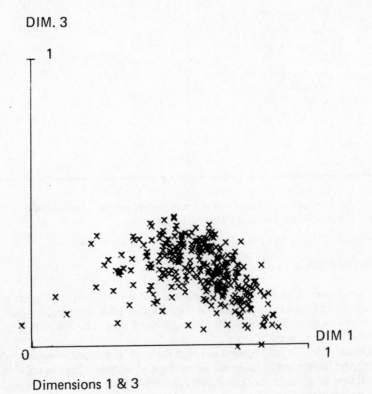

Dimensions 1 & 3

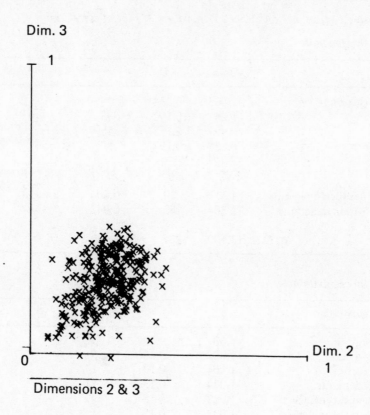

Dim. 3

Dim. 2

Dimensions 2 & 3

Fig. T.3.4 INDSCAL subject space

There are three occurrences of negative weights, all of which are close to zero. Two occur for dimension III (−.010 and −.007), and one for dimension I (−.032). In this last case, the subject's data are singularly ill-fit by this model (or any distance model), and are discussed further under the heading of 'deviant cases'. In the other two cases the subject's data are very well fit, and the values may be taken as equivalent to zero weights.

T.3.18 Goodness-of-fit analysis: individual correlations (INDSCAL 3-D solution)

Analysis of variance on Fisher's Z-transform of subject correlations

A. *By Quadrant*

		Mean	S.D.	n
Quadrant:	A	1.003	0.234	95
	B	1.062	0.192	83
	C	0.991	0.175	48
	D	0.839	0.197	60

	SS	df	MSQ	F
Between quadrants	1.815	3	0.605	14.358
Within quadrants	11.884	282	0.042	
TOTAL	13.699	285		$(p \ll .001)$

B. *By occupation*

Occupation

	Mean	S.D.	n
Clergy	1.007	0.229	32
Teachers	1.002	0.250	51
Actuaries	1.104	0.191	17
Accountants	1.024	0.136	11
Chemical engineers	1.027	0.181	22
Electrical engineers	1.092	0.185	16
Business students	1.064	0.244	17
Nurses	1.069	0.132	19
Ambulance drivers	0.910	0.168	16
Police	0.977	0.198	13
Engineers/Fitters	0.836	0.201	55

	SS	df	MSQ	F
Between occupations	2.071	10	0.207	4.830
Within occupations	11.063	258	0.043	
TOTAL	13.134	268		$(p < .001)$

Note: This excludes Journalists and Printers, whose numbers are too small for stable estimates to be made.

T.3.19 Similarities data badly fit by the INDSCAL model

ID	(1) UMI	(2) TI	(3) 1s	(4) Stress$_1$	Comment
6740	.55	.09	18	.245	Worst fit; negative weight
6729	.58	.08	41	.157	
4243	.54	.13	24	.243	
4235	.50	.12	2	.211	Circular configuration, centred on RP, BSL
6701	.59	.10	5	.210	Displacement of C
6730	.53	.17	18	.183	
J271	.63	.05	7	.157	Displacement of CST
4170	.55	.07	0	.171	Displacement of MIN and CSE
4242	.05	.00	112	.000	Degenerate; isolates BM
M136	.06	.00	107	.000	Degenerate; isolates BM and C
4174	.45	.02	48	.186	
4135	.19	.03	95	.010	Degenerate; isolates BM
AVERAGE	.39	.04		.080	

Cols: (1) Ultrametric inequality value
(2) Triangle inequality value
(3) Number of 1s in data
(4) Stress$_1$ value of individual MDS scaling

T.3.20 Multivariate Analysis of Variance of INDSCAL Subject Weights

In this appendix, we present analysis of variance tables which show significant differences in the averaged similarity judgements of occupational sub-groups. The cognition of each individual was summarised by his judgements of overall similarity for all pairs of 16 occupations. These similarity judgements were in turn summarised in terms of the INDSCAL model (see above). In sum, each individual's cognitive biases are summarised by the three INDSCAL weights, and by the relationships between those weights.

For reasons discussed in Chapter 3 of *Images* (and also by MacCallum 1977), it is desirable to analyse the *ratios* of the INDSCAL weights, rather than the weights themselves. This makes the test one of the *relative* salience of dimensions to any individual. The distribution of ratios of weights is markedly skew (positively). This was corrected to some extent by making a logarithmic transformation of the weight ratios.

TABLE T.3.20.1   Multivariate analysis of variance of INDSCAL subject weights

A. For 11 occupational groups

	INDSCAL Dimensions						
	I		II		III		
Occupational Groups	Mean	S.D.	Mean	S.D.	Mean	S.D.	*n*
1. Clergy	0.61	0.18	0.28	0.09	0.25	0.10	32
2. Teachers	0.63	0.16	0.25	0.08	0.25	0.10	51
3. Actuaries	0.67	0.12	0.26	0.07	0.26	0.12	17
4. Accountants	0.66	0.09	0.27	0.10	0.23	0.09	11
5. Nurses	0.67	0.09	0.28	0.07	0.24	0.09	19
6. Ambulance drivers	0.57	0.11	0.29	0.07	0.27	0.08	16
7. Police	0.58	0.14	0.31	0.08	0.28	0.07	13
8. Chem. engineers	0.65	0.12	0.25	0.10	0.22	0.10	22
9. Elect. engineers	0.68	0.12	0.26	0.10	0.23	0.09	16
10. Engineers, Fitters	0.51	0.13	0.30	0.09	0.27	0.07	55
11. Business students	0.68	0.14	0.23	0.06	0.21	0.10	17
TOTAL	0.61	(0.14)	0.27	(0.08)	0.25	(0.09)	269

MANOVA   H1: For equality of dispersions, $F_{60,25803} = 1.920$ ($p < .01$)

H2: For equality of centroids, $F_{30,752} = 2.140$ ($p < .01$); $\eta = .46$

(Univariate ANOVA:

Dimension I: $F_{10,258} = 5.42, p < .01$

Dimension II: $F \quad\quad = 1.90, p < .05$

Dimension III: $F \quad\quad = 1.23$, n.s.   )

B. For 4 quadrants

*Quadrants**						
A	0.62	0.16	0.27	0.09	0.25	0.10
B	0.67	0.12	0.25	0.09	0.23	0.10
C	0.61	0.12	0.29	0.07	0.26	0.08
D	0.51	0.13	0.30	0.08	0.27	0.07

*See Table 3.2 (*Images*, p. 69)

MANOVA   H1: $F_{18,169106} = 3.373$ ($p < .01$)

H2: $F_{9,681} = 5.690$ ($p < .01$); $\eta = .40$

(Univariate ANOVA:

Dimension I: $F_{3,282} = 16.23$ ($p < .01$)

Dimension II: $F \quad\quad = 4.04$ ($p < .01$)

Dimension III: $F \quad\quad = 2.91$ ($p < .05$)   )

TABLE T.3.20.2 Multivariate analysis of variance of logarithmic transformation of ratios of subject weights

In order to normalise the variance of the distributions, the natural logarithm of the weight ratios was taken. A constant of 2 was added to make all values positive.

A. For 11 occupational groups

	Log. Ratios of Weights + 2					
	I/II		I/III		II/III	
Occupational Group	Mean*	S.D.	Mean*	S.D.	Mean*	S.D.
1. Clergy	2.76	0.70	2.93	0.71	2.17	0.44
2. Teachers	2.90	0.53	3.02	0.85	2.12	0.75
3. Actuaries	2.97	0.50	3.08	0.69	2.11	0.46
4. Accountants	2.99	0.62	3.14	0.64	2.15	0.38
5. Nurses	2.88	0.37	3.09	0.56	2.21	0.38
6. Ambulance drivers	2.67	0.35	2.79	0.58	2.12	0.60
7. Police	2.62	0.40	2.72	0.49	2.11	0.27
8. Chem. engineers	3.01	0.59	3.18	0.73	2.17	0.47
9. Elect. engineers	3.02	0.54	3.13	0.57	2.11	0.32
10. Engineers/Fitters	2.54	0.51	2.62	0.41	2.08	0.40
11. Business students	3.11	0.44	3.30	0.68	2.19	0.51
TOTAL	2.82	0.53	2.95	0.65	2.13	0.51

*This is equivalent to the *geometric mean* of the ratios, plus the constant of 2.

MANOVA H_1 $F_{60,25803} = 1.89 \ (p < .01)$
       H_2 $F_{30,752} = 39.07 \ (p \ll .01) \ (\eta = .97)$

Univariate ANOVA
    I/II $F_{10,258}$ $= 3.34 \ (p < .01)$
    I/III $= 2.89 \ (p < .01)$
    II/III $= 0.20$ ns

B. For 4 quadrants

Quadrants	I/II		I/III		II/III	
A	2.85	0.60	2.99	0.79	2.14	0.65
B	3.00	0.55	3.14	0.65	2.14	0.41
C	2.74	0.38	2.89	0.56	2.15	0.44
D	2.54	0.51	2.62	0.41	2.08	0.40

MANOVA H_1 $F_{18,161429} = 2.978 \ (p < .01)$
       H_2 $F_{9,598} = 106.69 \ (p \ll .01) \ (\eta = .95)$

Univariate ANOVA
    I/II $F_{3,248}$ $= 7.94 \ (p < .01)$
    I/III $= 6.76 \ (p < .01)$
    II/III $= 0.31$ ns

T.3.21 Summaries of triadic similarities scalings of selected individuals' data

Case	Solution	Fit: Prentice Global Stress$_1$	Dimensional standard deviation			Main constructs employed
			DIM1	DIM2	DIM3	
6707	3D	.015	.689	.580	.436	Working with people
	2D	.053	.744	.668		Have/have not degree/further education.
	1D	.244				Drivers, have no manual skill.
6711	3D	.061	.668	.531	.520	Working with people (welfare, as individuals).
	2D	.098	.789	.602		With figures not people, manual, travelling.
	1D	.220				
6712	3D	.003	.799	.472	.374	Working with people (helping)
	2D	.011	.875	.487		Qualifications
	1D	.069				Law, drivers, builders.
6713	3D	.005	.685	.559	.468	Deal with people (problems)
	2D	.033	.756	.655		Training, skilled/ unskilled, manual
	1D	.163				Mobile
6715	3D	.011	.718	.573	.394	Need higher education
	2D	.043	.801	.599		Working with people, for good of community
	1D	.163				Skilled, drive, need mathematical brains
6718	3D	.018	.655	.614	.440	People, professional, unskilled
	2D	.053	.769	.639		Manual, drive, selling —see *Images*, p. 107
	1D	.186				

Case	Solution	Fit Prentice Global Stress$_1$	Dimensional standard deviation			Main constructs employed
			DIM1	*DIM2*	*DIM3*	
6748	3D	.001	.650	.543	.532	Income, status
	2D	.055	.786	.618		Work for welfare of community, people
	1D	.206				Skilled, qualified.
M205	3D	.024	.670	.554	.494	Could swap jobs, come into contact with each other
	2D	.057	.759	.651		Deal with public,
	1D	.198				qualified Education, Apprenticeship
M206	3D	.015	.660	.584	.473	Dealing with people, Profession *v.* Trade
	2D	.061	.793	.601		Unskilled, dealing with figures
	1D	.231				Drive
M207	3D	.003	.744	.507	.435	Professions *vs.* just jobs trades, labouring
	2D	.008	.853	.523		(see *Images,* p.107)
	1D	.109				
M208	3D	.022	.673	.551	.494	Education, Qualifications, training, apprenticeships
	2D	.063	.811	.586		Dealing with public, manual
	1D	.192				
V851	3D	.025	.764	.495	.413	Status, Public service, Manual/ Non-manual
	2D	.063	.875	.485		Drive, skills, social class
	1D	.101				(see *Images,* p. 107)

4 Rankings and Ratings Data: Appendices to Chapter 4 of *The Images of Occupational Prestige*

T.4.1 Elementary Analysis for means and standard deviations of ratings and rankings

Rankings and ratings data for the standard set of 16 occupational titles were briefly described in Chapter 4 of *Images*. When several groups of people judge a number of stimuli in terms of a variety of criteria, a vast proliferation of statistical tables can result. We coped with this problem in *Images* by transforming rank orders into directional data (see section T.4.7). However this is such a novel procedure in the social sciences that we think it desirable to report more conventional analyses of the data as well.

The main purpose of this section is to make available the basic data on means and standard deviations. However, we also include supplementary analysis and discussion. The basic data on means and standard deviations for the judgements of 16 occupational titles on five criteria, by eight sub-groups of subjects yields ten tables, each with sixteen rows and eight columns (five tables for the means and five for the standard deviations). These ten tables are shown at the end of this section, as Tables T.4.1.9 to T.4.1.18.

The eight sub-groups of subjects were as follows:
1. Clergy and theological students
2. Teachers and student teachers
3. Actuaries
4. Chartered accountants
5. Ambulance drivers
6. Policemen
7. Joiners, fitters and turners
8. Electrical engineering students

The occupational titles to be judged by the subjects were the standard set of 16, which have been described in table T.2.2 earlier in this book.

The five criteria of judgement were:
1. 'Social usefulness'
2. 'Prestige and rewards'
3. 'Cognitive distance'

4. 'Social standing'
5. 'Monthly earnings'
They are more fully described in Chapter 4 of *Images*.

TABLE T.4.1.1 Profile correlations between pairs of occupational groups, over means for the judgements of 16 occupations on 5 criteria of judgement

Pairs of occupational groups	(a) Social useful- ness	(b) Prestige and rewards	(c) Cognitive distance	(d) Social standing	(e) Monthly earnings
Clergy and teachers	0.93	0.96	0.69	0.98	0.98
Clergy and actuaries	0.84	0.86	−0.13	0.95	0.97
Clergy and accountants	0.89	0.93	0.05	0.97	0.94
Clergy and ambulance drivers	0.86	0.87	0.01	0.97	0.97
Clergy and policemen	0.94	0.89	0.16	0.97	0.94
Clergy and fitters	0.83	0.88	−0.06	0.91	0.95
Clergy and engineers	0.91	0.93	0.54	0.97	0.99
Teachers and actuaries	0.92	0.96	0.14	0.98	0.99
Teachers and accountants	0.94	0.98	0.18	0.98	0.96
Teachers and ambulance drivers	0.88	0.94	0.29	0.97	0.94
Teachers and policemen	0.93	0.97	0.47	0.98	0.89
Teachers and fitters	0.91	0.87	0.29	0.89	0.92
Teachers and engineers	0.97	0.98	0.63	0.98	0.97
Actuaries and accountants	0.96	0.98	0.56	0.99	0.98
Actuaries and ambulance drivers	0.89	0.95	−0.04	0.94	0.94
Actuaries and policemen	0.94	0.95	−0.08	0.95	0.86
Actuaries and fitters	0.83	0.78	−0.17	0.82	0.91
Actuaries and engineers	0.86	0.93	−0.12	0.97	0.96
Accountants and ambulance drivers	0.90	0.95	−0.37	0.95	0.90
Accountants and policemen	0.93	0.96	−0.22	0.96	0.80
Accountants and fitters	0.83	0.82	−0.41	0.87	0.84
Accountants and engineers	0.91	0.95	−0.14	0.98	0.92
Ambulance drivers and policemen	0.95	0.94	0.86	0.98	0.94
Ambulance drivers and fitters	0.84	0.83	0.69	0.93	0.94
Ambulance drivers and engineers	0.84	0.94	0.30	0.97	0.98
Policemen and fitters	0.85	0.80	0.76	0.90	0.96
Policemen and engineers	0.88	0.95	0.44	0.97	0.94
Fitters and engineers	0.92	0.93	0.37	0.90	0.95

The traditional sociological method of comparing aggregated occupational judgements between sub-groups has been to calculate a 'profile correlation' between each pair of sub-groups. As we argued in *Images*, we find this procedure to be insensitive to important differences between sub-groups, and therefore potentially misleading. However, we present such profile correlations in the first table of this appendix, in order that the sceptical reader may see how our data show the usual rather high values that such correlations seem always to attain. Table T.4.1.1 shows the 28 profile correlations for each of the five criteria of judgement. If we discount the 'cognitive distance' criterion as being a rather special case, we find that the profile correlations range from a lowest value of 0.78 to a high of 0.99 and that the majority of them have values above 0.90. There is a clear tendency for the profile correlations for the two evaluative criteria ('social usefulness' and 'prestige and rewards') to be in the range 0.80 to 0.90, while those for the two descriptive criteria ('social standing', and 'monthly earnings') are mostly above 0.90. These results establish that our data give similar results to those in the previous literature. We shall now show an alternative method of analysis which is a little more sensitive to differences between sub-groups.

It provides considerable aid to summarisation and interpretation if we can re-express each of tables T.4.1.9 to T.4.1.18 by the contributions from row effects, column effects and a typical value. This is called 'fitting an additive model'. So far as the applications in this appendix are concerned, the row effects are always the contributions from the 16 occupational titles, and the column effects are always associated with the eight occupational sub-groups. The data of any table are decomposed as:

$$\text{Response} = \frac{\text{typical}}{\text{value}} + \frac{\text{row}}{\text{effect}} + \frac{\text{column}}{\text{effect}} + \text{residual}$$

Depending upon which table we are summarising, the 'response' which is decomposed is either a mean value, or a standard deviation for judgements of an occupational title by a particular occupational group. The 'typical value' indicates the overall tendency for the responses to be high or low. The 'row effect' for any occupational title indicates the general tendency for that sub-group to have high or low responses. Finally, the particular and possibly idiosyncratic tendency for a certain occupational sub-group to judge a particular occupational title especially high or especially low is captured in the 'residual' term. We find that a display of these residuals is an invaluable tool for testing hypotheses about systematic differences in occupational judgements. The hypothesis of 'egoism', for example, predicts that people will judge their own jobs more favourably than might be expected from a prediction based on an additive model alone. Similarly a 'values' hypothesis implies that subcultures who hold (say) highly nurturant people-oriented values will judge people-oriented jobs more favourably than would be expected from an additive model's prediction. These (and other) hypotheses predict that statistical interactions ought to be observable in the data. Standard F-tests are available for testing such hypotheses, but their usefulness is limited to problems in which the row and column layout is balanced. We prefer to search for interactions by examining the residuals from an additive model.

The method we choose to fit this additive model is called 'median polishing'. Starting with the data in the form of a two-way table, the 'polishing' technique proceeds by successively removing medians, alternately by rows and then by columns. The method has been described by Mosteller and Tukey (1977) by Erickson and Nosanchuk (1977) and by McNeil (1977). We used McNeil's computer program.

It is equally possible to use the polishing method with the arithmetic mean. We chose to use the median because of our interest in the residuals from the fit of the additive model. It is a well-known feature of the median that it tends to give more very small residuals and more very large residuals than the mean does (Mosteller and Tukey 1977, p. 186). Mosteller and Tukey also conclude:

> Such analysis by medians leaves unusual perturbations in the data much more clearly delineated in the residuals than does analysis by means, which tends to smear the consequences of isolated perturbations quite widely. (p. 201)

Any attempt at an additive fit to some real data will result in the estimation of row effects, column effects and a set of residuals. The goodness of fit of the model is indicated by some totalising function of the residuals, but more importantly by the absence of any 'outlier' residuals. The next two tables (T.4.1.2 and T.4.1.3) show the estimates of row effects, column effects and typical value, for each of the five criteria of judgement. Table T.4.1.2 fits an additive model to the data on average judgements of occupational titles. Table T.4.1.3 does the same for data on the *spread* (standard deviations) of such judgements. In both cases, the median polishing procedure finds the estimates which minimise the sum of absolute deviations between data points and fitted values.

TABLE T.4.1.2   Summary of 5 analyses by median polishing, estimating row effects, column effects and typical value for the fitting of an additive model to the mean values for judgements of 16 occupational titles
Positive values indicate high judgements; negative values indicate low judgements.

	Criteria of judgement				
	Social usefulness	Prestige and rewards	Cognitive distance	Social standing	Monthly earnings
Row effects					
1 MIN	9.51	2.30	4.57	4.80	−5.81
2 CST	22.18	3.56	15.44	3.91	8.70
3 QA	−.01	1.72	−17.83	4.24	141.03
4 CA	.62	1.79	−2.74	4.57	104.77
5 MPN	9.88	.97	−7.12	.51	−27.32
6 AD	10.77	−.97	6.15	−.51	−32.14
7 BSL	−12.66	−6.07	4.89	−5.32	−1.14
8 MTO	−5.11	−3.17	−13.05	−2.04	1.14
9 SOL	4.90	1.69	−3.46	4.66	103.35

TABLE T.4.1.12 *continued*

	Criteria of judgement				
	Social usefulness	*and rewards*	*Cognitive distance*	*Social standing*	*Monthly earnings*
10 CSE	−1.26	1.07	−4.86	4.09	78.24
11 CT	−18.90	−3.94	−4.49	−.82	22.13
12 PM	20.43	1.57	12.75	2.41	−9.44
13 C	.01	−2.38	−2.48	−1.14	−6.91
14 LO	−6.77	−4.31	10.60	−3.42	5.91
15 RP	−27.44	−6.60	2.48	−5.28	−48.40
16 BM	−26.55	−7.15	12.42	−4.07	−38.09
Column effects					
1 Clergy	4.05	−.06	−.73	−.42	12.81
2 Teachers	.66	−.12	−2.29	.12	−3.45
3 Actuaries	−2.22	.05	10.50	−.04	1.64
4 Accountants	1.76	.53	−.40	.03	2.22
5 Ambulance drivers	−.72	−.26	−.34	−.59	−1.85
6 Policemen	2.18	−.19	12.72	.65	−1.83
7 Fitters etc.	−.89	.80	−3.02	.56	−11.04
8 Engineers	−3.76	.10	6.12	−.11	6.41
Typical value	60.86	10.26	46.80	8.62	143.98

The tendency to rate or rank particular occupational titles high or low is indicated by the 'row effects' in table T.4.1.2. Comprehensive School Teacher (CST) has an estimated 'effect' of 22.18 for the social usefulness criterion, and this is the largest of all the row effects in this column of the table. On the average, CST is judged most socially useful. As it happens, CST is also judged the most deserving of prestige and rewards, and the best known. However CST falls to sixth place when judged on the two 'descriptive' criteria of social standing and monthly earnings. The 'column effects' of Table T.4.1.2 are to be interpreted as the general tendency of the sub-group concerned to rank (or rate) *all* of the 16 stimuli high or low. Finally, the 'typical value' is meant to indicate the overall average of the judgements after row and column effects have been subtracted. The residuals which correspond to the five analyses (summarised as the columns of Table T.4.1.2) are graphically displayed in Tables T.4.1.4 to T.4.1.8.

Before proceeding to the search for patterns in residuals from the analysis of *average* judgements, it is instructive to use the median polishing technique on the standard deviation data, i.e. on the spread of judgements.

Here, the row effects and column effects reflect the contributions of occupational titles and of the judging sub-groups to the amount of *dispersion*

TABLE T.4.1.3 Summary of 5 analyses by median polishing, estimating row effects, column effects and typical value, for the fitting of an additive model to the standard deviations for judgements of occupational titles
Positive values indicate dissensus; negative values indicate consensus.

	Criteria of judgement				
	Social usefulness	Prestige and rewards	Cognitive distance	Social standing	Monthly earnings
Row effects					
1 MIN	3.10	.14	.17	−.21	.58
2 CST	−5.69	−.92	2.15	−.68	4.08
3 QA	2.87	.29	−1.37	.34	43.75
4 CA	−1.29	.29	−1.95	−.14	43.85
5 MPN	.23	.02	.34	.20	−7.70
6 AD	−1.14	.36	−1.09	.21	−10.70
7 BSL	2.51	.08	1.86	.36	7.56
8 MTO	−1.07	−.47	−.17	−.33	−.58
9 SOL	−.13	−.02	−.55	−.26	31.41
10 CSE	1.26	.25	1.80	.40	50.49
11 CT	−.46	−.20	−.89	.16	2.56
12 PM	−2.12	.00	.71	.06	−9.47
13 C	−.60	−.27	−1.81	−.32	−2.09
14 LD	.13	−.08	−.24	−.06	4.78
15 RP	.61	−.12	1.25	−.09	−17.67
16 BM	3.25	−.00	4.96	.39	−10.60
Column effects					
1 Clergy	−2.67	−.27	−2.26	.29	16.05
2 Teachers	.23	.15	−.15	.12	−.43
3 Actuaries	−.26	−.37	−4.66	−.26	1.17
4 Accountants	−.65	.03	3.53	−.33	−11.82
5 Ambulance drivers	1.70	.52	.40	−.25	−2.32
6 Policemen	−2.09	−.48	−.45	−.14	−11.46
7 Fitters etc.	3.93	1.00	2.88	1.14	.43
8 Engineers	2.91	−.03	.15	.41	4.61
Typical value	17.86	3.03	24.11	2.55	35.55

(indicated by the standard deviation) of the judgements. For example, Civil Servant (Executive Grade) has relatively large and positive 'effects' for all five criteria of judgement. This reflects the high degree of dissensus in judgements about this occupation. The effects for Building Site Labourer show a similar pattern indicating dissensus over each of the five criteria. At the other extreme there is consensus about the judgements of Carpenter and of Machine Tool Operator, and this is indicated by row effects which are negative.

The 'column effects' in the table reflect the contributions of the different sub-groups to the dispersion of judgements. Both actuaries and policemen are consistently more homogeneous than other sub-groups (that is, their judgements are less dispersed). By contrast, the sub-group of fitters and joiners is consistently less homogeneous than other sub-groups (across all five criteria of judgement.

Finally (and not before time), we revert to discussion of the average (mean) ratings and rankings of occupational titles, and we come to the display of residuals from fitting row effects, column effects and typical value. The rationale for this method is that it provides a direct test of hypotheses about certain sub-groups having systematically different evaluations of occupations. Subtracting out the components of the additive model leaves the residuals easily available for inspection. Tables T.4.1.4 to T.4.1.8 are each concerned with one of the five criteria of judgement, and they each show the residuals coded into a simple scheme.

Key to symbols in residual plots

+++   signifies an upper outlier.

+   signifies an upper adjacent value; — a residual which is not an outlier, but whose value is above the upper quartile point.

.   signifies a residual which is between the upper and lower quartile points.

-     signifies a lower adjacent value — a residual which is not an outlier, but whose value is below the lower quartile point.

---   signifies a lower outlier.

Definition of outlier: if the midspread is the difference between the upper and the lower quartile points, an upper outlier is a residual greater than 1½ midspread units above the upper quartile, and a lower outlier is a residual less than 1½ midspread units below the lower quartile.

(a) Social usefulness criterion (Table T.4.1.4)

Excessively high ratings are made when Church of Scotland Minister is judged by the ambulance driver and police sub-groups, Barman is judged over-generously by joiners-fitters.

There are eight 'negative outliers' (conjunctions of occupational title and judging sub-group where the average rating was markedly lower than an additive model would predict). Church of Scotland Minister is marked down by the two young sub-groups of joiners-fitters and student engineers. In their turn, the sub-group of clergy and theology students make especially low ratings of the social usefulness of Qualified Actuary and Policeman. The actuaries' sub-group marks down Railway Porter and Ambulance Driver. As well as rating Church of Scotland Minister especially high, the ambulance drivers rate Building Site Labourer extra low.

TABLE T.4.1.4   Display of residuals from fitting an additive model (row effects, column effects and typical value) to the mean ratings of occupational titles on the 'social usefulness' criterion (data of Table T.4.1.9)

Residuals

1	MIN	•	−	+	•	+++	+++	---	---
2	CST	•	•	•	+	•	+	•	•
3	QA	---	•	•	•	+	−	•	•
4	CA	−	•	+	+	•	−	•	•
5	MPN	+	•	−	−	•	+	+	•
6	AD	−	•	---	−	+	•	+	+
7	BSL	+	+	•	•	---	•	•	+
8	MTO	•	+	−	•	•	•	•	+
9	SOL	−	•	−	+	+	•	−	−
10	CSE	•	+	•	•	•	+	−	•
11	CT	•	•	•	•	•	•	•	---
12	PM	---	•	•	−	−	+	+	•
13	C	+	•	•	+	−	•	−	•
14	LC	•	−	−	•	•	•	−	+
15	RP	+	•	---	−	+	•	+	−
16	BM	•	•	•	•	•	•	+++	•

CLERGY AND THEOL. STUDENTS
TEACHERS AND STUDENT TEACHER
QUALIFIED ACTUARIES
CHARTERED ACCOUNTANTS
AMBULANCE DRIVERS
POLICEMEN
JOINERS, FITTERS, ETC.
ELECTRICAL ENGINEERS (STU)

(b) Prestige and rewards criterion (Table T.4.1.5)
Some of the patterns of outliers that were apparent for the 'social usefulness' criterion can be observed here. Church of Scotland Minister is again marked down by joiners-fitters and by engineering students — the two youngest sub-groups. Again, the joiners and fitters evaluate Barman extra high, and this time they are joined by the ambulance drivers sub-group. Again, the clergy and theological students have an extra-low opinion of Qualified Actuary; and this time they also mark down Chartered Accountant, and mark up Male Psychiatric Nurse. The actuaries sub-group indulges in occupational

egoism by giving excessively generous rating to Qualified Actuary (the actuaries are also generous to Chartered Accountant, though only sufficiently, to make the relevant residual a positive 'adjacent value' rather than an outlying one). A final point to note is that the sub-group of joiners-fitters systematically marks down all six middle-class occupational titles in the set of 16. Surely this is evidence of an 'upside-downer' evaluation of occupations.

TABLE T.4.1.5   Display of residuals from fitting an additive model (row effects, column effects and typical value), to the mean rankings of occupational titles on the 'prestige and rewards' criterion (data of Table T.4.1.11)

Residuals

1	MIN	•	•	•	•	•	+	---	---
2	CST	+	+	-	•	---	+	---	•
3	QA	---	•	+++	+	•	+	---	-
4	CA	---	•	+	•	-	+	---	•
5	MPN	+++	+	-	•	-	-	•	•
6	AD	•	•	-	-	+	-	+	+
7	BSL	+	+	•	-	•	•	+	•
8	MTO	•	•	•	•	•	-	•	•
9	SOL	•	•	+	+	•	•	---	•
10	CSE	-	•	•	•	+	+++	---	•
11	GT	-	•	+	+	•	•	•	-
12	PM	+	•	•	•	•	+	•	+
13	C	+	•	•	•	•	-	•	-
14	LD	-	•	•	-	•	+	•	•
15	RP	•	•	-	•	•	•	+	-
16	BM	•	•	+	•	+++	•	+++	•

CLERGY AND THEOL. STUDENTS
TEACHERS AND STUDENT TEACHER
QUALIFIED ACTUARIES
CHARTERED ACCOUNTANTS
AMBULANCE DRIVERS
POLICEMEN
JOINERS, FITTERS, ETC.
ELECTRICAL ENGINEERS (STU)

(*c*) *Cognitive distance criterion* (Table T.4.1.6)
For this type of judgement, subjects were asked to rate occupations in terms of how much they felt they knew about the job. One interesting feature of the display of residuals is that only positive outliers occur (there are negative adjacent values, but no negative outliers). As might be expected, positive outliers among the residuals tend to occur when an occupational title is judged by a sub-group whose members have experience of that occupation. Some exceptions to this rule are that not one of the sub-groups of teachers,

TABLE T.4.1.6   Display of residuals from fitting an additive model (row effects, column effects and typical value) to the mean ratings of occupational titles on the 'cognitive distance' criterion (data of Table T.4.1.3)

Residuals

1	MIN	+++	+	•	+	-	-	-	•
2	CST	•	+	•	•	-	-	-	•
3	QA	•	•	+++	+++	•	-	•	•
4	CA	•	•	+	+++	-	-	-	•
5	MPN	+	+	-	•	•	-	•	•
6	AD	•	•	-	-	+++	+	•	•
7	BSL	-	•	•	-	+	+	+	•
8	MTO	•	•	•	•	•	-	+++	+
9	SOL	•	•	•	+++	-	•	-	•
10	CSE	•	•	•	+	-	-	-	•
11	CT	•	+	+	+++	•	•	•	-
12	PM	•	•	-	-	•	+	•	•
13	C	•	•	•	•	•	•	+++	•
14	LD	-	•	•	•	+	+	+	-
15	RP	-	•	+	•	+	•	•	-
16	BM	-	•	•	+	•	+	+	-

CLERGY AND THEOL. STUDENTS
TEACHERS AND STUDENT TEACHER
QUALIFIED ACTUARIES
CHARTERED ACCOUNTANTS
AMBULANCE DRIVERS
POLICEMEN
JOINERS, FITTERS, ETC.
ELECTRICAL ENGINEERS (STU)

policemen or engineering students has any outlier in its column. On the other hand, the sub-group of accountants marks up not only Chartered Accountant, but also Qualified Actuary, Solicitor and Commercial Traveller. The patterning of the positive and negative (mostly negative) adjacent values in the table is much as expected.

(*d*) *The social standing criterion* (Table T.4.1.7)
There are comparatively few outlying residuals here. The sub-group of joiners

TABLE T.4.1.7   Display of residuals from fitting an additive model (row effects, column effects and typical value) to the mean rankings of occupational titles on the 'social standing' criterion (data of Table T.4.1.15)

Residuals

1	MIN	•	–	+	+	+	•	–––	–
2	CST	+	•	–	•	+	+	–	–
3	QA	•	•	+++	+++	•	–	–––	•
4	CA	•	•	+	+	–	•	–––	•
5	MPN	+	•	–	•	+	–	+	•
6	AD	•	–	–	–	+	•	+	•
7	BSL	–	•	•	•	•	•	+	•
8	MTO	+	•	•	+	•	–	+	•
9	SOL	•	•	+	+	•	•	–––	–
10	CSE	+	•	•	+	•	•	–––	•
11	CT	+	•	+	+	•	•	–	–
12	PM	–	–	•	•	•	•	+	•
13	C	•	•	•	+	•	•	•	•
14	LD	•	•	•	–	•	+	•	•
15	RP	•	•	•	–	•	•	+	•
16	BM	–	•	+	–	•	•	+	•

CLERGY AND THEOL. STUDENTS
TEACHERS AND STUDENT TEACHER
QUALIFIED ACTUARIES
CHARTERED ACCOUNTANTS
AMBULANCE DRIVERS
POLICEMEN
JOINERS, FITTERS, ETC.
ELECTRICAL ENGINEERS (STU)

and fitters maintains its exceptionally unfavourable evaluation of Minister, Qualified Actuary, Chartered Accountant, Solicitor and Civil Servant (Executive). The title Qualified Actuary is judged extra favourably by the sub-group of accountants and also by actuaries themselves.

(*e*) *The monthly earnings criterion* (Table T.4.1.8)
The display of residuals for this 'descriptive' criterion of judgement shows the presence of 19 outlier residuals (seven of them being 'lower' (negative)

TABLE T.4.1.8   Display of residuals from fitting an additive model (row effects, column effects and typical value) to the means of the judgements of monthly earnings (data of Table T.4.1.17)

Residuals									
1	MIN	•	•	•	+	+++	•	•	-
2	CST	+	•	•	•	•	•	-	•
3	QA	•	-	+++	+++	•	---	---	+
4	CA	+	•	+	•	•	---	---	+++
5	MPN	•	•	+	•	•	+++	+++	-
6	AD	•	•	•	•	+++	+	+	•
7	BSL	•	+	•	+++	-	•	-	•
8	MTO	•	•	•	•	•	•	•	•
9	SOL	•	•	•	-	+	---	---	+
10	CSE	+++	-	-	-	+++	+	-	+++
11	CT	•	•	+	+++	•	---	-	•
12	PM	+	•	-	•	+	•	•	-
13	C	•	-	•	+	-	•	•	-
14	LD	•	+	•	•	-	-	•	+
15	RF	-	•	-	-	+	•	+	•
16	BM	•	•	•	•	-	-	•	-

CLERGY AND THEOL. STUDENTS
TEACHERS AND STUDENT TEACHER
QUALIFIED ACTUARIES
CHARTERED ACCOUNTANTS
AMBULANCE DRIVERS
POLICEMEN
JOINERS, FITTERS, ETC.
ELECTRICAL ENGINEERS (STU)

outliers). This indicates substantial departure from the additive row and column effects model, and shows that there are systematic differences between sub-groups in the accuracy of their occupational information.

The two sub-groups of policemen and joiners-fitters share a similar pattern of outlier residuals. Both underestimate the earnings for Qualified Actuary, Chartered Accountant, and Solicitor, and both overestimate the earnings for Male Psychiatric Nurse. (By under- and overestimate here, we mean to imply comparison with values fitted by the additive model, and *not* any comparison with the true earnings for these occupations.) The

TABLE T.4.1.9 'Social usefulness' criterion: mean ratings on a scale from 0 to 100, for 16 occupational titles by 8 occupational groups

MIN	65.4	74.6	63.5	71.8	71.6	80.4	85.2	56.4	56.3
CST	83.2	85.6	83.6	80.6	92.0	82.5	90.4	80.5	82.0
QA	59.9	54.4	61.6	61.6	62.9	65.9	59.9	59.8	56.7
CA	61.3	58.8	63.1	62.9	70.7	53.9	59.4	51.0	57.5
MPN	72.3	78.4	71.6	61.9	67.4	68.9	76.4	75.3	67.2
AD	73.7	72.5	72.8	59.4	69.0	76.3	73.3	79.2	72.9
BSL	51.0	60.1	56.0	45.6	48.1	36.5	48.5	47.6	51.3
MTO	56.5	60.2	59.7	48.2	53.7	53.9	56.0	54.0	57.6
SOL	63.5	63.6	64.1	66.6	72.9	67.4	70.5	61.7	53.3
CSE	59.9	61.8	64.5	57.6	63.1	58.7	69.5	55.4	54.7
CT	41.0	45.9	40.8	42.6	43.4	42.9	43.5	41.3	27.8
PM	81.6	75.4	81.0	80.3	79.1	78.6	88.2	86.4	78.5
C	60.3	67.9	60.5	57.4	67.7	57.4	64.7	56.7	58.5
LD	52.5	58.5	52.3	44.7	56.7	55.4	55.5	49.8	53.8
RP	35.1	43.6	35.2	20.4	26.9	40.4	34.5	36.1	25.7
BM	38.1	39.2	34.3	33.7	34.4	32.1	37.0	46.7	30.3
	211	28	55	16	9	14	10	66	19

Key to columns OVERALL ROW MEANS
CLERGY AND THEOL. STUDENTS
TEACHERS AND STUDENT TEACHER
QUALIFIED ACTUARIES
CHARTERED ACCOUNTANTS
AMBULANCE DRIVERS
POLICEMEN
JOINERS, FITTERS, ETC.
ELECTRICAL ENGINEERS (STU)

ambulance drivers' sub-group gives extra high estimates to Minister, Civil Servant (Executive) and to Ambulance Driver. The sub-group of accountants gives extra high estimates to Actuary, Commercial Traveller and to Building Site Labourer. The engineering students give extra high estimates to Accountant and to Civil Servant (Executive).

The basic data on means and standard deviations of occupational titles (for the sub-groups we have been discussing) are given as Tables T.4.1.9 to T.4.1.18.

TABLE T.4.1.10 'Social usefulness' criterion: standard deviations of the ratings, for 16 occupational titles by 8 occupational groups

MIN	22.6	17.1	23.2	20.2	20.9	13.9	15.6	27.4	26.3
CST	14.2	10.4	15.1	17.4	4.7	11.5	9.4	17.6	13.1
QA	19.8	18.5	16.9	21.1	19.8	17.4	22.0	21.5	24.0
CA	18.7	17.2	16.7	16.1	15.9	15.6	20.0	23.3	17.3
MPN	16.9	12.6	18.4	22.7	24.8	21.2	13.2	20.3	20.7
AD	18.2	11.3	15.0	21.8	12.7	20.0	17.9	24.0	17.7
BSL	20.7	15.0	19.5	20.6	21.1	22.8	18.4	24.2	21.0
MTO	17.9	11.7	17.1	22.6	12.7	18.3	14.5	20.6	20.6
SOL	18.6	16.5	17.1	15.9	17.9	15.1	20.8	20.4	24.1
CSE	19.6	15.7	19.7	11.4	16.6	21.0	16.9	23.2	22.4
CT	18.3	17.1	18.3	18.0	16.2	19.3	10.6	21.0	15.7
PM	16.4	12.7	16.3	15.5	9.3	18.5	13.9	16.4	20.4
C	17.7	14.9	15.9	16.9	16.9	20.7	17.5	20.8	16.5
LD	19.1	13.2	18.2	17.7	17.3	19.1	17.4	22.6	22.0
RP	19.8	16.5	20.6	15.1	17.9	22.6	15.1	22.3	13.1
BM	23.0	20.9	20.5	19.1	21.3	15.6	16.5	29.1	25.4
	211	28	55	16	9	14	10	60	19

Key to columns OVERALL ROW MEANS
CLERGY AND THEOL. STUDENTS
TEACHERS AND STUDENT TEACHER
QUALIFIED ACTUARIES
CHARTERED ACCOUNTANTS
AMBULANCE DRIVERS
POLICEMEN
JOINERS, FITTERS, ETC.
ELECTRICAL ENGINEERS (STU)

TABLE T.4.1.11   'Rewards' criterion: means of rankings on a scale from 1 to 16, by 8 occupational groups

MIN	11.2	12.7	12.1	12.6	13.3	12.3	13.8	8.2	13.6
CST	13.5	14.9	14.1	12.9	14.6	10.6	15.2	12.5	13.7
QA	11.5	10.0	12.1	14.6	13.0	11.5	12.8	10.3	11.3
CA	11.4	10.0	12.0	13.4	12.6	11.1	12.9	10.0	12.4
MPN	11.6	13.8	11.7	10.5	11.7	9.4	9.8	12.0	11.6
AD	9.7	9.3	9.1	8.3	8.6	10.4	8.0	11.4	9.8
BSL	4.8	4.7	4.9	5.9	3.4	3.9	3.7	5.8	4.4
MTO	7.3	7.0	7.1	7.1	7.7	6.7	6.5	8.0	7.2
SOL	11.7	11.7	11.8	13.1	13.8	12.0	11.8	10.5	12.1
CSE	11.0	10.2	10.8	11.2	12.0	11.5	13.2	10.5	11.6
CT	6.5	5.3	6.2	7.7	7.6	6.1	6.1	7.1	5.4
PM	12.1	12.2	11.5	11.8	11.4	11.3	13.1	12.7	13.3
C	8.0	9.0	7.5	8.2	8.8	7.9	7.1	8.2	7.1
LD	6.0	5.3	5.5	6.2	4.9	5.7	6.5	6.8	6.1
RP	3.9	3.8	3.7	3.1	2.7	3.6	3.3	5.2	2.8
BM	4.0	2.8	3.0	4.0	3.2	4.5	2.9	6.1	3.1
	190	21	53	17	9	10	13	50	17

Key to columns	OVERALL ROW MEANS
	CLERGY AND THEOL. STUDENTS
	TEACHERS AND STUDENT TEACHER
	QUALIFIED ACTUARIES
	CHARTERED ACCOUNTANTS
	AMBULANCE DRIVERS
	POLICEMEN
	JOINERS, FITTERS, ETC.
	ELECTRICAL ENGINEERS (STU)

TABLE T.4.1.12   'Rewards' criterion: standard deviations of rankings, by 8 occupational groups

MIN	3.6	3.0	3.5	2.3	3.1	2.2	2.1	5.2	3.7
CST	2.6	1.5	2.1	1.8	2.1	4.7	1.0	4.1	2.2
QA	3.5	3.1	3.5	2.5	4.3	3.8	2.6	3.9	3.6
CA	3.6	2.7	3.5	2.8	4.0	4.6	2.9	4.3	3.2
MPN	3.3	2.7	3.0	2.2	2.6	4.2	3.7	4.2	3.1

TABLE T.4.1.12 *continued*

AD	3.4	3.4	3.2	3.2	3.4	4.2	2.3	3.9	3.4
BSL	3.4	2.9	3.4	3.1	3.3	2.9	2.4	4.1	3.0
MTO	2.8	2.1	3.0	3.0	2.7	2.2	2.3	3.4	2.0
SOL	3.2	3.0	3.4	1.8	1.9	4.3	3.5	3.5	2.7
CSE	3.5	3.5	3.1	2.5	3.4	3.9	2.7	4.1	3.6
CT	3.1	2.4	3.0	2.6	2.3	2.8	2.9	3.8	3.2
PM	3.3	2.7	3.2	2.6	2.1	4.2	2.9	4.4	2.6
C	2.8	2.6	2.6	2.7	3.2	1.5	2.1	3.5	2.8
LD	3.1	1.7	3.0	2.7	3.2	2.9	3.3	4.2	2.5
RP	3.2	2.7	3.1	3.1	2.8	3.3	2.4	4.1	2.6
BM	3.3	2.8	2.5	2.6	3.1	3.8	2.8	5.2	2.1
	190	21	53	17	9	10	13	50	17

Key to columns

OVERALL ROW MEANS
CLERGY AND THEOL. STUDENTS
TEACHERS AND STUDENT TEACHER
QUALIFIED ACTUARIES
CHARTERED ACCOUNTANTS
AMBULANCE DRIVERS
POLICEMEN
JOINERS, FITTERS, ETC.
ELECTRICAL ENGINEERS (STU)

TABLE T.4.1.13 'Cognitive distance' criterion: mean ratings on a scale from 0 to 100, by 8 occupational groups

MIN	54.2	89.5	57.9	63.6	63.3	37.5	52.4	33.7	53.5
CST	64.7	67.7	78.1	75.6	58.8	43.1	58.7	52.1	71.1
QA	35.4	26.8	28.4	95.8	58.3	24.7	20.9	24.8	39.2
CA	44.8	43.6	41.7	73.8	93.3	33.6	36.7	28.6	53.2
MPN	42.7	58.0	43.9	35.3	33.4	45.0	45.8	32.6	49.6
AD	56.4	47.8	47.8	57.2	37.1	90.9	84.4	53.5	61.3
BSL	56.9	42.8	43.3	64.6	39.9	69.6	85.5	67.7	53.2
MTO	42.9	35.2	29.8	35.3	32.8	34.7	40.0	57.5	51.0
SOL	41.8	43.7	38.1	60.0	68.9	29.1	55.8	27.7	48.6
CSE	41.4	47.0	45.7	50.0	49.3	23.6	40.4	29.5	43.2

TABLE T.4.1.13 *continued*

CT	44.6	41.6	47.2	59.4	63.2	39.0	55.3	37.1	39.6
PM	61.4	58.8	54.4	57.2	46.7	59.5	91.0	59.6	69.8
C	52.0	42.6	40.9	52.5	40.7	48.5	60.3	66.5	50.3
LD	58.3	41.8	56.2	64.3	56.6	74.0	84.3	63.1	49.5
RP	49.2	41.5	43.3	73.6	49.3	65.8	68.2	47.5	41.1
BM	60.4	47.2	57.0	68.0	70.0	58.6	81.9	67.4	50.0
	195	25	38	16	9	10	12	51	34

Key to columns
OVERALL ROW MEANS
CLERGY AND THEOL. STUDENTS
TEACHERS AND STUDENT TEACHER
QUALIFIED ACTUARIES
CHARTERED ACCOUNTANTS
AMBULANCE DRIVERS
POLICEMEN
JOINERS, FITTERS, ETC.
ELECTRICAL ENGINEERS (STU)

TABLE T.4.1.14 'Cognitive distance' criterion: standard deviations of the ratings for 16 occupational titles by 8 occupational groups

NIM	24.0	9.2	25.1	25.0	25.9	21.4	27.1	26.1	29.4
CST	25.3	19.5	18.3	14.0	33.4	26.2	25.8	33.9	26.6
QA	22.6	21.0	24.4	5.8	29.3	19.7	15.1	25.1	27.4
CA	22.5	24.3	22.1	17.4	8.1	21.2	26.0	24.4	24.1
MPN	25.2	21.3	23.9	23.3	30.3	19.6	24.0	27.4	28.2
AD	22.5	20.9	19.7	19.9	29.8	8.9	15.3	28.7	23.1
BSL	25.6	23.5	25.7	25.0	33.8	27.9	15.9	28.9	23.0
MTO	24.5	22.3	19.0	15.1	20.3	27.3	29.6	32.4	23.6
SOL	23.1	15.5	20.7	23.4	26.6	23.4	26.3	25.9	24.3
CSE	26.0	20.4	25.6	25.5	30.5	27.2	25.4	28.8	25.2
CT	23.4	19.4	23.8	17.4	26.0	28.2	25.5	27.5	20.0
PM	24.9	21.5	24.6	20.2	27.0	25.8	16.2	29.7	25.0
C	22.5	24.2	22.6	15.6	25.4	26.9	24.6	23.9	19.5
LD	23.4	22.5	23.9	23.2	27.2	16.1	16.3	27.7	20.3
RP	25.8	25.1	25.3	20.6	29.1	21.5	31.6	27.4	25.3
BM	28.5	27.8	30.3	23.5	15.2	32.1	26.7	29.4	32.4
	195	25	38	16	9	10	12	51	34

TABLE T.4.1.14 *continued*

Key to columns   OVERALL ROW MEANS
CLERGY AND THEOL. STUDENTS
TEACHERS AND STUDENT TEACHER
QUALIFIED ACTUARIES
CHARTERED ACCOUNTANTS
AMBULANCE DRIVERS
POLICEMEN
JOINERS, FITTERS, ETC.
ELECTRICAL ENGINEERS (STU)

TABLE T.4.1.15   'Social standing' criterion: means of rankings on a scale from 1 to 16, by 8 occupational groups

MIN	12.4	12.8	13.0	14.3	14.7	14.0	14.2	10.0	12.7
CST	12.3	12.8	12.8	11.6	12.3	12.7	14.5	12.1	11.1
QA	12.4	12.0	13.3	15.0	14.8	12.3	12.3	10.7	12.5
CA	12.8	12.6	13.4	14.2	14.0	11.9	13.2	11.6	13.4
MPN	9.8	10.1	9.3	8.1	9.1	10.1	9.1	11.3	9.6
AD	8.5	7.6	7.4	7.2	7.0	9.3	6.8	10.2	3.3
BSL	3.5	2.4	3.5	3.3	2.6	2.8	3.9	4.7	2.9
MTO	6.9	7.6	6.2	6.5	7.1	5.7	6.3	7.7	6.5
SOL	12.7	13.0	13.2	14.2	14.4	12.4	14.1	11.4	12.5
CSE	12.3	12.9	12.8	12.6	12.2	12.9	13.3	10.9	12.9
CT	7.8	8.1	7.8	8.6	8.8	6.9	3.5	7.3	6.9
PM	11.0	9.9	10.0	10.0	11.1	10.9	11.9	12.2	10.9
C	7.6	7.1	7.8	7.6	8.1	6.9	7.8	7.9	7.3
LO	5.3	4.8	5.0	5.1	4.6	4.6	6.4	5.9	5.1
RP	3.7	2.9	3.5	3.1	2.4	2.7	4.0	4.6	3.6
BM	4.9	3.4	4.7	5.1	4.0	3.9	4.9	6.2	4.5
	223	30	40	18	9	15	13	63	35

Key to columns   OVERALL ROW MEANS
CLERGY AND THEOL. STUDENTS
TEACHERS AND STUDENT TEACHER
QUALIFIED ACTUARIES
CHARTERED ACCOUNTANTS
AMBULANCE DRIVERS
POLICEMEN
JOINERS, FITTERS, ETC.
ELECTRICAL ENGINEERS (STU)

TABLE T.4.1.16 'Social standing' criterion: standard deviations of rankings, by 8 occupational groups

MIN	3.4	2.7	3.8	1.9	1.7	2.0	2.1	5.1	2.8
CST	2.5	2.1	1.9	1.7	1.4	2.2	1.3	3.6	2.9
QA	3.2	4.2	3.2	1.2	2.4	3.1	2.4	3.5	3.7
CA	2.9	2.4	2.5	1.3	3.0	3.0	2.0	3.5	3.4
MPN	3.1	3.2	3.1	2.3	4.3	2.4	2.4	3.3	3.6
AD	3.2	3.1	2.7	2.8	2.4	3.3	2.0	4.0	3.0
BSL	3.1	1.8	3.1	2.7	2.6	1.9	3.4	3.9	3.4
MTO	2.6	2.4	2.3	2.6	2.0	2.0	2.6	3.2	2.6
SOL	2.8	3.2	2.5	1.2	1.7	3.1	1.3	3.7	2.6
CSE	3.2	3.3	2.5	1.8	2.9	2.6	3.1	4.4	3.1
CT	2.9	2.6	3.0	2.4	2.4	2.5	2.8	3.5	2.8
PM	3.1	3.5	3.6	2.4	2.3	3.0	2.0	3.5	2.4
C	2.5	2.1	2.4	2.9	2.1	2.0	2.2	3.2	2.5
LD	2.8	2.9	2.3	2.6	2.1	1.1	2.7	3.7	2.7
RP	2.9	1.8	2.2	2.8	2.1	1.8	3.3	3.6	3.4
CM	3.3	2.6	2.5	2.3	2.8	2.5	3.0	4.6	3.9
	223	30	40	18	9	15	13	63	35

Key to columns

OVERALL ROW MEANS
CLERGY AND THEOL. STUDENTS
TEACHERS AND STUDENT TEACHER
QUALIFIED ACTUARIES
CHARTERED ACCOUNTANTS
AMBULANCE DRIVERS
POLICEMEN
JOINERS, FITTERS, ETC.
ELECTRICAL ENGINEERS (STU)

TABLE T.4.1.17 'Monthly earnings' criterion: means of subjects' estimates, by 8 occupational groups

MIN	137.4	150.0	132.2	138.9	144.8	163.7	137.4	129.3	136.0
CST	151.9	177.9	150.0	153.4	153.3	149.8	154.6	135.3	159.4
QA	260.5	293.6	269.8	308.5	343.5	266.8	192.7	190.0	297.4
CA	243.7	270.4	247.6	264.7	247.3	244.2	197.8	203.4	280.9
MPN	124.0	129.0	109.7	126.5	118.1	114.7	132.3	142.8	112.7
AD	112.9	121.9	104.1	115.3	110.3	127.7	120.2	109.5	116.2

TABLE T.4.1.17 *continued*

BSL	139.1	157.2	147.4	147.3	164.0	123.3	137.0	114.7	147.5
MTO	144.5	157.4	141.6	147.1	150.8	139.3	143.0	134.4	154.1
SOL	237.4	261.9	244.4	243.7	238.1	251.6	214.4	198.6	264.5
CSE	230.4	265.8	203.6	213.1	210.4	277.4	230.2	201.6	285.4
CT	162.4	176.0	162.1	175.5	188.1	164.4	133.8	144.4	174.7
PM	134.1	154.6	131.1	131.1	134.8	137.5	133.0	127.0	134.2
C	134.0	150.4	126.8	138.2	156.3	130.0	136.3	127.3	136.3
LD	151.3	158.1	155.8	150.0	153.4	136.9	142.6	141.1	163.1
RP	95.6	103.3	92.4	91.1	89.4	98.7	94.2	92.7	101.7
BM	102.1	121.5	103.9	108.0	108.9	90.7	96.2	94.5	96.9
	226	29	54	19	8	13	9	53	36

Key to columns	OVERALL ROW MEANS
	CLERGY AND THEOL. STUDENTS
	TEACHERS AND STUDENT TEACHER
	QUALIFIED ACTUARIES
	CHARTERED ACCOUNTANTS
	AMBULANCE DRIVERS
	POLICEMEN
	JOINERS, FITTERS, ETC.
	ELECTRICAL ENGINEERS (STU)

TABLE T.4.1.18 'Monthly earnings' criterion: standard deviations of subjects' estimates, by 8 occupational groups

MIN	40.4	45.0	30.3	41.1	21.8	42.9	24.8	51.5	40.6
CST	34.5	55.2	31.1	27.5	14.6	29.1	19.9	31.9	40.7
QA	106.9	105.0	160.1	59.1	57.8	197.8	46.7	61.2	120.9
CA	83.3	100.9	87.3	52.5	17.3	145.1	45.4	84.8	79.0
MPN	36.8	43.8	23.7	33.1	16.1	20.7	23.4	58.2	32.1
AD	25.3	41.0	15.9	26.3	12.9	27.1	10.3	24.8	32.6
BSL	43.5	53.8	47.9	41.6	47.9	38.8	43.7	31.5	49.7
MTO	32.8	35.0	35.6	39.5	26.0	20.3	43.3	25.4	38.5
SOL	73.0	70.4	86.0	66.0	57.3	105.5	25.4	61.2	82.3
CSE	92.3	103.9	84.9	98.8	48.8	187.4	59.9	87.2	82.4
CT	45.2	50.2	52.6	53.6	24.7	35.8	26.5	45.9	36.9
PM	27.3	47.8	23.9	28.8	20.2	20.1	24.8	21.4	29.2
C	36.2	58.2	31.9	34.6	43.5	21.0	25.2	32.1	38.2
LD	43.9	45.4	39.0	33.9	20.6	42.4	29.8	51.9	51.4

TABLE T.4.1.18 *continued*

RP	20.4	27.2	17.4	19.1	18.1	11.1	13.1	18.3	23.8
BM	28.4	42.4	32.5	21.8	29.1	13.1	12.0	25.8	29.2
	226	29	54	19	8	13	9	58	36

Key to columns OVERALL ROW MEANS
CLERGY AND THEOL. STUDENTS
TEACHERS AND STUDENT TEACHER
QUALIFIED ACTUARIES
CHARTERED ACCOUNTANTS
AMBULANCE DRIVERS
POLICEMEN
JOINERS, FITTERS, ETC.
ELECTRICAL ENGINEERS (STU)

T.4.2 Internal Analysis with MDPREF and MINIRSA: Evaluative Maps

In *The Images of Occupational Prestige,* we stressed the importance of investigating cognitive maps before investigating invidious comparisons. As discussed in the fourth chapter of *Images,* it is quite possible to use vector or distance models with evaluative data, and to obtain configurations of stimulus points of the kind we call 'evaluative maps'. Evaluative maps can be obtained from 'internal' analysis of descriptive or evaluative ratings and rankings of occupations. This appendix will show that such evaluative maps are not very closely related to the cognitive map derived from INDSCAL analysis of similarities data. It is misleading, therefore, to take evaluative maps and to imply that they might yield valid estimates of cognitive maps. (See Seligson, 1977, for a case in point.)

The 48-case quadrant subset

Appendices T.4.2, T.4.3 and T.4.4 required data analyses to be made on a comparatively small number of cases. We selected 48 cases (12 from each of the four quadrants) for each of whom we had data on all five ranking and rating criteria (Social usefulness, Prestige and rewards, Cognitive distance, Social standing and Monthly earnings). The 48 cases were each identified by a four-character number. There were 8 Church of Scotland ministers (initial letter A), 3 Episcopalian ministers (initial letter C) one comprehensive school teacher (initial letter B), 6 actuaries (initial letter F), 6 chartered accountants (initial letter G), 2 male psychiatric nurses (initial letter K), 8 ambulance drivers (initial letter M), 2 policemen (initial letter N), 3 joiners (numbers 4166 to 4168), 3 plasterers (numbers 4169 to 4171), 5 turner-fitters (numbers 4172 to 4178) and one ship's joiner (number 4248). Each of the 48 respondents judged the standard set of 16 occupational titles on the five criteria already mentioned. It seems desirable to make this small set of data available for future analysis by yet-to-be-perfected methods. We therefore show the data as Tables T.4.2.1 to T.4.2.5

TABLE 4.2.1   Social usefulness ratings for the balanced set of 48 subjects

A211	95	95	30	30	75	75	30	50	50	50	25	60	50	60	40	20
A263	78	84	30	66	54	54	90	30	66	36	12	72	96	24	18	6
A266	50	99	80	80	99	50	50	80	80	90	30	75	99	60	20	20
A267	75	90	75	80	75	90	40	65	80	80	60	90	60	55	50	20
A268	75	99	30	50	99	60	50	70	90	60	50	99	70	60	60	20
A305	70	75	65	65	70	70	65	65	65	70	55	70	65	65	60	50
A306	57	72	70	72	85	91	60	52	62	57	70	90	43	40	37	42
A307	55	90	60	60	80	70	65	70	60	65	55	75	70	65	40	50
B144	90	95	95	70	70	80	90	90	90	80	30	95	45	80	50	45
C295	50	80	40	50	60	70	65	60	60	50	20	70	70	60	10	25
C298	90	90	50	60	90	80	80	60	70	70	50	90	80	70	40	5
C299	99	90	80	80	75	80	70	70	80	80	65	90	75	75	60	60
F128	60	60	50	50	60	40	30	50	60	40	30	70	50	30	20	30
F204	85	75	65	60	95	85	10	50	50	40	30	90	60	35	10	15
F247	80	85	70	80	85	85	75	75	80	60	50	85	80	60	50	50
F257	90	99	75	75	60	60	80	90	90	50	40	95	85	70	20	40
F294	65	90	75	75	60	65	75	50	75	60	50	90	60	60	50	50
F312	70	99	70	80	20	60	60	60	80	60	20	80	60	60	10	10
G213	50	90	60	70	50	75	70	70	70	70	55	75	70	70	10	40
G216	75	90	75	80	70	60	65	65	70	60	50	70	65	60	50	55
G264	90	99	75	80	90	90	30	40	90	80	60	99	90	80	20	5
G265	80	90	90	90	90	70	20	70	90	50	50	80	60	30	20	20
G269	80	90	80	80	70	70	70	60	80	80	20	70	70	70	10	45
G318	60	95	40	80	70	60	70	70	80	80	40	80	90	70	50	50

TABLE 4.2.1 *continued*

K310	50	75	65	55	70	50	35	40	65	45	10	75	40	40	10	25
K313	90	88	65	54	70	60	50	50	85	55	53	70	50	50	50	45
M155	83	88	60	60	85	75	60	45	60	60	25	90	45	55	40	30
M156	99	70	50	25	65	80	15	35	55	60	5	80	40	20	10	30
M159	80	80	65	60	70	70	45	50	75	75	50	70	60	60	50	30
M196	50	99	93	80	99	97	80	80	94	50	70	97	90	80	70	40
M209	75	60	75	60	50	30	20	25	60	50	20	30	25	20	20	20
M210	60	75	65	45	60	75	40	55	55	45	45	80	60	50	45	40
M214	90	80	50	50	85	90	30	55	75	45	65	90	88	70	70	5
M215	75	80	30	40	20	80	10	25	40	60	30	99	25	50	10	20
N114	90	99	80	60	99	99	70	50	99	50	50	99	80	70	40	50
N115	70	80	70	70	70	70	50	60	70	70	50	70	70	60	40	40
4166	50	90	60	50	90	60	40	50	50	50	40	99	50	30	35	20
4167	50	99	99	99	99	99	50	75	99	50	25	99	99	50	10	50
4168	25	99	75	75	99	99	60	60	75	60	40	99	60	50	40	60
4169	10	70	50	30	90	99	60	50	60	30	40	70	55	50	35	35
4170	20	50	25	75	65	25	20	30	75	70	15	75	30	10	15	20
4171	50	80	90	50	60	99	20	50	60	70	1	99	30	40	30	1
4172	50	99	50	75	50	75	20	20	40	60	20	99	75	20	20	75
4173	50	70	45	50	65	30	25	60	75	50	45	99	55	45	40	30
4175	45	35	55	60	30	42	25	25	50	60	55	25	15	15	35	5
4176	60	75	70	70	50	30	20	25	50	40	20	90	25	10	10	10
4178	35	99	20	60	80	99	70	20	55	50	40	99	50	80	2	70
4248	40	70	30	60	80	60	10	30	60	70	20	80	50	20	40	10

TABLE 4.2.2 Prestige and rewards rankings for the balanced set of 48 subjects

A211	16	16	10	10	13	7	3	6	12	11	2	8	6	5	1	1
A263	12	15	7	10	16	8	6	9	11	13	4	14	9	7	5	3
A266	15	15	8	8	16	11	2	8	15	1	4	12	8	4	9	10
A267	12	16	10	10	15	15	2	5	11	10	4	15	6	7	3	1
A268	9	16	7	8	14	6	2	10	13	12	5	15	11	4	4	1
A305	0	16	13	13	15	11	7	5	14	12	5	12	7	7	7	3
A306	12	13	11	10	14	15	4	6	5	7	8	16	9	3	1	2
A307	4	16	13	12	14	7	3	10	8	15	5	11	10	6	2	1
B144	15	16	11	9	13	4	1	8	14	10	5	12	7	6	3	6
C295	14	16	4	6	15	9	9	9	14	14	3	14	2	5	2	2
C298	14	16	11	8	15	9	5	6	12	13	2	10	7	4	3	1
C299	0	15	14	14	9	6	4	7	16	14	10	11	8	3	6	4
F128	13	12	16	15	8	5	1	7	14	11	10	9	6	3	2	4
F204	15	11	16	14	13	8	3	4	10	9	7	12	5	6	3	2
F247	12	13	15	16	11	8	3	4	14	9	6	10	7	5	2	1
F257	14	13	15	11	9	8	3	6	14	12	5	10	7	4	1	2
F294	15	15	16	16	14	13	11	13	15	16	13	14	13	12	11	11
F312	9	13	16	16	9	10	3	4	16	13	9	13	9	9	1	2
G213	12	16	16	16	12	13	10	13	16	15	12	14	13	13	10	11
G216	15	16	16	4	12	11	8	10	15	7	6	13	10	5	2	2
G264	13	16	10	9	15	7	3	4	11	12	8	14	6	5	2	1
G265	14	14	16	16	14	8	1	7	16	12	9	9	15	2	1	1
G269	13	11	15	12	8	6	2	5	14	16	9	10	7	4	1	3
G318	15	11	15	15	10	5	1	7	15	16	8	9	6	3	2	4

TABLE 4.2.2 continued

K310	8	5	8	9	13	10	12	16	7	6	11	12	16	15	13	14
K313	2	3	5	9	13	12	7	15	8	9	5	13	14	10	10	16
M155	5	5	5	5	14	1	12	10	7	7	15	16	9	9	12	13
M156	3	1	4	8	11	5	15	16	7	2	10	9	6	12	14	13
M159	2	3	4	6	10	7	16	14	5	1	9	8	15	12	11	13
M196	13	12	10	7	2	11	5	3	6	9	2	1	4	3	1	8
M209	3	1	4	9	8	7	13	14	5	2	6	10	15	16	12	11
M210	2	1	5	8	11	4	16	16	7	3	11	6	16	16	9	12
M214	1	3	12	9	15	6	11	7	8	2	16	14	5	10	4	13
M215	5	3	5	9	15	7	9	11	5	1	9	9	11	11	13	15
N114	3	2	4	7	12	5	10	14	8	3	9	6	13	11	15	16
N115	3	1	9	9	10	9	13	13	9	4	9	9	15	15	14	13
4166	3	5	5	7	16	10	13	12	8	3	6	14	11	13	15	9
4167	6	2	4	10	9	11	13	15	8	3	7	5	16	14	12	1
4168	7	2	4	10	9	11	13	15	8	3	6	5	16	14	12	1
4169	7	5	6	8	13	11	9	12	4	13	16	14	2	10	15	1
4170	12	5	8	11	15	12	13	15	13	7	14	13	12	13	12	7
4171	5	3	4	8	16	1	14	11	6	1	9	15	12	13	10	2
4172	3	2	5	7	4	6	14	8	13	2	12	16	9	10	15	11
4173	1	3	4	11	16	5	10	8	12	6	9	14	6	7	15	13
4175	1	3	2	4	8	11	16	9	10	3	7	12	15	13	0	14
4176	2	2	4	7	14	6	10	11	5	9	12	8	15	16	13	9
4178	2	1	3	9	16	5	9	11	9	9	15	16	4	10	14	6
4248	2	6	5	8	16	4	14	12	3	1	10	15	13	9	11	7

TABLE 4.2.3 Cognitive distance ratings for the balanced set of 48 subjects

A211	99	90	40	40	80	70	60	60	60	50	50	60	60	60	20	20
A263	95	50	40	60	60	50	40	50	60	60	40	50	70	50	40	50
A266	90	35	1	25	80	50	25	35	35	35	10	35	35	10	20	20
A267	99	55	75	75	60	40	45	60	45	60	70	75	30	50	50	25
A268	85	50	1	10	45	25	50	35	50	25	40	60	50	40	20	30
A305	80	60	40	45	65	60	65	65	50	48	45	55	65	60	48	55
A306	90	63	30	70	85	42	40	30	52	73	40	85	30	40	62	75
A307	95	80	30	35	75	70	40	30	50	60	40	75	45	35	35	25
B144	95	99	70	95	40	90	70	20	75	80	85	98	80	60	50	95
C295	90	75	40	30	50	40	5	20	50	20	10	20	10	10	5	10
C298	90	70	20	50	40	70	65	30	40	50	60	60	70	75	80	70
C299	90	75	5	40	40	35	25	30	45	40	30	60	30	40	20	20
F128	75	80	99	90	75	50	60	40	50	80	70	60	50	60	60	50
F204	75	65	95	85	30	30	25	20	75	35	25	45	55	20	35	40
F247	65	75	99	85	40	75	50	40	40	50	50	50	60	50	75	90
F257	90	90	99	90	5	25	70	40	80	60	60	70	70	40	90	80
F294	25	75	85	55	30	70	80	25	35	35	40	65	35	75	75	75
F312	50	70	99	90	60	70	80	50	80	90	90	70	70	99	90	50
G213	60	85	80	99	20	40	65	45	80	50	70	70	45	70	55	85
G216	20	5	15	90	1	5	10	5	5	40	30	25	1	70	15	60
G264	75	70	60	99	50	10	10	10	80	20	99	20	20	30	70	80
G265	80	99	80	99	99	99	99	70	90	99	99	90	70	99	99	90
G269	20	20	20	80	20	50	20	30	40	20	40	20	50	20	20	40
G318	90	85	95	99	1	15	10	40	95	95	95	15	10	70	40	60

TABLE 4.2.3 continued

K310	75	80	30	70	98	90	90	60	45	45	75	80	60	65	45	90
K313	92	85	45	68	98	85	70	80	75	50	60	85	85	80	80	80
M155	25	35	30	30	45	98	96	40	30	55	30	70	65	65	88	40
M156	70	60	25	40	30	99	95	40	25	35	55	75	50	80	70	85
M159	55	80	20	50	50	99	80	40	25	30	60	85	70	75	80	80
M196	60	60	60	60	70	99	90	80	70	80	90	80	90	90	70	90
M209	30	10	1	10	30	99	80	30	20	10	50	20	20	90	90	90
M210	60	70	25	50	70	80	70	75	40	40	60	65	70	65	60	90
M214	20	10	5	5	15	80	5	30	5	5	5	80	10	80	20	60
M215	10	1	1	1	30	90	50	1	1	1	10	30	30	75	50	10
N114	99	99	1	99	80	99	99	80	99	90	99	99	99	99	99	1
N115	50	50	40	40	50	90	90	30	50	50	60	90	90	90	90	99
4166	50	90	70	60	75	50	25	65	60	60	50	99	60	40	25	90
4167	50	99	25	5	5	50	99	99	25	10	10	99	99	99	50	10
4168	30	99	25	5	10	30	99	99	25	8	15	99	99	99	30	99
4169	10	30	10	10	10	30	99	10	10	10	10	50	30	10	20	99
4170	10	25	10	10	15	10	50	50	10	10	25	25	50	15	10	10
4171	50	20	3	1	1	30	90	1	1	1	20	50	50	70	10	85
4172	75	99	10	25	50	99	90	99	20	90	25	99	90	90	60	50
4173	65	85	50	50	90	60	25	80	75	70	35	99	70	40	40	99
4175	45	25	70	45	45	75	30	65	75	65	65	50	80	55	55	45
4176	20	30	20	30	40	60	50	70	20	40	40	30	50	50	60	75
4178	20	90	1	1	10	1	20	99	1	1	1	50	10	40	20	80
4248	10	10	40	60	20	10	10	90	10	30	40	10	90	30	40	50

Rankings and Ratings Data

93

TABLE 4.2.4 Social standing rankings for the balanced set of 48 subjects

Subject																
A211	16	15	12	12	13	10	5	8	14	6	2	9	8	5	5	1
A263	13	12	11	16	8	6	1	4	14	15	10	9	7	2	3	5
A266	9	10	15	14	7	3	2	11	13	16	8	6	11	5	1	4
A267	11	15	5	9	14	16	2	7	12	3	6	13	8	10	4	1
A268	14	12	4	11	10	6	1	8	16	15	10	13	8	3	2	5
A305	7	15	15	15	14	5	3	8	15	16	13	1	9	8	5	1
A306	12	14	5	11	15	13	4	7	3	10	9	16	8	6	2	1
A307	5	11	16	14	12	6	3	10	13	15	4	9	8	7	2	1
B144	12	11	16	15	6	13	1	8	13	14	10	9	7	4	2	5
C295	11	12	15	14	10	7	3	5	13	16	6	8	9	4	2	1
C298	14	15	16	11	10	5	1	8	13	12	9	6	7	2	3	4
C299	16	14	11	11	12	5	3	8	15	11	7	13	6	3	3	4
F128	13	10	16	15	6	4	2	8	14	11	12	9	7	3	1	5
F204	16	11	15	14	8	7	1	5	12	13	10	9	6	4	2	3
F247	16	13	12	15	9	8	4	5	14	10	7	11	6	1	2	3
F257	16	11	15	12	10	7	2	4	13	14	8	9	6	3	1	5
F294	15	15	15	16	13	12	11	13	16	16	14	15	13	12	11	11
F312	12	12	16	16	5	7	5	7	16	12	8	12	13	6	5	5
G213	16	14	16	16	10	10	9	11	13	15	13	12	11	10	8	10
G216	14	12	16	16	10	5	1	6	16	7	8	11	9	3	2	4
G264	16	12	9	8	15	10	3	6	13	11	5	14	7	4	2	1
G265	16	15	16	16	15	8	1	7	16	12	10	14	11	3	2	2
G269	14	13	15	10	5	8	3	6	11	16	9	12	7	4	1	2
G318	12	11	16	15	8	3	1	6	15	15	11	9	5	2	2	7

TABLE 4.2.4 continued

K310	10	9	12	11	9	5	2	6	13	14	7	8	6	3	1	4
K313	16	15	8	12	13	7	7	3	14	11	6	13	7	5	4	2
M155	16	14	12	12	10	8	6	6	15	14	10	8	7	6	6	6
M156	13	12	15	6	9	11	1	8	16	14	5	11	6	4	2	3
M159	16	15	11	10	12	8	6	6	14	13	7	9	7	6	6	6
M196	14	15	13	10	16	8	3	6	11	9	5	12	6	4	2	1
M209	16	12	15	13	10	8	3	2	14	11	6	9	7	4	1	5
M210	9	12	15	15	6	11	1	7	15	16	4	11	7	5	3	3
M214	15	14	13	12	7	8	4	6	3	16	10	9	8	5	1	11
M215	15	9	13	15	9	5	1	7	11	15	9	15	2	3	3	5
N114	16	15	10	12	9	8	1	7	13	11	6	14	9	3	2	4
N115	14	14	14	14	9	9	2	4	14	11	9	10	5	9	2	3
4166	9	15	13	11	14	6	4	8	9	13	10	16	9	5	5	3
4167	1	12	14	16	5	7	3	8	15	13	11	9	7	4	2	6
4168	1	12	14	16	5	6	3	8	15	13	11	9	10	4	2	7
4169	2	14	12	6	15	16	1	4	10	11	9	13	10	5	7	3
4170	7	14	13	14	13	7	7	13	15	13	12	13	8	7	4	13
4171	12	10	11	14	13	8	4	5	9	15	2	16	13	7	3	1
4172	12	16	6	14	9	10	1	13	5	15	2	11	6	3	4	8
4173	12	13	8	8	15	11	1	10	14	9	5	16	7	4	3	2
4175	15	12	11	14	9	5	2	7	13	16	10	8	10	3	6	1
4176	9	12	16	15	10	8	5	10	14	11	6	13	6	4	3	2
4178	5	15	14	9	13	16	11	9	7	9	10	16	10	11	1	11
4248	1	13	9	12	15	10	2	7	11	14	6	16	6	4	5	3

TABLE 4.2.5 Monthly earnings ratings for the balanced set of 48 subjects

Subject																
K310	100	146	292	250	96	133	250	104	183	417	183	158	150	175	79	108
K313	87	217	347	260	108	152	238	173	433	217	282	195	173	329	195	152
M155	130	173	260	217	108	152	217	173	260	195	217	152	87	260	108	78
M156	156	147	165	104	104	121	121	139	238	195	121	139	147	117	95	95
M159	130	147	173	173	78	113	130	130	173	260	152	130	130	130	113	78
M196	173	121	173	130	121	100	100	130	217	173	152	100	121	87	82	91
M209	250	208	500	292	167	167	100	125	250	208	167	167	125	100	100	100
M210	130	139	195	173	95	104	87	113	173	182	143	139	108	113	87	82
M214	130	108	173	139	113	113	74	113	139	152	130	121	121	130	78	108
M215	130	130	195	195	113	189	87	152	173	217	130	130	152	152	95	87
N114	130	130	217	260	130	100	173	152	260	130	130	108	130	173	91	95
N115	172	152	217	217	130	121	152	130	217	217	130	130	130	130	87	108
4166	108	117	152	152	152	113	102	130	173	126	173	130	130	113	126	108
4167	65	152	173	433	65	78	100	113	303	260	130	95	113	108	78	87
4168	30	130	195	433	65	78	100	113	260	260	130	87	113	108	74	87
4169	82	101	260	247	106	127	98	115	217	195	130	142	113	100	89	82
4170	0	108	173	173	126	87	100	130	173	130	152	130	113	87	87	65
4171	65	152	173	217	173	126	100	130	199	152	87	139	113	130	74	87
4172	130	130	173	173	173	87	87	173	173	173	130	108	108	130	78	65
4173	182	173	152	130	121	113	102	130	152	195	130	156	130	130	100	91
4175	139	143	173	130	113	82	117	74	134	139	108	117	117	74	85	91
4176	0	130	260	260	152	130	173	173	260	173	173	130	130	173	87	65
4178	108	152	173	217	152	121	100	139	195	260	217	139	173	130	108	156
4248	87	130	87	126	130	87	61	108	195	152	87	152	117	78	78	65

TABLE 4.2.5 continued

A211	130	195	173	173	108	108	130	173	217	173	163	119	108	130	78	108
A263	152	173	173	520	130	121	130	195	260	260	173	130	217	173	130	152
A266	133	150	208	208	130	108	130	152	167	250	208	125	150	152	87	130
A267	139	152	195	173	117	108	130	195	217	325	152	130	130	152	87	108
A268	139	173	238	173	108	121	130	147	173	247	173	152	139	156	121	139
A305	130	147	217	195	121	108	152	152	238	347	173	152	130	165	108	130
A306	186	195	273	225	161	121	311	152	260	181	212	186	325	229	108	130
A307	165	238	347	303	152	130	173	217	260	303	195	130	173	195	108	130
B144	200	208	500	375	133	100	167	183	233	292	250	142	167	167	100	150
C295	130	173	520	347	98	95	152	152	433	607	152	130	121	130	78	108
C298	130	195	303	260	152	152	217	238	266	217	260	260	195	173	130	217
C299	138	167	250	333	125	108	167	167	292	250	150	208	167	117	108	100
F128	104	125	292	250	75	67	83	146	229	104	146	83	125	125	67	83
F204	173	160	282	247	139	108	186	186	208	238	195	130	178	195	100	91
F247	104	117	295	250	104	104	167	125	208	146	167	108	104	167	75	100
F257	165	195	238	217	139	130	130	152	217	238	152	173	139	173	108	104
F294	195	195	347	347	195	152	173	152	347	520	260	173	217	217	108	152
F312	130	173	303	260	143	152	130	130	260	195	165	165	173	152	108	108
G213	167	150	417	250	150	108	87	108	250	208	167	133	87	152	78	87
G216	117	130	347	243	121	130	173	152	347	260	173	139	152	165	108	104
G264	133	146	292	233	125	104	130	130	167	292	208	104	130	173	52	108
G265	121	173	433	217	95	95	130	152	173	152	165	130	152	130	95	108
G269	138	150	333	250	117	117	208	150	250	0	225	133	150	167	83	100
G318	173	152	260	260	121	95	217	173	260	195	217	121	152	117	95	87

There are three instances of a 'missing data point' in Table T.4.2.5 (for cases G269, 4170, and 4176). These are indicated by a 'guessed monthly income' of zero.

Vector model analysis

The formal properties of vector model analysis were discussed in Chapter 4 of *Images* (see also Carroll and Chang 1964). The model is a vector model. because each rank-ordering or set of ratings is transformed into a direction (or vector) over an evaluative map of the stimuli (in this case, occupations). The analysis is called 'internal' analysis because the locations of the stimuli in the evaluative map are determined at the same time as the subject-vectors are estimated. (In 'external' analysis, the map of the stimuli is provided by the researcher, and may indeed be an estimate of a cognitive map.)

Each internal analysis yields an evaluative map and a set of subject-vectors. We used Carroll's MDPREF computer program to estimate evaluative maps over the 48 subjects, for each of the five criteria of judgement. The coordinates of the stimulus points are shown in Tables T.4.2.6 to T.4.2.10. We defer commentary upon them until the evaluative maps derived from analysis using the distance model have been discussed.

TABLE T.4.2.6   Evaluative map from the social usefulness ratings based on a vector model analysis, using MDPREF with the 48 quadrant cases

		Dimensions		
		I	*I*	*III*
1	MIN	.116	−.556	−.101
2	CST	.393	+.141	.023
3	QA	.050	−.349	.251
4	CA	.078	−.132	.375
5	MPN	.210	+.137	−.334
6	AD	.201	+.228	−.390
7	BSL	−.193	+.402	.391
8	MTO	−.092	−.015	.208
9	SOL	.165	−.093	.205
10	CSE	−.000	−.249	.086
11	CT	−.349	−.118	−.242
12	PM	.383	+.120	−.252
13	C	.041	+.243	.175
14	LD	−.134	+.192	.007
15	RP	−.441	−.203	−.346
16	BM	−.429	+.251	−.055

TABLE T.4.2.7   Evaluative map from the prestige and rewards rankings, based on a vector model analysis, using MDPREF with the 48 quadrant cases

		Dimensions		
		I	*II*	*III*
1	MIN	+.154	+.158	.926
2	CST	+.300	+.226	−.183
3	QA	+.229	−.398	−.072
4	CA	+.196	−.501	.024
5	MPN	+.203	+.437	−.097
6	AD	+.018	+.282	−.174
7	BSL	−.369	+.084	−.066
8	MTO	−.124	+.072	.051
9	SOL	+.267	−.164	−.042
10	CSE	+.215	−.192	−.117
11	CT	−.161	−.277	.010
12	PM	+.213	+.284	−.187
13	C	−.047	+.048	−.068
14	LD	−.270	+.010	.016
15	RP	−.417	+.024	−.003
16	BM	−.406	−.093	−.018

TABLE T.4.2.8   Evaluative map from the cognitive distance ratings, based on a vector model analysis, using MDPREF with the 48 quadrant cases

		Dimensions		
		I	*II*	*III*
1	MIN	.139	.466	.047
2	CST	−.012	.389	−.403
3	QA	.419	−.247	−.197
4	CA	.386	−.188	−.062
5	MPN	.101	.314	.490
6	AD	−.283	−.033	.529
7	BSL	−.384	−.152	−.000
8	MTO	−.124	.160	−.302
9	SOL	.310	.053	.014
10	CSE	.218	.009	.137
11	CT	.204	−.225	.115
12	PM	−.240	.284	−.093
13	C	−.198	.013	−.166
14	LD	−.286	−.179	−.008
15	RP	−.061	−.324	.180
16	BM	−.188	−.340	−.283

TABLE T.4.2.9   Evaluative map from the social standing criterion, based on a vector model analysis using MDPREF with the 48 quadrant cases

		Dimensions		
		I	*II*	*III*
1	MIN	+.233	.181	−.885
2	CST	+.258	.212	.087
3	QA	+.271	−.343	.113
4	CA	+.272	−.266	.064
5	MPN	+.088	.458	.143
6	AD	−.079	.363	.192
7	BSL	−.408	−.021	−.126
8	MTO	−.129	−.058	.132
9	SOL	+.277	−.165	.002
10	CSE	+.262	−.245	.090
11	CT	−.064	−.265	.001
12	PM	+.135	.416	.184
13	C	−.083	−.055	.185
14	LD	−.295	.029	.036
15	RP	−.400	−.010	−.123
16	BM	−.336	−.231	−.094

TABLE T.4.2.10   Evaluative map from the monthly earnings ratings, based on a vector model analysis using MDPREF with the 48 quadrant cases

		Dimensions		
		I	*II*	*III*
1	MIN	−.160	−.019	−.296
2	CST	−.037	−.027	−.028
3	QA	.508	−.520	−.526
4	CA	.412	−.013	.679
5	MPN	−.194	.011	−.045
6	AD	−.222	.020	−.036
7	BSL	−.095	−.110	.043
8	MTO	−.085	−.025	.090
9	SOL	.344	−.054	.225
10	CSE	.367	.827	−.303
11	CT	.021	−.124	−.004
12	PM	−.129	−.001	−.026
13	C	−.108	.008	.105
14	LD	−.068	−.075	.059
15	RP	−.303	.027	.051
16	BM	−.252	.075	.014

Distance model analysis

The differences between vector and distance models in the analysis of rank orders and sets of ratings are discussed in Chapter 4 of *Images*. The essential difference is that vector model analysis transforms each rank order into a direction over an evaluative map, while distance model analysis transforms each rank order into a point, located along with the stimuli in the evaluative map. The distance model is less restrictive than the vector model. It fits more parameters, and therefore uses more degrees of freedom in the data. We used Roskam's MINIRSA computer programme, which uses a quasi-non-metric approach in order to estimate stimulus points in the evaluative map, and the 'ideal point' corresponding to each subject. MINIRSA finds a metric solution but avoids treating the data as anything other than rank ordered. (MDPREF by contrast treats the data as being real numbers.) All quasi-non-metric scaling methods run into difficulties when there are ties in the data, and MINIRSA is no exception. When there are many ties in the data, a solution can sometimes be found which has a low stress-value (appears to be a good fit

TABLE T.4.2.11   'Social usefulness' rating criterion: internal analysis by the simple distance model (multidimensional unfolding using Roskam's MINIRSA algorithm): coordinates of stimulus points

	Dimensions		
	I	*II*	*III*
MIN	−0.663	−0.156	0.013
CST	0.315	−0.303	−0.474
QA	−0.696	−0.111	0.076
CA	−0.684	−0.141	0.025
MPN	0.045	−0.159	0.589
AD	0.955	0.133	−0.120
BSL	0.177	0.429	−1.080
MTO	−0.661	−0.142	0.114
SOL	−0.642	−0.163	0.095
CSE	−0.660	−0.149	0.094
CT	0.594	1.099	0.579
PM	0.402	−0.273	0.327
C	−0.663	−0.135	0.135
LD	0.190	0.435	−1.077
RP	0.592	1.089	0.572
BM	1.400	−1.453	0.133
Sigma	0.662	0.572	0.484

Stress_2 (*d*-hat) = 0.125 Stress_2 (*d*-star) = 0.207

TABLE T.4.2.12 'Cognitive distance' rating criterion: internal analysis by the simple distance model (multidimensional unfolding using Roskam's MINIRSA algorithm): coordinates of stimulus points

| | *Dimensions* | | |
	I	*II*	*II*
MIN	−1.051	−0.338	0.133
CST	−0.566	−0.633	−0.127
QA	−1.518	0.069	0.622
CA	−0.873	0.826	0.727
MPN	−0.354	−0.665	−0.230
AD	0.418	−0.363	−0.131
BSL	0.693	0.094	0.075
MTO	−0.850	1.048	−1.327
SOL	0.110	−0.560	−0.150
CSE	0.452	−0.320	−0.071
CT	0.723	0.346	0.184
PM	−0.024	−0.612	−0.191
C	0.681	−0.008	−0.042
LD	0.723	0.291	0.153
RP	0.727	0.259	0.131
BM	0.709	0.567	0.245
Sigma	0.740	0.516	0.432

Stress $_2$ (*d*-hat) = 0.183 Stress $_2$ (*d*-star) - 0.269

to the data), but upon closer inspection turns out to be degenerate. Another consequence of having many ties in the data can be that the iterative computations in the MINIRSA algorithm may fail to converge. Our analyses showed that the presence of many ties in the data gave rise to degenerate solutions for the social usefulness, cognitive distance and social standing criteria, and to the impossibility of obtaining any plausible solution at all for the rewards and earnings criteria. The stimulus coordinates for the three solutions which could be obtained are shown as Tables T.4.2.11-13.

Congruence between the overall cognitive map and various evaluative maps

Eight evaluative maps for the 16 occupational titles have been reported in this appendix. How similar or different are they, when compared one to another? A number of methods are available for testing the degree of congruence between configurations (see Green and Rao 1972). The most straightforward method is to take a configuration in which one has some

TABLE T.4.2.13 'Social standing' ranking criterion: internal analysis by the simple distance model (multidimensional unfolding using Roskam's MINIRSA algorithm): coordinates of stimulus points

	Dimensions		
	I	*II*	*III*
MIN	−0.285	0.246	0.426
CST	0.385	−0.167	−0.471
QA	0.037	0.077	0.368
CA	0.071	0.044	0.372
MPN	0.397	−0.204	−0.444
AD	0.381	−0.212	−0.559
BSL	−1.619	0.430	−0.875
MTO	0.001	0.049	0.446
SOL	0.081	0.022	0.364
CSE	0.089	0.031	0.356
CT	−0.113	0.156	0.454
PM	0.389	−0.186	−0.457
C	0.006	0.048	0.434
LD	−1.233	0.607	0.012
RP	−0.141	−1.937	−0.047
BM	1.556	0.994	−0.380
Sigma	0.676	0.588	0.444

Stress $_2$ (*d*-hat) = 0.150 Stress $_2$ (*d*-star) = 0.253

confidence, and to use INDSCAL in order to test the extent to which the interpoint distances for each of the evaluative maps can be approximated by a differentially stretched or shrunken version of that 'target' configuration.

We used the two-dimensional configuration which is given in T.3.15 as a target. This 'cognitive map' was derived from similarities judgements, and we have some confidence in its being correct. The interpretation of the dimensions is available in Chapter 3 of *Images*. Table T.4.2.14 shows the 'pseudo subject' weights and the goodness-of-fit correlation for each of the eight evaluative maps.

The 'goodness-of-fit correlations' in the far right-hand column are a useful indicator of the congruence between the various 'evaluative map' configurations, and the fixed two-dimensional 'cognitive map'. They range from 0.681 (for the evaluative map derived from vector model analysis of social standing judgements) to a lowest extreme of 0.214 (for distance model analysis of monthly earnings judgements). These values are comparatively low, especially if it is borne in mind that our congruence testing method (INDSCAL) chooses weights on the dimensions of the fixed cognitive map, so as to make each goodness-of-fit correlation

TABLE T.4.2.14   Use of INDSCAL to compare stimulus configurations derived from internal analysis with the fixed two-dimensional configuration of T.3.15 as a target

Criterion for internal MDPREF *analysis, using the 48-case quadrant set*	*Pseudo-subject weights on dimensions*		*Goodness-of-fit correlations*
	I	*II*	
Social usefulness	0.435	0.489	0.662
Prestige and rewards	0.535	0.309	0.624
Cognitive distance	0.493	0.325	0.597
Social standing	0.552	0.386	0.681
Monthly earnings	0.373	0.075	0.383
Criterion for internal MINIRSA analysis, using the 48-case quadrant set			
Social usefulness	0.288	0.105	0.309
Cognitive distance	0.333	0.287	0.445
Social standing	0.154	0.144	0.214

Note: The unfolding algorithm failed to converge for the 'rewards' and 'earnings' criteria.

as large as possible. So far as the first dimension of the fixed space is concerned the weights for the three evaluative maps derived from distance model analysis (MINIRSA) are all smaller than any of the weights for the five maps derived from vector model analysis (MDPREF). The same pattern comes close to being repeated for the weights on the second dimension. The single exception is the monthly earnings evaluative map (derived from vector model analysis), which has a very low weight on dimension two. The goodness-of-fit correlations are higher for the evaluative maps derived from vector model analysis than for those derived from the distance model — though the monthly earnings criterion again provides an exception to the perfect pattern. Finally, we can look at the ratios of weights on the fixed dimensions (see MacCallum 1977). Out of the eight evaluative maps compared, only the first (social usefulness criterion analysed by the vector model) has a larger weight on the second dimension. The remaining seven evaluative maps have larger weights on the first dimension, though in only one case of the vector model applications (monthly earnings) is the ratio greater than 3 : 1.

The main conclusions from this analysis are

(*a*) Technical difficulties can sometimes make it impossible to find an acceptable solution when making an internal analysis of rank order data with a quasi-non-metric distance model. No such problems arise with the metric vector model.

(*b*) Evaluative maps derived from internal analysis of rankings and ratings

by the vector model are different from those derived from internal analysis
by the distance model in that they are more congruent with the cognitive
map that was discussed in chapter three of *Images* (see T.3.15).

(c) The evaluative maps were only moderately congruent with the cognitive
map that had been taken as a fixed comparison point (the highest goodness-
of-fit correlation was 0.68). It seems true that evaluative maps can sometimes
give a rough approximation to a cognitive map, but it would be difficult to
argue that any single evaluative map would give a good approximation.

Internal analyses were also carried out within each of the four quadrants.
We used the vector model, and focused on two ratings criteria, social
usefulness and monthly earnings. Each of the 'within quadrants' analyses is
based on 12 cases. The resulting evaluative maps were transformed into sets
of interpoint distances, and thus tested for congruence with the fixed two-
dimensional cognitive map of T.3.15.

TABLE T.4.2.15   Use of INDSCAL to compare stimulus configurations
derived from internal MDPREF analysis with the fixed two-dimensional
configuration of T.3.15 as a target

Source of internal MDPREF analysis	Pseudo-subject weights on dimensions		Goodness-of-fit correlations
	I	*II*	
Social usefulness, quadrant A	0.197	0.412	0.461
Social usefulness, quadrant B	0.198	0.319	0.379
Social usefulness, quadrant C	0.373	0.328	0.502
Social usefulness, quadrant D	0.415	0.188	0.460
Social usefulness, all quadrants	0.435	0.489	0.662
Monthly earnings, quadrant A	0.370	0.107	0.388
Monthly earnings, quadrant B	0.369	0.117	0.390
Monthly earnings, quadrant C	0.442	0.109	0.458
Monthly earnings, quadrant D	0.488	0.184	0.526
Monthly earnings, all quadrants	0.373	0.075	0.383

Note: It is curious that the figures for 'all quadrants' are so different from
those for the quadrants.

The results shown on T.4.2.15 are interesting because they show the
range of variation that can occur when internal analyses are carried out in
different sub-groups. So far as the social usefulness criterion is concerned,
evaluative maps from quadrants A and B have greater weight on the second
dimension of the fixed cognitive map than on the first. This pattern is
reversed for the quadrant D evaluative map, and the weights on the two
dimensions are about equal for quadrant C. As before, the degree of congruence
between evaluative maps and the fixed cognitive map is only moderate.

T.4.3 Internal Analysis with MDPREF and MINIRSA: Goodness-of-fit Tests

The estimation procedures for the MDPREF algorithm that we used in estimating evaluative maps by the vector model are quite different from the estimation procedures used by the MINIRSA distance model algorithm. A major difference is that MDPREF is a metric scaling procedure, while MINIRSA operates by quasi-non-metric methods. (It is of course possible to estimate the distance model by metric methods, but we chose not to do so.) Since the two programs minimise different badness-of-fit functions, it is difficult to compare the overall goodness of fit between data and fitted values between MDPREF and MINIRSA.

The following method was used to estimate the goodness of fit. The evaluative map configurations shown in the previous appendix (T.4.2) were used as the 'externally provided' configurations in PREFMAP analysis, and in this way correlations were computed between data and fitted values. The simple vector model of PREFMAP was used with the five configurations estimated by MDPREF. The simple distance model of PREFMAP was used with the three configurations estimated by MINIRSA. The results are shown (in summary form) in Table T.4.3.1, and they may be compared with the results from PREFMAP analysis with the same data, but using the INDSCAL-derived cognitive map, as shown in Table T.4.4.6.

TABLE T.4.3.1   Summary of goodness of fit between rankings and ratings data and the 'evaluative maps' derived from internal analysis

	Goodness of fit (Root Mean Square Correlations)	
	Linear fit	*Monotone fit*
Vector model configurations (estimated by MDPREF)		
Social usefulness	0.84	0.95
Prestige and rewards	0.89	0.96
Cognitive distance	0.73	0.90
Social standing	0.90	0.96
Monthly earnings	0.87	0.97
Distance model configurations (estimated by MINIRSA)		
Social usefulness	0.82	0.98
Cognitive distance	0.69	0.97
Social standing	0.75	0.98

Note: Carroll's PREFMAP computer program was used to compute correlations between data and fitted values. The vector phase of PREFMAP was used with the five configurations estimated by MDPREF. The simple distance phase of PREFMAP was used with the three configurations estimated by MINIRSA.

T.4.4 External Analysis with PREFMAP (using group space from INDSCAL analysis)

A scaling analysis of rank orderings or sets of ratings is said to be an 'external analysis' when the 'cognitive map' (or similarities space) into which the scaling will take place is derived from some source other than the rankings or ratings themselves. Sometimes a cognitive map can be derived *a priori*, from rational considerations, (see Coxon 1974). More usually, it will arise from a separate scaling analysis of similarities data. In this appendix, we discuss the fitting of rankings and ratings data to a cognitive map derived from individual differences scaling (see T.3.15 and Chapter 3 of *Images*).

Carroll's scheme for the external analysis of preference data can be seen as four neatly nested sub-models (see Chapter 4 of *Images*). The four models are referred to as: (*a*) the rotated-and-weighted distance model; (*b*) the weighted distance model; (*c*) the simple distance model; and (*d*) the simple vector model. The sub-models are said to be 'nested' because (*d*) is a special case of (*c*), which is in its turn a special case of (*b*), which is itself a special case of the most general model, (*a*). When the parameters of the models are estimated, they are easily seen to be functions of regression coefficients (see below) and the 'nested' nature of the four sub-models comes out in the fact that the more general models contain the same parameters as the less general ones, but also contain extra parameters. Familiar statistical tests (F-tests) are available to help the researcher decide whether or not a more complex model explains a significantly greater amount of variation in the data than is accounted for by a special case of that more general model.

In the first three phases of the (metric) PREFMAP procedure, the model is:

$$s_{ij} = a_i d^2{}_{ij} + b_i + e_{ij} \ (a_i \geqslant 0)$$

i.e. preference values are related linearly to the (squared) distance between the subject's ideal point and the stimulus point.

These three distance models differ in how the $d^2{}_{ij}$ are defined.

(*a*) *In phase 1 (Generalised Unfolding)* the model involves

$$d^2{}_{ij} = \sum_t w_{it}(x^*_{jt} - y^*_{it})^2$$

where x^*_{jt} is the coordinate of the stimulus point x_j on dimension t, orthogonally rotated by the subject's idiosyncratic transformation of the reference axes.

y^*_{it} is the coordinate of the subject's ideal point on dimension t, similarly transformed.

Carroll (1972) shows (p. 132) that the model may be written

$$s_{ij} = \sum_{tt'} r^i_{tt'} (x_{jt} x_{jt'}) + \sum_t b_{it} x_{jt} + c_i$$

(where the $r_{tt'}^i$ coefficient incorporates the weights and the transformation of the subject).

The cross-product-term $(x_{jt}x_{jt'})$ includes both the *squared* terms x_t^2 (when $t = t'$) and the *cross-product* terms $(x_t.x_{t'})$.

This formulation makes it clear that the model assumes a *quadratic* regression (with squared, linear and cross-product terms) between the preferences (s_{ij}) and the x_{jt}.

For any individual, therefore, there will be the following unknown parameters to estimate:

(1) $t\ b_{it}$ coefficients for the linear terms
(2) $t\ r_{tt}$ (not $r_{tt'}$ as in Carroll (1972: 132, bottom line))
(3) $\binom{t}{2}\ r_{tt'}$ coefficients for the cross-product terms
(4) $1\ c_i$ constraint

In toto, $2t + \binom{t}{2} + 1$ 'beta' coefficients.

Thus for $t = 2$ dimensions, there are obviously coefficients for 2 linear, 2 squared, 1 cross-product terms and constant term.

(b) Phase II (Weighted Unfolding)

The model involves:

$$d_{ij}^2 = \sum_t w_{it}(x_{jt} - y_{jt})^2$$

i.e. no idiosyncratic rotation.

The model is expressible as:

$$s_{ij} = \sum_t w_{it}x_{jt}^2 + \sum_t b_{it}x_{jt} + c_i$$

This model still involves a quadratic regression, but without cross-product terms.

It involves estimation of:

(i) $t\ b_{it}$ (linear)
(ii) $t\ w_{it}$ (squared)
(iii) $1\ c_i$ (constant)

In toto, $2t + 1$ 'beta' coefficients; output in this order.

(c) Phase III (Simple Unfolding)

This model involves:

$$d_{ij}^2 = \sum_t (x_{jt} - y_{jt})^2$$

i.e. no idiosyncratic weights.

The model is expressible as:

$$s_{ij} = a_i(\sum_t u_t x_{jt}^2) + \sum_t b_{it}x_{jt} + c_i$$

In this phase, the weights w_{it} of Phase II are independent of the subject, and may equal only ± 1. They are called u_t.

The model still involves a quadratic regression, but *only one* squared-term variable.

It involves estimating:

(i) $t\, b_{it}$ (linear)

(ii) $1\, a_i$ (squared)

(iii) $1\, c_i$ (constant)

In toto, $t + 2$ 'beta' coefficients, output in this order.

(d) Phase IV (Vector)

The model is *not* a distance model, but the linear model:

$$s_{ij} = \sum_t b_{it} x_{jt} + c_i$$

This involves only a *linear* regression, between the s_{ij} and the x_{jt}, and the only parameters to be estimated are:

(i) $t\, b_{it}$ (linear)

(ii) $1\, c_i$ (constant)

i.e. $t + 1$ 'beta' coefficients, in that order.

The hierarchical nature of the models

Each model/phase is embedded in the one immediately above it, in the sense of a lower model being derivable by setting regression terms to zero in the 'higher' model. It is for this reason that it is justifiable to test for the goodness of fit of a model to the data by standard significance procedures, and test for significant increases in the variance explained by an F test between models (although models are clearly not independent).

PREFMAP is usually used by entering a higher phase, and dropping down to a lower phase (S-PHASE and E-PHASE). Carroll argues, with considerable plausibility, that the solution for the 'average subject' of the highest phase entered should form the basis for the succeeding phases (p. 135).

e.g.   S-PHASE = 1, E-PHASE = 4

(a) After Phase I, the rotated reference axes of the *average subject* form the 'canonical reference frame' for Phase II.

(b) The subjects' weights and ideal points are fitted in *this* reference frame (rather than the one initially input in Phase I) in Phase II.

(c) Similarly, the average subject's dimensional weights are applied to the rotated configuration for analysis in Phase III.

This is not always desirable, and the remedy is simply to enter at a lower phase — i.e.

(a) If it is desired to help the orientation of the input configuration, enter at Phase II,

(b) If it is desired to keep the dimensions unweighted, then enter at Phase III.

The parameters for the four sub-models can be estimated through regression and regression-like methods. Three classes of estimation procedure are feasible at the present time:

(*a*) Isotonic (monotone) regression

(*b*) Linear regression (ordinary least squares)

(*c*) Bisquare weighted linear least squares

The first of these allows the data and the fitted values to be related by any monotone function, but only permits very approximate statistical testing. The second allows statistical testing, but requires data and fitted values to be linearly related. The third is resistant in the sense that badly fitted data points are not allowed to affect parameter estimates.

This appendix reports the analysis of rankings and ratings of the standard set of 16 occupational titles, on five criteria of judgement, as made by 48 subjects taken from the four 'quadrant' sub-groups. The five criteria of judgement have been described in Chapter 4 of *Images,* and in T.4.1 of this book. The data themselves are shown as Tables T.4.2.1 to T.4.2.5.

Tables T.4.4.1 to T.4.4.5 show goodness-of-fit correlations between data and fitted values for each of the five criteria of judgement. Each table uses the fixed 3-dimensional INDSCAL cognitive map from T.3.15 and reports the results of fitting the four nested PREFMAP models to the data by isotonic (monotone) regression (with a weak approach to ties in the data). Given the same data, the goodness of fit correlation should always be at least as large in a more complex model as it is in a simpler model. These tables show some exceptions to this rule, but this is because the estimation procedure for isotonic regression operates iteratively, and is subject to problems of local minima. Therefore it can happen that a more complex sub-model of PREFMAP can have a lower goodness-of-fit correlation than a simpler sub-model, even where precisely the same data points are being fitted.

TABLE T.4.4.1 'Social usefulness' rating criterion: correlations between data and fitted values, for the four nested sub-models of PREFMAP, with the fixed 3-dimensional INDSCAL cognitive map.

	MODELS			
	(1)	*(2)*	*(3)*	*(4)*
	Rotated weighted distance	*Weighted distance*	*Simple distance*	*Simple vector*
Case				
A211	1.00	1.00	.96	.96
A263	.99	.96	.92	.86
A266	.99	.94	.91	.89
A267	1.00	.99	.98	.96
A268	.98	.97	.96	.96
A305	1.00	1.00	.98	.98
A306	1.00	.95	.95	.88
A307	.99	.92	.92	.92

TABLE T.4.4.1 *continued*

Case	(1) Rotated weighted distance	(2) Weighted distance	(3) Simple distance	(4) Simple vector
B144	1.00	.98	.66	.70
C295	.99	.92	.88	.88
C298	1.00	1.00	.96	.96
C299	1.00	.99	.96	.95
F128	1.00	.99	1.00	.99
F204	1.00	1.00	1.00	.99
F247	1.00	1.00	.98	.97
F257	.99	.95	.93	.84
F294	.99	.98	.81	.78
F312	1.00	.95	.93	.92
G213	1.00	.86	.76	.76
G216	1.00	1.00	.97	.92
G264	1.00	.99	.98	.98
G265	1.00	.99	.99	.97
G269	1.00	1.00	.97	.97
G318	.97	.94	.82	.80
K310	1.00	.99	.98	.96
K313	.99	.99	.99	.99
M155	1.00	.99	.95	.95
M156	.99	.99	.96	.96
M159	1.00	1.00	.98	.97
M196	.95	.91	.86	.85
M209	1.00	1.00	1.00	1.00
M210	.99	.96	.91	.90
M214	1.00	.96	.93	.93
M215	.98	.98	.86	.84
N114	1.00	.97	.97	.94
N115	1.00	1.00	.99	.99
4166	.99	.99	.99	.97
4167	1.00	.99	.99	.96
4168	.99	.97	.96	.88
4169	.99	.97	.96	.88
4170	.99	.98	.97	.94
4171	1.00	.99	.96	.93
4172	1.00	.94	.86	.85
4173	.98	.97	.96	.96
4175	.98	.98	.96	.93
4176	1.00	.99	.99	.99
4178	1.00	.90	.86	.86
4248	.99	.94	.93	.91

TABLE T.4.4.2 'Prestige and rewards' ranking criterion: correlations between data and fitted values for the four nested sub-models of PREFMAP, with the fixed 3-dimensional INDSCAL cognitive map

	MODELS			
	(1)	*(2)*	*(3)*	*(4)*
	Rotated weighted distance	*Weighted distance*	*Simple distance*	*Simple vector*
Case				
A211	1.00	1.00	.99	.98
A263	1.00	.99	.99	.97
A266	.98	.96	.91	.91
A267	1.00	.99	.97	.97
A268	.99	.99	.98	.98
A305	.93	.87	.84	.82
A306	1.00	.97	.97	.97
A307	.96	.91	.87	.86
B144	1.00	.99	.99	.98
C295	1.00	.99	.98	.97
C298	1.00	1.00	.98	.98
C299	.96	.92	.90	.90
F128	1.00	1.00	1.00	.99
F204	1.00	1.00	.99	.99
F247	1.00	1.00	.99	.98
F257	1.00	1.00	1.00	.99
F294	1.00	1.00	1.00	1.00
F312	1.00	.99	.98	.97
G213	1.00	.96	.93	.91
G216	1.00	.97	.94	.93
G264	.99	.99	.98	.98
G265	1.00	.99	.98	.97
G269	1.00	1.00	.99	.99
G318	1.00	1.00	1.00	1.00
K310	1.00	.99	.99	.99
K313	.97	.92	.85	.85
M155	1.00	1.00	.98	.96
M156	1.00	1.00	.97	.96
M159	1.00	1.00	.99	.99
M196	1.00	.99	.99	.95
M209	1.00	1.00	1.00	.99
M210	1.00	.99	.97	.91
M214	1.00	.99	.99	.93
M215	1.00	1.00	1.00	1.00
N114	.99	.99	.97	.97
N115	1.00	1.00	1.00	1.00
4166	.97	.97	.95	.95
4167	.98	.98	.97	.94
4168	.98	.98	.97	.94

TABLE T.4.4.2 *continued*

Case	(1) Rotated weighted distance	(2) Weighted distance	(3) Simple distance	(4) Simple vector
4169	.96	.86	.85	.85
4170	1.00	.81	.81	.73
4171	.95	.87	.87	.80
4172	1.00	.95	.90	.87
4173	.99	.99	.99	.99
4175	.98	.87	.85	.81
4176	1.00	.99	.98	.96
4178	.99	.97	.94	.88
4248	.98	.96	.95	.91

TABLE 4.4.3 'Cognitive distance' rating criterion: correlations between data and fitted values, for the four nested sub-models of PREFMAP, with the fixed 3-dimensional INDSCAL cognitive map

	MODELS			
Case	(1) Rotated weighted distance	(2) Weighted distance	(3) Simple distance	(4) Simple vector
A211	1.00	.99	.99	.98
A263	.99	.95	.92	.92
A266	1.00	.98	.99	.98
A267	.85	.85	.82	.74
A268	1.00	.94	.77	.75
A305	1.00	.98	.98	.93
A306	1.00	.99	.95	.94
A307	1.00	.99	.97	.95
B144	1.00	.88	.70	.69
C295	1.00	1.00	.99	.99
C298	1.00	.84	.83	.73
C299	1.00	.98	.96	.87
F128	.99	.99	.93	.92
F204	.97	.91	.88	.88
F247	.96	.77	.74	.74
F257	.95	.89	.87	.86
F294	.94	.91	.89	.86
F312	.94	.93	.87	.87
G213	.99	.95	.87	.85
G216	.98	.96	.93	.91
G264	1.00	.94	.85	.85
G265	1.00	1.00	.97	.95

TABLE 4.4.3 *continued*

Case	(1) Rotated weighted distance	(2) Weighted distance	(3) Simple distance	(4) Simple vector
G269	1.00	.99	.83	.82
G318	1.00	1.00	.99	.99
K310	.99	.94	.86	.84
K313	1.00	.99	.99	.99
M155	.99	.92	.87	.86
M156	1.00	.92	.92	.88
M159	1.00	.90	.88	.89
M196	1.00	.97	.89	.89
M209	.99	.99	.98	.98
M210	1.00	.99	.99	.99
M214	1.00	1.00	1.00	.97
M215	1.00	.99	.99	.98
N114	1.00	1.00	1.00	.99
N115	1.00	.99	.98	.96
4166	1.00	.99	.98	.97
4167	1.00	.99	.99	.99
4168	1.00	.99	.99	.99
4169	1.00	.99	.97	.96
4170	1.00	1.00	.93	.93
4171	.99	.88	.84	.79
4172	.99	.93	.91	.86
4173	.99	.99	.97	.97
4175	.98	.97	.72	.66
4176	.99	.99	.97	.97
4178	.99	1.00	.97	.93
4248	1.00	.99	.94	.92

TABLE T.4.4.4   'Social standing' ranking criterion: correlations between data and fitted values, for the four nested sub-models of PREFMAP, with the fixed 3-dimensional INDSCAL cognitive map

	MODELS			
Case	(1) Rotated weighted distance	(2) Weighted distance	(3) Simple distance	(4) Simple vector
A211	1.00	1.00	.97	.97
A263	1.00	1.00	1.00	.99
A266	1.00	1.00	1.00	.98
A267	.98	.96	.93	.93
A268	.98	.98	.94	.93

TABLE T.4.4.4 *continued*

Case	(1) Rotated weighted distance	(2) Weighted distance	(3) Simple distance	(4) Simple vector
A305	.99	.98	.95	.94
A306	1.00	.99	.98	.95
A307	1.00	.97	.92	.90
B144	1.00	1.00	.99	.93
C295	1.00	1.00	.99	.99
C298	1.00	1.00	.99	.99
C299	1.00	1.00	1.00	1.00
F128	1.00	1.00	.97	.96
F204	1.00	1.00	1.00	.99
F247	1.00	.99	.99	.99
F257	1.00	1.00	1.00	1.00
F294	1.00	1.00	1.00	1.00
F312	.99	.99	.99	.95
G213	1.00	1.00	1.00	.99
G216	1.00	1.00	.96	.96
G264	1.00	1.00	.99	.99
G265	.99	1.00	.99	.99
G269	.99	.97	.97	.96
G318	1.00	1.00	1.00	1.00
K310	1.00	1.00	1.00	1.00
K313	1.00	1.00	.98	.96
M155	1.00	1.00	1.00	1.00
M156	1.00	.99	.99	.95
M159	1.00	1.00	1.00	1.00
M196	1.00	1.00	1.00	.99
M209	1.00	1.00	.99	.99
M210	1.00	.99	.98	.92
M214	.92	.85	.81	.81
M215	1.00	1.00	.99	.99
N114	1.00	1.00	1.00	1.00
N115	1.00	1.00	1.00	1.00
4166	.97	.97	.95	.94
4167	.98	.98	.95	.94
4168	.98	.98	.95	.94
4169	.98	.92	.90	.88
4170	1.00	.96	.95	.95
4171	1.00	.99	.97	.95
4172	.97	.87	.86	.85
4173	.99	.99	.99	.98
4175	1.00	.99	.99	.98
4176	.99	.99	.97	.96
4178	.99	.87	.79	.75
4248	.92	.85	.82	.78

TABLE T.4.4.5 'Monthly earnings' rating criterion: correlations between data and fitted values, for the four nested sub-models of PREFMAP, with the fixed 3-dimensional INDSCAL cognitive map

| | MODELS | | | |
| | *(1)* | *(2)* | *(3)* | *(4)* |
Case	*Rotated weighted distance*	*Weighted distance*	*Simple distance*	*Simple vector*
A211	1.00	.98	.96	.94
A263	1.00	.99	.98	.96
A266	.98	.97	.94	.93
A267	1.00	.95	.91	.89
A268	1.00	.98	.97	.97
A305	1.00	.97	.96	.95
A306	.89	.76	.74	.72
A307	1.00	.98	.98	.95
B144	.98	.98	.97	.97
C295	1.00	.97	.96	.96
C298	.99	.90	.87	.82
C299	.99	.97	.97	.94
F128	.96	.93	.93	.91
F204	1.00	.98	.98	.94
F247	−.93	.91	.91	.85
F257	1.00	.98	.96	.95
F294	.99	.98	.97	.94
F312	1.00	.99	.98	.93
G213	1.00	.99	.99	.96
G216	1.00	.97	.96	.91
G264	.95	.92	.91	.90
G265	.97	.93	.92	.92
G269	.92	.88	.88	.79
G318	.97	.94	.93	.93
K310	.99	.94	.94	.87
K313	.91	.86	.86	.85
M155	.92	.83	.82	.80
M156	.99	.94	.87	.85
M159	1.00	1.00	.99	.98
M196	1.00	.99	.93	.93
M209	1.00	1.00	1.00	1.00
M210	1.00	.98	.97	.97
M214	1.00	.99	.98	.94
M215	1.00	1.00	.92	.80
N114	.97	.95	.89	.87
N115	1.00	1.00	.99	.99
4166	.99	.90	.75	.73
4167	.99	.98	.96	.94
4168	.99	.98	.97	.94
4169	1.00	.98	.98	.90

TABLE T.4.4.5 *continued*

	MODELS			
	(1)	*(2)*	*(3)*	*(4)*
	Rotated			
	weighted	*Weighted*	*Simple*	*Simple*
Case	*distance*	*distance*	*distance*	*vector*
4170	.98	.97	.94	.89
4171	.97	.93	.93	.85
4172	1.00	.98	.98	.94
4173	.96	.96	.94	.92
4175	1.00	.99	.97	.96
4176	1.00	.98	.98	.92
4178	1.00	.98	.90	.89
4248	.99	.99	.98	.97

Since the goodness-of-fit correlations are only concerned with monotone fit in these tables, it seems reasonable to demand very high correlations. As a rough rule of thumb, we would say that a goodness-of-fit correlation lower than 0.90 is unsatisfactory, and one below 0.80 is highly unsatisfactory. Such unsatisfactory goodness-of-fit correlations give clues about which cases are 'deviant', and should be given special attention.

Table T.4.4.6 summarises the previous five tables, by giving average (root mean square) correlations between data and fitted values for each criterion of judgement and for each of the sub-models of PREFMAP.

As mentioned above, it is possible to carry out statistical tests for each case, between the four sub-models of PREFMAP. Table T.4.4.7 shows these 'step-down' F tests for the (monotone fit) comparison between the simple

TABLE T.4.4.6   Averaged correlations (root mean square) between data and fitted values, for the four nested sub-models of PREFMAP with the fixed 3-dimensional INDSCAL cognitive map. Root mean square correlations are given for each of the five criteria of judgement

	MODELS			
	(1)	*(2)*	*(3)*	*(4)*
	Rotated			
	weighted	*Weighted*	*Simple*	*Simple*
	distance	*distance*	*distance*	*vector*
Social usefulness	0.98	0.96	0.93	0.91
Prestige and rewards	0.98	0.96	0.95	0.93
Cognitive	0.98	0.95	0.91	0.89
Social standing	0.98	0.97	0.96	0.95
Monthly earnings	0.97	0.95	0.93	0.90

Note: The results in this table should be compared with those in Table T.4.3.1.

distance model and the simple vector model. The F-ratios here are merely approximate, since the monotone fitting algorithm is subject to local minima. This results in some of the F-ratios being negative (an impossible result if a linear fit was used), and in some being infinite. These difficulties are part of the price paid for the convenience of having monotone rather than linear fit.

TABLE T.4.4.7 Statistical tests (approximate) between the simple distance model and the simple vector model (external analysis with PREFMAP, with the fixed 3-dimensional INDSCAL cognitive map). The table shows 'step-down' F-ratios at 1 and 11 degrees of freedom (critical value for the 1% level is 9.65).

| | \multicolumn{5}{c}{CRITERIA OF JUDGEMENT} |
	Social usefulness	*Prestige and rewards*	*Cognitive distance*	*Social standing*	*Monthly earnings*
A211	1.27	4.35	21.71	1.25	5.38
A263	8.37	15.07	negative	1.01	9.19
A266	2.43	negative	1.16	136.95	1.76
A267	8.32	negative	3.84	negative	1.41
A268	.11	negative	.66	.06	.32
A305	.64	1.28	19.54	2.23	3.21
A306	15.40	1.55	4.34	21.14	.51
A307	.31	.89	3.87	2.08	11.34
B144	negative	5.32	.55	61.97	negative
C295	negative	9.47	1.66	4.05	.50
C298	negative	5.43	5.65	1.36	3.30
C299	4.19	.02	20.52	negative	11.31
F128	.42	12.85	1.27	1.10	2.65
F204	36.02	6.79	.10	7.59	22.22
F247	5.94	6.72	.00	2.93	6.95
F257	11.91	1.27	.70	infinite	4.79
F294	1.41	7.81	2.26	71.05	10.65
F312	1.49	12.81	negative	31.63	22.90
G213	.01	2.14	1.51	7.29	23.36
G216	20.29	3.02	2.96	.90	13.55
G264	1.29	negative	.18	.06	.83
G265	20.50	5.69	6.44	negative	negative
G269	.27	3.81	.13	4.82	7.20
G318	.78	negative	.48	negative	1.40
K310	8.34	2.82	.96	infinite	10.59
K313	2.19	negative	negative	11.81	.25
M155	.04	5.68	.47	negative	.89
M156	negative	2.65	4.03	57.45	1.57
M159	1.50	6.20	negative	infinite	.94
M196	.48	24.76	.45	7.02	.61

TABLE T.4.4.7 *continued*

	CRITERIA OF JUDGEMENT				
	Social usefulness	*Prestige and rewards*	*Cognitive distance*	*Social standing*	*Monthly earnings*
M209	negative	11.48	2.17	3.43	negative
M210	.80	23.53	3.42	37.89	2.29
M214	.34	51.72	61.87	negative	18.14
M215	1.37	8.03	3.02	negative	16.06
N114	12.00	negative	12.66	negative	1.74
N115	.03	.23	8.07	negative	11.98
4166	16.56	negative	2.61	1.66	.76
4167	48.87	7.40	negative	2.81	6.35
4168	21.74	7.39	negative	2.84	7.15
4169	21.90	.16	5.69	1.80	35.57
4170	11.19	3.56	.20	.07	8.80
4171	5.81	4.79	3.48	6.49	10.91
4172	.83	2.36	4.84	.52	21.85
4173	.14	.33	.53	12.26	3.83
4175	8.35	2.72	1.85	1.60	1.11
4176	9.25	13.67	.05	2.53	33.97
4178	.01	11.15	17.57	1.71	1.18
4248	3.14	10.39	3.40	2.19	5.29

Note: 'negative' means that a negative F-ratio was calculated: see text for explanation.

The F-ratios are approximate because the monotone fitting algorithm is subject to local minima. When the linear fit option is used, F-ratios are exact.

It is obviously desirable to have a better-behaved statistical test. We therefore re-analysed the data using a linear fit rather than a monotone fit. With a linear fit, the estimation proceeds by ordinary least squares, so that problems of negative F-ratios cannot arise. Of course the linear-relationships model gets lower goodness-of-fit correlations. Statistical tests between the simple distance model and the simple vector model, and between the weighted distance model and the simple distance model are shown as Tables T.4.4.8 and T.4.4.9. Both tables refer to analyses using a linear fit, and cover all five criteria of judgement for the 48 cases. While some of the F-ratios are significant at the 1 per cent level, the overall pattern supports our view (in *Images*) that the simple vector model is adequate for most cases.

TABLE T.4.4.8   Statistical tests between the simple distance model and the simple vector model (external analysis with PREFMAP, with the fixed 3-dimensional INDSCAL cognitive map). The table shows 'step-down' F-ratios at 1 and 11 degrees of freedom (critical value for the 1% level is 9.65). A linear fit was used to estimate the models.

CRITERIA OF JUDGEMENT

Case	Social usefulness	Prestige and rewards	Cognitive distance	Social standing	Monthly earnings
A211	36.07	.33	1.54	.31	2.77
A263	.72	.01	.03	2.06	1.36
A266	.30	.16	.09	9.46	.00
A267	.40	1.39	.01	1.00	.05
A268	1.57	.45	6.23	.86	.17
A305	7.44	1.46	1.12	.23	.00
A306	2.19	2.24	.52	.18	.06
A307	.94	.52	1.24	.36	.49
B144	8.89	7.55	.89	20.91	1.55
C295	4.35	.47	1.22	1.49	1.58
C298	1.78	.05	2.02	.16	.00
C299	7.21	.10	7.29	1.63	3.01
F128	.05	.01	.33	2.03	1.26
F204	.08	2.71	.39	2.84	.98
F247	.66	3.51	.28	.10	2.63
F257	3.53	.32	1.71	.76	.08
F294	1.50	3.18	.01	2.29	.71
F312	6.87	1.26	1.61	3.84	5.23
G213	1.18	.06	3.23	5.01	2.64
G216	13.77	3.04	.01	.00	2.83
G264	.51	1.20	1.51	.21	.39
G265	.34	3.58	.01	.11	1.12
G269	6.02	.01	1.76	2.90	.37
G318	3.24	.39	9.31	1.40	.47
K310	2.06	1.71	.44	3.04	.71
K313	5.81	.00	.42	3.41	.00
M155	6.08	3.11	3.83	.00	.01
M156	4.37	.37	.77	5.97	.29
M159	6.99	1.91	.53	1.12	.00
M196	.01	3.71	.05	4.39	.08
M209	2.77	5.05	.03	.08	2.98
M210	.47	5.41	1.07	9.03	.26
M214	.12	4.70	.44	.03	.59
M215	3.85	.28	6.09	.31	4.99
N114	1.25	.70	1.68	.13	1.27
N115	2.57	.04	.06	3.43	2.27
4166	.08	.10	.00	1.46	.62
4167	.02	.22	5.65	3.23	1.35
4168	.01	.08	6.38	2.65	2.73

TABLE T.4.4.8 *continued*

| | CRITERIA OF JUDGEMENT | | | | |
Case	Social usefulness	Prestige and rewards	Cognitive distance	Social standing	Monthly earnings
4169	.04	.00	.01	.58	13.89
4170	.13	.28	2.58	.07	1.63
4171	1.37	3.84	.90	.32	3.19
4172	.00	.08	2.32	.08	.65
4173	.00	.99	.20	1.05	3.15
4175	.78	3.96	1.02	.04	.00
4176	.02	3.32	.00	.06	2.94
4178	.86	.86	5.93	.01	.01
4248	.00	4.13	.59	.00	.00

TABLE T.4.4.9   Statistical tests between the weighted distance model and the simple distance model, (external analysis with PREFMAP, with the fixed 3-dimensional INDSCAL cognitive map). The table shows 'step-down' F-ratios at 2 and 9 degrees of freedom, (critical value at the 1% level is 8.02). A linear fit was used to estimate the models.

| | CRITERIA OF JUDGEMENT | | | | |
Case	Social usefulness	Prestige and rewards	Cognitive distance	Social standing	Monthly earnings
A211	.01	21.55	1.57	4.80	.85
A263	.79	3.68	.26	1.35	.13
A266	.79	.33	.78	.53	1.80
A267	2.06	4.39	.32	1.23	1.07
A268	1.25	.04	.22	1.85	1.02
A305	2.83	.38	1.62	.04	.56
A306	.63	.33	2.32	.10	.03
A307	.11	.04	1.54	1.82	.83
B144	1.23	1.16	.17	1.08	.29
C295	.50	1.13	2.24	3.45	.88
C298	.68	10.02	.37	.73	1.51
C299	.08	.21	1.86	1.95	.04
F128	.21	1.80	1.75	3.29	.53
F204	3.38	.24	.12	.16	.22
F247	2.80	.55	.01	.09	.03
F257	.16	3.62	.14	.04	1.93
F294	.62	1.68	1.05	.42	.83
F312	.44	1.32	.20	.18	.77
G213	.50	2.58	.04	1.21	.09
G216	8.07	.90	.04	.59	.86
G264	1.44	1.23	1.13	1.54	.59
G265	.84	1.60	1.22	1.97	.06

TABLE T.4.4.9 *continued*

		CRITERIA OF JUDGEMENT			
Case	*Social usefulness*	*Prestige and rewards*	*Cognitive distance*	*Social standing*	*Monthly earnings*
G269	1.21	2.81	1.42	.32	.10
G318	.02	1.10	4.11	5.53	.24
K310	1.59	.37	1.45	.50	.07
K313	1.04	.85	1.04	1.47	.68
M155	9.12	8.11	1.07	2.70	.75
M156	.44	4.18	.64	.75	1.88
M159	1.34	5.42	.15	7.53	1.26
M196	.84	.67	3.49	1.56	1.03
M209	1.95	.92	1.73	.58	.01
M210	.46	9.27	.09	4.01	2.52
M214	.70	2.04	3.70	.73	3.70
M215	1.34	.43	5.20	1.23	12.12
N114	.46	3.64	.06	2.52	.53
N115	2.87	3.01	.04	.47	1.53
4166	1.46	.75	.03	.42	3.20
4167	1.51	2.39	1.33	.93	.31
4168	.63	2.32	.53	1.04	.25
4169	.77	.49	1.43	.63	1.31
4170	.39	.45	1.18	2.07	.91
4171	3.11	.45	.40	2.79	.24
4172	.02	.40	1.46	.41	.03
4173	.36	.06	.03	.21	1.50
4175	.79	.67	11.64	.11	1.18
4176	1.01	.36	.35	1.45	.10
4178	.03	.09	1.17	.03	3.90
4248	.87	.08	3.80	.61	.18

T.4.5 External Analysis with PREFMAP: Scaling Ratings and Rankings in Private Spaces

Four cases were selected from those with deviant cognitive maps (see T.3.19), and their similarities data were scaled using a quasi-non-metric 'smallest space analysis' programme (Roskam's MINISSA). These cases were J271, 4170, 4135 and 6701. The scalings with MINISSA led to our having an idiosyncratic 'private space' for each of the four subjects, and it seemed desirable to test whether or not it was easier to map ratings and rankings judgements made by these subjects into the overall INDSCAL group space of T.3.15, or into the 'private space' for the subject concerned.

To the extent that an individual's 'private' cognitive map has been correctly estimated from his similarity judgements, it should be easier to represent his rankings and ratings in that 'private space' than in the common 'group' space derived from INDSCAL analysis. On the other hand, 'No man is an island, entire of itself . . .', and there may be some subjects whose similarity judgements were, for one reason or another, a poor representation of their thinking.

Tables T.4.5.1 to T.4.5.4 show the comparisons between goodness-of-fit correlations in the four sub-models of PREFMAP, when fitting rankings and ratings judgements either to the INDSCAL group space or to the MINISSA private space for the subject concerned.

A linear rather than a monotonic fitting procedure was used. Broadly speaking, J271 is better fit in his private space than in the INDSCAL group space. The same goes for case 4170. However, cases 4135 and 6701 seem to be as well (or as badly) fit in their private spaces as in the INDSCAL group space.

TABLE T.4.5.1   Rankings and ratings made by J271; comparison of goodness-of-fit correlations for relating rankings and ratings to (*a*) the INDSCAL group cognitive map of T.3.15, and (*b*) the idiosyncratic cognitive map obtained with MINISSA. Linear fit.

	INDSCAL group space	*MINISSA* private space
Rotated and weighted distance model		
Social usefulness	0.71	0.87
Prestige and rewards	0.82	0.97
Cognitive distance	0.85	0.78
Social standing	0.91	0.96
Monthly earnings	0.73	0.78
Weighted distance model		
Social usefulness	0.56	0.79
Prestige and rewards	0.76	0.92
Cognitive distance	0.79	0.65
Social standing	0.81	0.95
Monthly earnings	0.54	0.63
Simple distance model		
Social usefulness	0.52	0.74
Prestige and rewards	0.74	0.89
Cognitive distance	0.77	0.64
Social standing	0.76	0.72
Monthly earnings	0.51	0.57
Simple vector model		
Social usefulness	0.30	0.74
Prestige and rewards	0.54	0.89
Cognitive distance	0.61	0.54
Social standing	0.74	0.63
Monthly earnings	0.37	0.53

TABLE T.4.5.2   Rankings and ratings made by 4170; comparison of goodness-of-fit correlations for relating rankings and ratings to (*a*) the INDSCAL group cognitive map of T.3.15, and (*b*) the idiosyncratic cognitive map obtained with MINISSA. Linear fit.

	INDSCAL *group space*	*MINISSA* *private space*
Rotated and weighted distance model		
Social usefulness	0.77	0.85
Prestige and rewards	0.92	0.75
Cognitive distance	0.83	0.91
Social standing	0.93	0.91
Monthly earnings	–	–
Weighted distance model		
Social usefulness	0.72	0.80
Prestige and rewards	0.49	0.58
Cognitive distance	0.78	0.72
Social standing	0.79	0.77
Monthly earnings	–	–
Simple distance model		
Social usefulness	0.70	0.80
Prestige and rewards	0.47	0.46
Cognitive distance	0.65	0.71
Social standing	0.74	0.76
Monthly earnings	–	–
Simple vector model		
Social usefulness	0.69	0.80
Prestige and rewards	0.37	0.45
Cognitive distance	0.63	0.71
Social standing	0.67	0.75
Monthly earnings	–	–

TABLE T.4.5.3   Rankings and ratings made by 4135: comparison of goodness-of-fit correlations for relating rankings and ratings to (*a*) the INDSCAL group cognitive map of T.3.15, and (*b*) the idiosyncratic cognitive map obtained with MINISSA. Linear fit.

	INDSCAL *group space*	*MINISSA* *private space*
Rotated and weighted distance model		
Social usefulness	0.78	0.81
Prestige and rewards	0.77	0.84
Cognitive distance	0.79	0.90
Social standing	0.86	0.79
Monthly earnings	0.60	0.71

TABLE T.4.5.3 *continued*

	INDSCAL group space	*MINISSA* private space
Weighted distance model		
Social usefulness	0.74	0.71
Prestige and rewards	0.69	0.70
Cognitive distance	0.71	0.71
Social standing	0.81	0.49
Monthly earnings	0.44	0.57
Simple distance model		
Social usefulness	0.73	0.69
Prestige and rewards	0.66	0.60
Cognitive distance	0.68	0.68
Social standing	0.74	0.49
Monthly earnings	0.39	0.56
Simple vector model		
Social usefulness	0.64	0.50
Prestige and rewards	0.54	0.24
Cognitive distance	0.54	0.61
Social standing	0.63	0.33
Monthly earnings	0.37	0.51

TABLE T.4.5.4   Rankings and ratings made by 6701: comparison of goodness-of-fit correlations for relating rankings and ratings to (*a*) the INDSCAL group cognitive map of T.3.15, and (*b*) the idiosyncratic cognitive map obtained with MINISSA. Linear fit.

	INDSCAL group space	*MINISSA* private space
Rotated and weighted distance model		
Social usefulness	0.93	0.92
Prestige and rewards	0.93	0.91
Cognitive distance	—	—
Social standing	0.92	0.87
Monthly earnings	0.79	0.82
Weighted distance model		
Social usefulness	0.79	0.88
Prestige and rewards	0.91	0.83
Cognitive distance	—	—
Social standing	0.87	0.73
Monthly earnings	0.74	0.69

TABLE T.4.5.4 *continued*

	INDSCAL group space	*MINISSA* private space
Simple distance model		
Social usefulness	0.76	0.86
Prestige and rewards	0.91	0.78
Cognitive distance	—	—
Social standing	0.84	0.72
Monthly earnings	0.70	0.66
Simple vector model		
Social usefulness	0.74	0.77
Prestige and rewards	0.89	0.72
Cognitive distance	—	—
Social standing	0.83	0.72
Monthly earnings	0.68	0.66

TABLE T.4.5.5 Rankings and ratings made by J271: comparison of goodness-of-fit correlations for relating rankings and ratings to (*a*) the INDSCAL group cognitive map of T.3.15, and (*b*) the idiosyncratic cognitive map obtained with MINISSA. Linear Fit.

	INDSCAL group space	*MINISSA* private space
Rotated and weighted distance model		
Social usefulness	0.71	0.87
Prestige and rewards	0.82	0.97
Weighted distance model		
Social usefulness	0.70	0.86
Prestige and rewards	0.82	0.97
Simple distance model		
Social usefulness	0.70	0.86
Prestige and rewards	0.82	0.96
Simple vector model		
Social usefulness	0.30	0.74
Prestige and rewards	0.54	0.89

The PREFMAP models all take an 'externally provided' cognitive map as given, but only the rotated and weighted distance model allows for a rotation of that given configuration. The remaining models take the given configuration unchanged. However, we carried out a further analysis, in which the two 'evaluative' criteria of social usefulness and prestige and rewards were the only rankings and ratings to be scaled. In this further analysis (shown in Tables T.4.5.5-8) the results for the rotated and weighted distance model are the same as before, but after that model has been estimated, the given configuration is changed by a rotation followed by a differential weighting of the axes (these being determined by the average subject). These changes to the given configuration mean that fitting the rankings and ratings data into the new configuration, by the weighted distance model, the simple distance model, and the simple vector model, all lead to different goodness-of-fit estimates. The private space analysis is still better than the INDSCAL group space for J271, but the picture is confused so far as the other cases are concerned. Overall it seems that scaling ratings and rankings into private spaces is a nice idea, but is by no means guaranteed to produce better results than using a carefully estimated INDSCAL group space.

TABLE T.4.5.6   Rankings and ratings made by 4170: comparison of goodness-of-fit correlations for relating rankings and ratings to (a) the INDSCAL group cognitive map of T.3.15, and (b) the idiosyncratic cognitive map obtained with MINISSA. Linear fit.

	INDSCAL group space	MINISSA private space
Rotated and weighted distance model		
Social usefulness	0.78	0.85
Prestige and rewards	0.92	0.75
Weighted distance model		
Social usefulness	0.76	0.83
Prestige and rewards	0.90	0.72
Simple distance model		
Social usefulness	0.76	0.83
Prestige and rewards	0.90	0.72
Simple vector model		
Social usefulness	0.69	0.80
Prestige and rewards	0.37	0.45

TABLE T.4.5.7   Rankings and ratings made by 4135: comparison of
goodness-of-fit correlations for relating rankings and ratings to (*a*) the
INDSCAL group cognitive map of T.3.15, and (*b*) the idiosyncratic cognitive
map obtained with MINISSA. Linear fit.

	INDSCAL *group space*	*MINISSA* *private space*
Rotated and weighted distance model		
Social usefulness	0.78	0.81
Prestige and rewards	0.77	0.84
Weighted distance model		
Social usefulness	0.76	0.78
Prestige and rewards	0.74	0.82
Simple distance model		
Social usefulness	0.74	0.77
Prestige and rewards	0.72	0.81
Simple vector model		
Social usefulness	0.64	0.50
Prestige and rewards	0.54	0.24

TABLE T.4.5.8   Rankings and ratings made by 6701: comparison of
goodness-of-fit correlations for relating rankings and ratings to (*a*) the
INDSCAL group cognitive map of T.3.15, and (*b*) the idiosyncratic cognitive
map obtained with MINISSA. Linear fit.

	INDSCAL *group space*	*MINISSA* *private space*
Rotated and weighted distance model		
Social usefulness	0.93	0.92
Prestige and rewards	0.93	0.91
Weighted distance model		
Social usefulness	0.92	0.89
Prestige and rewards	0.92	0.88
Simple distance model		
Social usefulness	0.90	0.87
Prestige and rewards	0.91	0.86
Simple vector model		
Social usefulness	0.74	0.77
Prestige and rewards	0.89	0.72

T.4.6 Deviant Case Analysis

Where our methods for analysing rank orderings and sets of ratings are concerned, deviant case analysis can mean a number of things. First, a case may be deviant because his data do not fit any of the alternative measurement models chosen by the investigator. Second, a subject's data may fit one of the investigator's measurement models (possibly very well), but the case may still be counted as deviant, either because the majority of cases have their data fit by some other model, or because his values in the measurement model he shares with other well-fit subjects may be markedly idiosyncratic. Finally, we may note that a mixture of these cases is possible, as when a subject's data fit the measurement model only barely satisfactorily, and the values estimated in that measurement model are slightly idiosyncratic, though not markedly so.

A priori, it is reasonable to suppose that a subject whose similarities judgements were badly fit by the overall INDSCAL group space would be a deviant case when his ratings and rankings data were subjected to external analysis in that INDSCAL group space. The *a priori* nature of the argument may be so strong that it might override mere empirical disconfirmation, so that all the cases itemised in T.3.19 should be classified as deviant cases of the first kind. This argument assumes that if evaluation depends on cognition, then deviant cognition implies deviant patterns of evaluation. As we saw in the preceding appendix (T.4.5), only one case out of four had his rankings and ratings data markedly better fit in his 'private space' than in the INDSCAL-derived group space.

Goodness-of-fit correlations for the data of the 48 subjects judging the 16 occupations on five criteria are shown in Tables T.4.4.1 to T.4.4.5. As remarked earlier, it seems reasonable to regard a case as 'deviant' in terms of goodness of fit, if his correlation is less than about 0.80.

T.4.7 Statistics for Directional Data

Social scientists use the notion of rank-ordering very frequently, particularly in studies of social inequality and social mobility, but also in such applied fields as market research. Sociologists have been interested in the prestige rankings that individuals make of such social categories as occupations. Market researchers have been interested in preference rankings. Not infrequently a crucial research problem arises, in the form of a question such as: 'How does the average rank ordering made by individuals in one sub-group compare with the average rank ordering made by individuals in other sub-group?' This turns out to be by no means a simple problem.

A rank ordering is a *relational* statement, and not merely a set of cardinal numbers. What we seek in attempting to make some kind of average of many rank orderings is a procedure in which the integrity of each rank ordering is preserved as much as possible. In short we seek a 'holistic' (though also a parsimonious) description of each rank ordering. The conventional survey analysis methods of presenting and analysing data on rank orders given by interviewees, or inferred from historical data, fail to maintain this integrity. Instead, they simply count the number of times each object is ranked first, the number of times it is ranked second, the number of times it is ranked third, and so forth. An average rank-ordering is produced which is the rank-ordering of the means (or some such function) of the rank numbers assigned to each of the objects. Clearly, the relational properties of each rank ordering are shattered at the first step of this aggregation procedure. The conventional approach usually continues by computing 'profile correlations' between the average rank-orderings of the sub-groups between which comparisons are to be made.

In *Images* we argued that it is more meaningful to average *parameters* derived from the fitting of a specified model to the individual rank-orderings. One possible model is called a vector model. In the vector model, a rank ordering is represented as a *direction* over a 'map' of the objects to be ranked. The 'map' may be in two or three (or more) dimensions. The mode of analysis is that rank orders are fitted as a whole (maintaining their integrity) into a 'map', in which they are represented by *metric* quantities, which are the direction cosines of the corresponding vectors. Efficient procedures are available for estimating both the 'map' and the directions over it. Tests of goodness of fit for the transformation from rank orders to direction cosines are also available (Carroll 1972, and sections T.4.3 and T.4.4 of this book). It is known that rank orders for some classes of objects are not well fit by a vector (directional) model. (Coxon (1974) showed that preference orders for family sizes and compositions are much better fitted by a different model.) However, the vector (directional) model is the most satisfactory for many other classes of objects, including occupational titles.

It seems plausible to suppose that a 'directional data' analysis would be more sensitive to differences between sub-groups than would a conventional analysis. Furthermore, the directional representation of rank orders makes it easier to pick out 'outlying' rank orders from a visual inspection, and therefore makes it possible to eliminate 'outliers' from confirmatory tests of hypotheses.

As an example, we may take the judgements of 16 occupational titles that were made by an ambulance driver (identified by the code M196). This man judged the occupational titles on five criteria, which we abbreviate as: (a) 'Social usefulness'; (b) 'Rewards'; (c) 'Cognitive distance'; (d) 'Social standing'; (e) 'Monthly earnings'. His judgements are shown in T.4.7.1 as rank orderings, with 16 indicating the highest rank and 1 indicating the lowest. The lower part of the same table shows the direction cosines which correspond to a vector representation for each of the rank orderings. A certain amount of 'data reduction' is achieved since 16 numbers are summarised by three direction cosines (whose sum of squares is constrained to unity). The data are also shifted to a higher level of measurement, since Carroll's (1972) 'quasi-non-metric' fitting procedure can estimate the (metric) direction cosines, while avoiding doing any arithmetic on the rank orderings. It must be emphasised that the 'external analysis' of rank orderings (which transforms them into a vector representation) takes a stimulus configuration (or 'cognitive map') for the occupational titles as *given*. In this analysis, we used the INDSCAL group space which is shown as T.3.15.

Once it is granted that a set of rank orderings can be satisfactorily represented by a corresponding set of directions over a 'map', it is desirable to be able to make statistical tests of the degree to which different sub-groups have a similar spread in their rank orderings, and of the degree to which they have similar averaged rank orderings. By analogy with the analysis of variance, it is desirable to test homogeneity of spread between various sub-groups, and also to test whether the various sub-groups have the same or different average rank orderings.

TABLE T.4.7.1   Rank orderings of 16 occupational titles on five criteria of judgement, and their representation as direction cosines in the INDSCAL group space of T.3.15. Data from an ambulance driver (M196)

Titles	Criteria of judgement				
	(a)	*(b)*	*(c)*	*(d)*	*(e)*
MIN	2	8	1	14	13
CST	15	1	1	15	7
QA	11	3	1	13	13
CA	6	4	1	10	10
MPN	15	1	5	16	7
AD	13	2	16	8	4
BSL	6	9	11	3	4
MTO	6	6	8	6	10
SOL	12	3	5	11	16
CSE	2	5	8	9	13
CT	4	11	11	5	12
PM	13	2	8	12	4
C	10	7	11	7	7
LD	6	10	11	4	2
RP	4	12	5	2	1
BM	1	13	11	1	3

Direction cosines in relation to dimensions of the INDSCAL group space of T.3.15.

	(a)	*(b)*	*(c)*	*(d)*	*(e)*
Dimension I	0.145	0.577	0.985	−0.781	−0.93
Dimension II	−0.950	0.758	−0.086	−0.617	−0.13
Dimension III	−0.275	−0.303	−0.149	0.097	0.33

Statistical techniques for the analysis of directional data were pioneered by Fisher (1953), Watson (1956) and Stephens (1962, 1969). What are directional data? One definition is that data may be viewed as directional whenever each observation is represented by a set of positive or negative numbers, the sum of whose squares is unity. Rank orderings can be represented as directions over a p dimensional stimulus configuration, (cognitive map). Each rank order can then be replaced by p 'direction cosines' (one for each dimension of the space), and the sum of squares for these direction cosines will be unity. Most of the statistical theory was initially developed for distributions on the circumference of a circle or on the surface of a sphere (i.e. for $p = 2$ or $p = 3$).

The present state of the statistical literature on the analysis of directional data is summarised in Pearson and Hartley (1972), and in Mardia (1972). One-sample, two-sample and multi-sample tests for mean direction (for which may be read, 'average rank ordering') have been devised, and their statistical properties are thoroughly known. Tests have also been devised for the homogeneity of the spread of directions within two or more populations.

Before the discussion of available tests of significance, it is desirable to introduce some terminology and notation.

(*a*) Each observation (direction) is called a *vector*.

(*b*) A single sample of vectors can be thought of as being drawn from a population distributed symmetrically around a most probable direction called the *polar vector* or the *modal vector*.

(*c*) The vector sum of a set of directions is called the *resultant vector*, and the square root of the sum of squares for this resultant vector is called its *length*, and given the symbol R. The larger the value of R (i.e. the greater the length of the resultant vector), the more clustered is the sample, and by inference the population from which it is drawn.

(*d*) The clustering of the distribution of vectors around the polar vector is given by a parameter called *kappa*. High values of *kappa* give a concentrated symmetrical distribution of observation vectors around the polar vector, while a zero value would generate a uniform distribution of directions over the surface of the sphere (or around the circumference of a circle, if we are dealing with a two-dimensional space). *Kappa* has been called a 'precision' parameter and a 'concentration' parameter. Many results in the theory of directional data can be proved for the case where *kappa* is large (the value of 1.0 is a widely recommended cutting point), but not for the case where *kappa* is small.

A useful approximation estimates *kappa* from sample data (k is used for *kappa*);

$$k = \frac{N-1}{N-R} \qquad \text{(Watson 1956, p. 156)}$$

where N is the total number of vectors (and also the sum of the lengths of the N unit vectors) and R is the length of the resultant vector for the sample. This approximation is only accurate if the ratio of R to N is above about 0.7 (when this is so, the formula gives $k = 3.3$).

(*e*) For multi-sample tests, we follow the notation of Stephens (1969). There are S samples; N_i is the number of vectors in the *i*th sample, R_i is the length (inner product) of the vector sum for the vectors in the *i*th sample; R is the length of the resultant (vector sum) of the entire set of vectors in all samples, treated as one large sample.

Tests of Significance

Watson's directional analogy to one-way analysis of variance is an approximate test for the comparison of polar vectors (population directions) for two or more samples.

A simple function of the concentration parameter *kappa* and of R namely $2k$ (N−R) is distributed approximately as chi-square with (p−1) $(N-1)$ degrees of freedom.

Since an F distribution is generated as the ratio of two chi-square distributions, an approximate F-test may be made for the comparison of *kappa* estimates from two independent samples of vectors. (See Brandt 1976, pp. 160, 162.)

If a sample is drawn from each of two populations, where both populations have the same concentration parameter, *kappa*, then analogy with the analysis of variance suggests that we should be able to partition the chi square for the concentration of vectors from both samples about a common estimated mean vector. This analogy is valid. The overall chi-square is equal to the sum of components from (i) the concentrations of vectors in each sample about their estimated mean vectors, and (ii) the concentration of the two estimated mean vectors.

The less the concentration of vectors, the greater their dispersion; and so it is possible to write down the partitioning in a form which makes the analogy with analysis of variance more apparent;

Dispersion of both samples about   =   Sum of the dispersions of each sample
a common estimated mean vector   about its estimated mean vector
                                      PLUS dispersion of the two estimated
                                      mean vectors.

An approximation to the F-test proceeds by comparing 'between-group' with 'within-group' components.

Watson's analysis of variance technique enables us to test whether all the samples have the same modal vector. When there are S samples, in three dimensions, the following test statistic

$$U = \frac{(N - S)(\overset{i=S}{\underset{i=1}{\Sigma}} R_i - R)}{(S - 1)(N - \overset{i=S}{\underset{i=1}{\Sigma}} R_i)}$$

is approximately distributed as an F distribution, with $2S$-2 and $2N$-$2S$ degrees of freedom. In two-dimensional case, the U-statistic is calculated by the same formula, but the F distribution has S-1 and N-S degrees of freedom.

Large values of U indicate that the samples do not have a common modal vector. Tests for the same dispersion parameter, *kappa* are given in Stephens (1969) and Pearson and Hartley (1972).

Several analyses of variance for directional data were presented in Chapter 4 of *Images*. Ratings and rank orderings of occupations were transformed into directions over the 'cognitive map' derived from INDSCAL analysis of direct similarity judgements, and the mean directions of vectors for different sub-groups were then compared. In this appendix, we give a somewhat different example. We use the same kinds of ratings and rank orderings of the standard set of 16 occupations (label set 06), but they are represented as an 'evaluative map' which is itself derived from an 'internal' vector model analysis of the ratings or rankings data. In Tables T.4.7.1. to T.4.7.5 we show summary statistics for five analyses of variance, each of which corresponds to a different criterion of judgement, and each of which refers to a different 'evaluative map'. The corresponding evaluative maps are shown as Tables T.4.2.6 to T.4.2.10. The data which are analysed are shown in full as Tables T.4.2.1 to T.4.2.5, one table for each criterion of judgement. Each table presents the data for 48 cases, in four subsets of size 12. These 'quadrant' subsets are referred to as quadrants A, B, C and D. The summary statistics presented are the sums of direction cosines with respect to each of the three dimensions.

TABLE T.4.7.2   Summary statistics for the average directions of 'Social Usefulness' vectors, as estimated from ratings by internal analysis: data of 48 cases in four equal-sized 'quadrant' subgroups

Quadrants (12 cases)	Sums of direction cosines			Resultant (length)
	I	*II*	*III*	
A	10.92	−0.60	0.18	10.94
B	10.88	−0.50	2.66	11.22
C	10.76	1.67	−1.66	11.02
D	9.97	−0.73	−0.94	10.04
Overall	42.54	−0.16	0.23	42.54

Sum of lengths of resultants = 43.22

Reference configuration from internal analysis of the 'social usefulness' ratings data with a vector model (estimated by MDPREF). F approximation at 6 and 88 degrees of freedom is 2.086 which is not significant at conventionally accepted levels.

TABLE T.4.7.3 Summary statistics for the average directions of 'prestige and rewards' vectors, as estimated from rank orders internal analysis: data of 48 cases in four equal-sized 'quadrant' subgroups

Quadrants 12 cases	Sums of direction cosines			Resultant (length)
	I	II	III	
A	−10.22	3.25	−0.86	10.76
B	−10.93	2.03	1.32	11.20
C	−9.09	0.69	2.20	9.38
D	−9.34	−0.15	−3.39	9.93
Overall	−39.58	−0.67	−0.73	39.59

Sum of lengths of resultants = 41.27

Reference configuration from internal analysis of the 'prestige and rewards' rankings data with a vector model (estimated by MDPREF). F approximation at 6 and 88 degrees of freedom is 3.661 which is significant at the 1% level.

TABLE T.4.7.4 Summary statistics for the average directions of 'cognitive distance' vectors, as estimated from rating data by internal analysis: data of 48 cases in four equal-sized 'quadrant' subgroups

Quadrants (12 cases)	Sums of direction cosines			Resultant (length)
	I	II	II	
A	0.34	9.22	0.90	9.27
B	5.85	−5.48	−2.64	8.44
C	−10.20	−0.02	3.79	10.88
D	−5.73	0.62	−3.69	6.84
Overall	−9.75	4.33	−1.63	10.79

Sum of lengths of resultants = 35.43

Reference configuration from internal analysis of the 'cognitive distance' ratings data with a vector model (estimated by MDPREF). F approximation at 6 and 88 degrees of freedom is 28.08 which is obviously significant.

TABLE T.4.7.5 Summary statistics for the average directions of 'social standing' vectors, as estimated from rank orders by internal analysis: data of 48 cases in four equal-sized 'quadrant' subgroups

Quadrants (12 cases)	Sums of direction cosines I	I	II	Resultant (length)
A	−10.46	0.50	0.45	10.48
B	−11.36	−1.44	−1.39	11.53
C	−11.37	0.65	−1.77	11.53
D	−9.16	1.42	4.31	10.22
Overall	−42.35	1.13	1.60	42.40

Sum of lengths of resultants = 43.76

Reference configuration from internal analysis of the 'social standing' rankings data with a vector model (estimated by MDPREF). F approximation at 6 and 88 degrees of freedom is 4.704 which is significant at the 1% level.

TABLE T.4.7.6 Summary statistics for the average directions of 'monthly earnings' vectors, as estimated from ratings, by internal analysis: data of 48 cases, in four equal-sized 'quadrant' sub-groups

Quadrants (12 cases)	Sums of direction cosines I	II	III	Resultant (length)
A	10.80	0.81	0.04	10.83
B	10.81	−2.60	−0.69	11.14
C	11.00	0.18	−1.38	11.09
D	10.49	0.90	1.96	10.71
Overall	43.10	−0.70	−0.08	43.10

Sum of lengths of resultants = 43.77

Reference configuration from internal analysis of the 'monthly earnings' data with a vector model (estimated by MDPREF). F approximation at 6 and 88 degrees of freedom is 2.323 which is significant at the 5% level.

The one-way analyses of variance shown in Tables T.4.7.2 to T.4.7.6 show that the quadrant classification is significantly associated with the directional representations of ratings and rankings of occupations for all of the five criteria of judgement except 'social usefulness'. These findings replicate those in Chapter 4 of *Images,* and since the analyses reported there were concerned with directions over a cognitive map, while the analyses reported here are concerned with directions over distinct evaluative maps, the observation that the findings stand up is encouraging.

5 Design and Methods of Research Used in *Class and Hierarchy*

Introduction

Although the methods of data collection and the rationale for the selection of subjects and objects differ considerably between the first and second parts of the Project (and hence between *Images* and *Class and Hierarchy*) the basic logic is essentially similar. This chapter has the same structure as the corresponding (chapter 2 (T.2)) and should be treated as an extension of it.

U.1.1 Selecting Occupational Titles and Descriptions

In section 1.3 of *Class and Hierarchy* we explain why we wish to avoid being accused of selection bias and nominalism in the choice of occupations to be judged — selection bias because we appear to rely over-heavily in *Images* upon a single set of 16 occupations, and nominalism in the sense that we only use names of occupations as objects of judgement. It is much easier to defend ourselves in describing the tasks of the second volume (*Class and Hierarchy*) for here we deliberately chose a number of different sets of occupations and several of those sets comprised not the names of occupations, but rather descriptions of them.

We have argued elsewhere (Coxon and Jones 1974b) that three general considerations apply in selecting objects for judgement: *comparability* with previous investigations, practical considerations of the number of objects which can reasonably be used, taking into account the varying cognitive complexity of methods of data collection (*operational feasibility*), and *representativeness* (in the sense of sampling from some notional universe of occupational terms). In the tasks reported in *Class and Hierarchy* feasibility has been especially relevant, for the methods we use there vary considerably in the number of objects that a subject can reasonably be expected to judge. The free-sorting task (Chapter 2) can easily be used with a large number of objects (certainly in excess of the 82 descriptions and titles we use), the hierarchies task (Chapter 3) by contrast is only feasible with a smallish number (probably up to 25), and the substitution task (Chapter 5) with some combination of sentence frames and occupational titles which does not require the subject to make more than about 450 judgements. We used 15 sentence frames and 25 titles, and we appeared to be exploring the upper limits of tolerance with the 375 combinations thus generated.

Names of Occupations and Occupational Descriptions

The decision to shift emphasis away from names of occupations to descriptions of them is of especial importance, and was influenced by two considerations. From the outset of the Project we had deliberately encouraged subjects to verbalise their thoughts whilst they were making their judgements about occupations. As a result we amassed a considerable number of descriptive and evaluative comments on occupations. These verbalisations provided good examples of occupational predication, which we have argued (cf. section 1.1 in *Class and Hierarchy*) is the fundamental structure for representing occupational meaning, and is one of the central organising features of this research project. Needless to say, many of the things which subjects said about occupations occurred with considerable (not to say monotonous) regularity. It was not difficult to collect an extensive stock of occupational predicates in this way. But to what extent was this commonality specific to the particular set of occupations being considered? We could not answer this question in advance. Fortunately, the same predicates did recur with reassuring frequency in the later free-sorting task, when a quite different set of titles was being employed.

The problem of representativeness was approached in a manner suited to the task concerned. The set of occupational titles used in the free-sorting task was originally developed in conjunction with colleagues at the University of California at Irvine for a cross-cultural study of occupational cognition, and the occupations were therefore chosen to correspond to the experience of the subjects in the cultures concerned: it thus represents a purposive selection. For the predicate set, we merged two sources – the descriptions elicited in earlier tasks, and others which constantly occurred in a range of newspapers and other media when occupational matters were being discussed (see *Class and Hierarchy*, pp. 139ff.). In this case, representativeness is based upon the salience of the predicates in both the research context and the non-reactive, more naturally occurring, context of specialist and everyday public discussion.

I The main sets of occupation titles (used in *Class and Hierarchy*)
(*a*) The *Basic Set* (Label set 06) of 16 occupational titles (described and defined in pages 11-12 above) was only used in the Hierarchies task (Chapters 3 and 4).
(*b*) The *Extended Set* (Label set 08) of 32 occupational titles (described and defined in pages 13-14 above) was only used in the Free-Sorting task (Chapter 2).
(*c*) The *Minor Extended Set* (Label set 15). This set of 20 occupational titles consists of the Basic Set (LABL06) together with four further titles drawn

from the Hall-Jones (1950) list. (The additions are starred in Table U.1.1.1.) This set was only used in the pilot investigations reported in Chapter 5 (*Class and Hierarchy*, pp. 139.)

TABLE U.1.1.1   Minor extended set of 20 occupational titles (Label set 15)

	Name	*Abbreviation*
1	Church of Scotland minister	MIN
2	Barman	BM
3	*Business manager (10 to 99 hands)	BMG
4	Carpenter	C
5	Civil Servant (executive grade)	CSE
6	Commercial traveller	CT
7	Solicitor (country practice)	SOL
8	Male psychiatric nurse	MPN
9	*Jobbing master builder	JMB
10	Lorry driver	LD
11	Policeman	PM
12	Railway porter	RP
13	*Works manager (industrial)	WMG
14	Comprehensive school teacher	CST
15	Qualified actuary	QA
16	Ambulance driver	AD
17	Building site labourer	BSL
18	Machine tool operator	MTO
19	*Newsagent and tobacconist (one man shop)	NT
20	Chartered accountant	CA

(*d*) The *Full SA Set* (Label set 17). This set of 25 occupational titles represents a quite novel approach to the problem of selecting occupational titles. The purpose was twofold (*Class and Hierarchy*, p. 144).

(1) to obtain a set of titles which would reflect the dispersion of characteristics (salary, education, people-contact) likely to be encountered by our subjects in their daily lives;

(2) to use the form of the occupational title used by the job-incumbent himself, and specified to the same extent as his self-description.

This was done by listing the precise self-description used by each of the 371 people who were interviewed in enumeration district 160 (see below, p. 147) and then randomly selecting 25 of them.

The occupational titles are listed in Table U.1.1.1. They were used as the substitutions in the smaller set of occupational descriptions (see below) in the main sentence-frame task reported in Chapter 5.

TABLE U.1.1.2 Full set of 25 occupational titles used in the main sentence-frames task (Label set 17)

	Name	Abbreviation
1	Architect	AR
2	Mini ambulance driver	ADM
3	Civil servant, assistant secretary	CSA
4	Wages clerk for engineering firm	WCK
5	Industrial compositor (typesetter)	ICR
6	Director of brass foundry (self-employed)	DBF
7	Engine driver (second man on diesel engine)	ED
8	Refrigeration engineer (self-employed)	RE
9	Engineering inspector (steel plant)	EI
10	Head groundsman	HGR
11	Inspector of taxes	IT
12	Master jeweller	MJ
13	Carpenter-joiner (self-employed)	CJR
14	Long-distance lorry driver	LLD
15	Trainee manager in Burton's tailors	TMG
16	Motor mechanic in garage	MMG
17	Nursery man (self-employed with two employees)	NM
18	Police sergeant	PS
19	Teacher in boys' boarding school	TBS
20	Laboratory technician trainee (brewery)	LTT
21	Tyre repairer	TR
22	Warehouseman (groceries)	WH
23	Shop floor superintendent (engineering factory)	SF
24	Turner and fitter	TF
25	Assistant office manager (stockbroker's office)	AOM

II The main sets of occupational descriptions
The basic set of occupational descriptons: Label set 36.
The basic set of 50 occupational descriptions arises from transcriptions of task verbalisations, from newspaper descriptions and − to a very limited extent − from the descriptions employed in the Department of Employment's *Classification of Occupations and Dictionary of Occupational Titles* (CODOT). (See *Class and Hierarchy,* pp. 136ff. *et seq.)* The statements express a general predicate, and usually have the form:

They [have a certain property].

The basic set is used in all the variants of the free-sorting task, reported in Chapters 2 and 5.
The modified set of occupational descriptions: Label set 45
After initial piloting on a student sample, it was found necessary to reduce the number of occupational descriptions drastically for use in a full-scale

TABLE U.1.1.3   Basic set of 50 occupational descriptions (Label set 36)

	Description	*Abbreviation*
1	They would receive very little public support if they went on *strike*	STRIKE
2	They work very long *hours*	HOURS
3	They are involved in *managing* people as part of their work	MANAGE
4	They spend a lot of time at work *clock-watching*	CLOCK-W
5	They are often *self-employed*	S-EMP
6	They have mainly *physical* skills	PHYS
7	They provide a *service* to the community	SERVE
8	They have their job organised as a *closed* shop	CLOSED
9	They have served their *appr*enticeships to become tradesmen	APPR
10	They have *irreg*ular hours	IRREG
11	They have to have a high standard of *acad*emic education	ACAD
12	They often *switch* their jobs	SWITCH
13	They earn a lot of their salary by working *overtime*	OTIME1
14	They often encourage their *sons* to go into the same work as themselves	SONS
15	They have a lot of fringe benefits and *'perks'* in their job	PERKS
16	*Most* people have thought of being one at some time in their lives	MOST
17	They get paid *overtime* for work they do out of normal hours	OTIME2
18	They usually do their work dressed in ordinary *casual* clothes	CASUAL
19	They have a strong *trade union*	TU
20	They often take the *day off* from work	DAYOFF
21	*Any*one with average intelligence could do the job for which they are paid	ANY
22	They often work at *weekends*	WKENDS
23	They are almost always *men*	MEN
24	They are *paid by the week*	PAYWK
25	They have to *clock in* and out of work with a time-card	CLOCKIN
26	You expect them to be over *30* years old	30
27	They regard themselves as *prof*essionals	PROF
28	They have to undertake a long arduous *training* for their job	TRAIN
29	They are involved in *help*ing other people	HELP
30	They have a *boring* repetitive job	BORING
31	They are paid by the *month*	MONTH
32	They earn a great deal of *money*	MONEY
33	They have a high *social standing* in the community	STATUS

TABLE U.1.1.3 *continued*

	Description	Abbreviation
34	They are not paid regularly, but earn *fees* for what they do	FEES
35	They often *move* into some other line of work after a few years	MOVE
36	They have often had experience of working in *various* lines of work	VARIOUS
37	They tend to be active in the affairs of their local *community*	CTY
38	They earn a lot when *young*, but their incomes don't rise much after that	YOUNG
39	They are paid by the *hour*	HOUR
40	They build up relationships with other *people* as part of their job	PEOPLE
41	They work in a very *spec*ialised field	SPEC
42	They are required to have high *educ*ational qualifications	EDUC
43	Society could not continue to *exist* without them	ESSE
44	*No special training* is required to be one	N-TRAIN
45	They do not earn much at first, but do have high incomes *later* on	LATER
46	They are mostly *younger* than 30	YOUNGER
47	They have to be physically *fit* to do their job	FIT
48	They have a *secure* job	SECURE
49	They have to pass difficult *exam*inations	EXAM
50	They have a tradition of *solidarity* with each other	SOLIDY

interview and make considerable changes in wording (see *Class and Hierarchy*, pp. 143ff.).

The 15 modified descriptions, having the general form:

'A ——————— would [have a certain property]

are detailed in Table U.1.1.4. The modified set of descriptions is used, in conjunction with the full SA set of occupational titles, in the main sentence-frame task reported in Chapter 5.

TABLE U.1.1.4   Modified set of 15 occupational descriptions (Label set 45)

	Description	Abbreviation
1	A — would have served a trade apprenticeship to get into the job	TRA
2	A — would have high educational qualification	EDQ
3	A — would have the opportunity of working at overtime rates	OVT

TABLE U.1.1.4 *continued*

Description	Abbreviation
4 A — would be a member of a strong trade union	STU
5 A — would have high social standing in the community	STA
6 A — would be paid by the week	PBW
7 A — would have to clock in and out of work with a time card	CLK
8 A — would regard himself as a professional	PRO
9 A — would be involved in meeting the public in his job	PUB
10 A — would have a boring, repetitive job	BOR
11 A — would vote labour	LAB
12 A — would own the house or flat he lived in	OWN
13 A — would have financial security in his job	SEC
14 A — would send his children to a fee-paying school	FEE
15 A — would regard himself as working class	CLA

U.1.2 Selecting and Sampling Subjects

The strategies used to select subjects in the second part of the Project are considerably different to those used in the first part, which are described in T.1.2 above. Since the difficulties we encountered in the earlier stages played a large part in our decision to switch to a more naturalistic sampling scheme, it is worth citing the more important problems we faced. It will be recalled (see T.1.2) that the sampling scheme of the Project involves gathering information from persons in occupations specified by four different 'quadrants' of the population of economically active males. Quadrants A and B were defined as follows:

A – Occupations which require a relatively high degree of formal education, and involve work directly with other people.

B – Occupations which require a high degree of formal education, and involve work primarily with data or machines.

From these groups we selected sample members through up-to-date lists published by the professional associations of such occupations as Church of Scotland ministers and chartered accountants. Quadrants C and D were defined as follows:

C – Occupations which require little formal education, and involve working directly with people.

D – Occupations which require little or no formal education and predominantly involve work with data or machines.

Here again, our original selection of occupations was intended to facilitate contact with our potential subjects. In quadrant C, male psychiatric nurses, ambulance drivers, policemen all spend at least some of their time on duty at a particular location. In the case of ambulance crews it was necessary to interview them in the ambulance station, whilst they were on call. Although we chose to interview them early on Sunday mornings in order to minimise the possibility of an emergency call occurring during the course of an interview, this eventuality happened from time to time, and it was then usually impossible to complete the interview. Moreover, despite the very considerable assistance extended to us by the ambulance station officer, the physical layout of the station often made it impossible to interview an ambulance driver alone, or at least out of the hearing of his mates.

In quadrant D, we had originally selected groups such as engineering and foundry workers, plumbers and domestic engineers, printers, machine-tool workers, and building trade workers. Letters were then sent out to the trade unions representing these occupations, asking for their assistance in arranging interviews with some of their members, on a voluntary basis. Some unions were so small or represented such limited crafts that they thought they could not be of help, and a few had even gone out of existence. In other cases, the 'occupation' was represented by so many separate unions that it was practically impossible to coordinate any selection procedure. In yet other cases the labour force was not unionised, and it seemed to be quite impossible to contact subjects on any systematic basis. Even where union officers were favourably inclined, we often found ourselves in a double bind well known to social researchers: both management and unions would give permission for workers to be interviewed — so long as it was in paid work hours (unions), or so long as it was in unpaid time (management).

For reasons such as these, the original plans to contact subjects through 'place of work sampling' and through their trade union turned out to be impossible in most cases, and we were forced to adopt the less satisfactory expedient of intervieweing day-release apprentices attending technical and craft courses at various colleges of further education.

Our main conclusion was that the only feasible, practical and economically realistic way of obtaining our types of subjects would be to find ways of contacting and interviewing them in their own houses.

But how does on locate, let alone sample, a member of, say, quadrant D in the population at large? One alternative — a probability sample of households in Edinburgh — was quickly rejected both on grounds of inordinate cost and because we had no intention of inferring any parameter estimate of the Edinburgh population. Instead, we decided to identify geographical areas of Edinburgh where individuals in quadrants C and D were likely to constitute a large proportion of the resident population,[1] using the information on occupational classification provided in the 1966 Census. Fortunately (at least for our purposes) Edinburgh neighbourhoods are fairly homogeneous with respect to occupational status. Figure U.1.1 shows the enumeration districts (EDs, 'census tracts') of Edinburgh raised to a height which represents the proportion of economically-active males in social classes I and II (professional and intermediate) in each ED. It can readily be seen that these

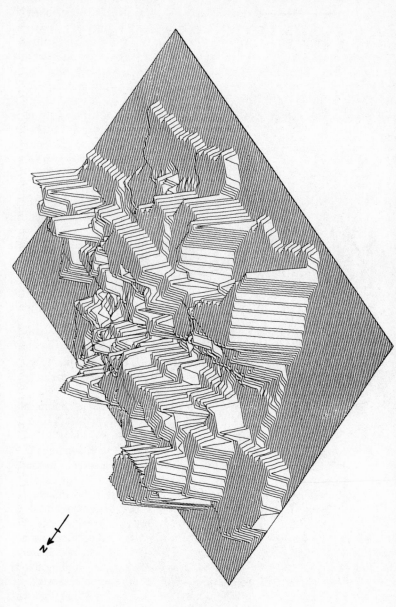

Fig. U.1.1: Social Classes I and II as a frequency surface over Edinburgh Enumeration districts (choropleth mapping)

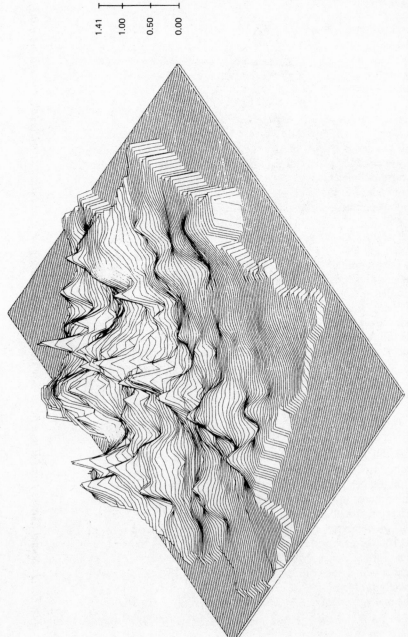

Fig. U1.2: Socio-Economic Group 11 as a frequency surface over Edinburgh Enumeration Districts (Isopleth mapping)

'middle-class' subjects are heavily concentrated in well-defined geographical areas, which resemble 'mountain chains'. Complementing this is a (smoothed) frequency surface representation[2] of socio-economic group 11 (unskilled manual workers). In both cases, the concentration of different social classes in particular areas of the city is very marked.

In view of this fact, the procedure we followed was:

(i) to equate quadrant types as closely as possible with census information on occupations (in effect, with the Registrar General's social classes and socio-economic groups);

(ii) to isolate those EDs with relatively high concentrations of the desired characteristics and then choose two which embodied best the contact between quadrants A and B *versus* C and D;

(iii) to carry out an entire census listing of households in these EDs;

(iv) to conduct a 'combing interview' at each household, designed to ascertain the occupation, age, etc., of each economically active male;

(v) to allocate each such person to a quadrant, and in this way produce a pool of potential subjects for the Project interviews.

Details of implementation[3]

(i) Data from the 1966 10 per cent census of population in Edinburgh — the most recent census data file available at the time — were processed in order to select enumeration districts with a relatively high proportion of male residents fitting into the quadrants of the typology. It was assumed that the quadrants and socio-economic groups would be best related in the following ways:

Quadrants C and D: to SEGs	8	— Foreman and Supervisors — manual,
	9	— Skilled manual workers,
	11	— Unskilled manual workers.
Quadrants A and B: to SEGs	3	— Professional workers — self-employed
	4	— Professional workers — employers
Or Social Classes	I	— Professional occupations
	II	— Intermediate occupations

With this assumption, frequency counts were obtained of the numbers of economically active males in suitable SEGs or social classes for each Edinburgh enumeration district. The enumeration districts were then rank-ordered in terms of the extent to which they exhibited these characteristics, making allowance for demolitions since 1966.

(ii) Two adjacent enumeration districts were eventually selected: ED 160 representing an area with a high proportion of males with little or no formal education (largely manual workers) and ED 161 representing an area with a high proportion of those with extensive formal education (mostly professionals).

The selected enumeration districts had the characteristics shown in Table U.1.2.1:

TABLE U.1.2.1   Characteristics of enumeration districts 160 and 161

		ED 160	ED 161	Edinburgh (221 EDs)
Number of households		700	620	157,900
Number of economically active males		700	700	132,360
Economically active males in SEGs 8 + 9 + 10 + 12	Number	259		47,400
	Per cent	37%		
Economically active males in SEG 11	Number	217		12,390
	Per cent	31%		
Economically active males in SEGs 3 + 4	Number		224	9,430
	Per cent		32%	
Economically active males in social classes I + II	Number		462	
	Per cent		66%	

TABLE U.1.2.2   Response rates in enumeration districts 160 and 161

SUMMARY OF RESPONSE RATES

	Enumeration District ED 160	ED 161	Total (N)
Households without any economically active residents	21.2%	28.4%	320
Net households eligible for interview	78.8%	71.6%	1023
Interviews	43.4%	45.0%	591
Refusals	12.5%	7.8%	145
Non-contacts (after 3 attempts)	8.6%	9.2%	118
On holiday	–	4.7%	23
Other non-interviews	7.0%	4.9%	84
Not attempted	7.3%	–	62
Households listed	N = 854	N = 489	N = 1343
SUBJECT POOL (N)			
Quadrant A	–	99	(99)
B	–	94	(94)
C	52	3	(55)
D	125	8	(133)
Total	177	204	381

(iii) Having selected the EDs, a census of households was made by listing systematically every dwelling unit satisfying the definition used by UK census enumerators, viz: 'A household comprises one person living alone, or a group of persons living together, partaking of meals prepared together and benefiting from a common house-keeping'. Interviewers were required to proceed systematically along street sides and around blocks paying particular attention to alleys, back doors, houses separated into flats, dwellings behind or above shops. Vacant households were listed, but not group quarters such as nursing-homes, doss-houses or transient dwellings such as guest houses or hotels.

(iv) Although the primary purpose of combing interviews was to obtain information regarding the number, age, sex and occupation of male residents, this information could not be obtained in isolation. We provided our subjects with a brief description of the purpose of the Project, and devised some standardised questions concerning occupations which demonstrated our interests and methods. These subsidiary questions served other purposes: they established a better rapport between interviewer and informant, they increased our chances of obtaining the personal information we needed, they provided us with some usable data.[4]

(v) Details of subject allocation to Project tasks are contained at the start of the relevant chapter in *Class and Hierarchy*.

U.1.3 Interviewing and the Interview

The general structure of the interview, and the instructions under which interviewers worked, do not differ significantly from those in the first

TABLE U.1.3.1   Summary of combination of tasks done by subjects (*Class and Hierarchy*)

| | TASK | | | |
Combination	Free sorting	Hierarchies	Sentence-frame	Percentage
1	+	+	+	4.5
2	+	+	−	33.1
3	+	−	+	16.0
4	+	−	−	27.4
5	−	+	+	10.8
6	−	+	−	7.6
7	−	−	+	0.6
8	−	−	−	−
				100.0
				N = 157 subjects

section of the Project (see T.2.3), except in the following ways:

(i) There was very much less experimentation with methods of data collection. Of the 157 individuals whose data are reported in *Class and Hierarchy,* four-fifths did at least one variety of free sorting (a number of these subjects had also done the ratings and pairwise similarities tasks reported in *Images*), three-fifths did the hierarchies task, and one-third did the sentence frame task.

(ii) Recording of subject's verbalisations was much more systematic, and edited transcripts were required of all interviewers. (The reliability of the scripts and the selection processes involved are discussed in section 4.1 of *Class and Hierarchy.*)

(iii) There were no group interviews among this group of subjects. Most interviews were done in the home of the subject; occasionally other members of the family were present, or within earshot. Their presence (and any interventions they made) were recorded by the interviewer.

U.1.4 Specification of Methods of Data Collection[5]

As in T.2.4, the methods used in the Project may best be described in terms of:

The object set(s) used
size and composition of the set(s) of occupational titles or descriptions
The judgement design
design and procedure for presenting objects to the subject
The method
task which the subject is asked to perform
In the second part of the Project, described in *Class and Hierarchy,* the *object sets* used (see U.1.1) are:

(i) *Occupational titles*
LABL06 (the basic set of 16 titles)
LABL08 (the extended set of 32 titles)
LABL15 (the minor extended set of 20 titles)
LABL17 (the full SA set of 25 titles)
(ii) *Occupational descriptions*
LABL36 (the basic set of 50 descriptions)
LABL45 (the modified set of 15 descriptions)
The *judgement designs* are:
complete set of titles and/or descriptions;
complete set of sentence frame (descriptions) by occupational titles;
randomised subsets of sentence frame by titles.
The *methods* used are:
free sorting (partition) into subject-chosen number of groups;
hierarchy construction;
substitution of titles (instances) into sentence frames (descriptions).

TABLE U.1.4.1   Specification of tasks done by subjects (*Class and Hierarchy*)

Brief name	Project abbreviation	Object set	Judgemental design	Method
Free-sorting	(i) FA	30 occupational titles (extended set)	Complete randomised set of cards	Sort into unspecified number of groups/piles on the basis of similarity
	(ii) FB	50 occupational descriptions (basic set of descriptions)	Complete randomised set of cards	Sort into unspecified number of groups/piles on the basis of similarity
	(iii) FC	Basic set of descriptions (50) *and* extended set of titles (32)	Complete randomised set of cards	Sort descriptions into groups and *then* sort titles (as instances) into already formed groups of descriptions
Hierarchies	HA	16 occupational titles (basic set of titles)	Complete randomised set of cards	Construct binary, rooted tree (or hierarchical clustering) by successive pairing, chaining or joining
Sentence frame substitution	SA	i) 50 sentence frames frames (basic set of descriptions) *with* 20 occupational titles (minor extended set of titles)	Randomised subsets of 15 sentence frames	Substitute titles into sentence frames, one by one; Resulting sentence judged as 'Always', 'Sometimes' or 'Never'
		ii) 15 sentence frames (modified set of descriptions) *with* 25 occupational titles) (full SA set of titles)	Complete frame x title presentation in fixed order	Same as (i) but with four response categories: 'Always', 'Usually', 'Seldom', 'Never'.

Free-sorting data

The free-sorting method has been used extensively by anthropologists and psychologists, usually to explore the semantic structure of social, cultural and linguistic domains (Berlin *et al.* 1968; Miller 1967, 1969; Anglin 1970; Jones and Ashmore 1973; Wish and Carroll 1974) and it has also been used previously in the study of occupations. Silverman (1966) had inhabitants of an Italian village sort 175 cards each bearing the name of a single family, into groups 'according to the level of *rispetto*' (p. 904) and used the information to describe the community status structure.[6] Burton (1972) asked student volunteers to sort a set of 60 occupational titles into piles on the basis of their similarity, and Burton and Romney (1975) use a set of sortings of 58 role terms. As we have commented elsewhere (Coxon and Jones 1974b:378), this technique has undoubted advantages when a large number of objects are involved, and it is a task which subjects often find interesting and thought-provoking (see also Miller 1969:170). Moreover,

since no single criterion or property is assumed, the hope is that this freedom
will permit conceptual bases which are culturally salient to emerge in a natural
manner, for whilst people certainly perform such sortings in different, often
individualistic, ways, it seems clear that strong cultural conditioning also
exists.

The length of time which an individual takes to complete a full sorting
increases, on average, with the number of cards (objects) they are presented
with, as one might expect. But the increase is not a simple linear function —
the mean time spent for sorting 32 titles (type A) is 31 minutes, for 50
descriptions (type B) is 33 minutes, and for the mixed set (type C) is
43 minutes. But the range of individual variation is very marked indeed,
especially within the type A sorting:

Type A sorting: from 5 minutes to 90 minutes
Type B sorting: 15 minutes to 55 minutes
Type C sorting: 30 minutes to 70 minutes

Similar variation has been noted by Miller (1969:170), who reports a range
between 5 and 30 minutes for sorting 48 English nouns.

The first two of the three types of free sorting (FA and FB) differ only
in that occupational titles are used in the former, and occupational descriptions in the latter case. (The basic method is described above in section
T.2.4.)

The third type of free-sorting data differs in that the subject was required,
first, to free-sort the 50 occupational descriptions. Having done so and
named the resulting groups, he was then handed 32 cards with the name of
an occupational title on it, and asked to allocate each as an instance of the
groups he had formed. (In several instances, some occupational titles did not
fit the pre-formed groups; in such cases the subject was allowed either to
put titles together to form new groups, or to leave them as single residual
instances.)

The subject was encouraged to verbalise, and his comments were recorded.
The data were transformed into individual co-occurrence matrices, available
as files DFA136AD and DFA139AD at the SSRC Archive.

Basic information gathered on the sortings of each individual included
the number of groups formed, the size of the largest group and the number
of cards left as singletons. Also calculated was the 'height' of each sorting —
a measure of the co-occurrence of pairs within each sorting, or the aggrega-
tiveness of a sorting.

In order to assess the similarity or dissimilarity between individual
sortings, a program FAIDPCO was developed to operationalise the 12 distance
measures proposed by Arabie and Boorman (1973). The use of a variety of
measures allowed us to focus on different aspects of dissimilarity between
the sortings. The measures were output as lower-half dissimilarity matrices
allowing subsequent multidimensional scaling of the variations between
sortings or hierarchical clustering of them. FAIDPCO also output the
'Z-matrix' associated with each pair of sortings, i.e. the groups of one sorting

were cross-classified with the groups of the other sorting allowing an assessment to be made of the extent of subset relations between the classifications.

Hierarchies Data

Hierarchical clustering is in effect another sorting task carried out with certain constraints. The subjects are asked to construct trees of naturally-belonging occupational titles, finally joining them up into one tree. The task restricts the size of the first cluster to only two stimuli. After that point the subject may add one title to an already existing group ('chaining'), or he may decide to merge ('join') two clusters at any later stage. Using a standard set of 16 occupational titles, this agglomerative strategy, starting from a single pair and merging upwards, has a standard 15 steps. At each step, subjects are encouraged to explain their decision.

Administration and instructions to interviewers

There were no standard instructions for this task but it was explained to interviewers in the following way:
   (i) For each administration you will need a kit consisting of:
   (*a*) 15 *sets* of matching numbered bracket cards
   (*b*) A set of randomised stimulus cards; sixteen computer-generated, randomly ordered, cards, each bearing an occupational title.
   (ii) Give the subject the occupation cards and ask him to read them through and lay them out on the table where he can see them. Note anything he says about any of the titles.
   (iii) Ask him to 'pick the *two* occupations which you think most naturally go together' — do not say 'most similar'. If asked 'on what basis?' say 'Whatever seems right to you', or 'we leave that up to you'.
   (iv) Lay them together on the table, so that they are clearly visible to the subject, with the opening first bracket card on top of them and the ending first bracket card below them.
   (v) Say 'Could you give me your reasons for choosing these two, or give me a name for the branch?', and record the answer for your report.
   (vi) At step 2, tell the subject that he now has two choices: to add *one* other stimulus to the existing group or branch *or* start a new branch (pair).
   (vii) At step 3, and subsequent steps, the subject can do one — and one only — of three things:
      (*a*) Start a new pair;
      (*b*) Chain *one* stimulus to an existing branch;
      (*c*) Join two existing branches.
   (viii) This 'nesting' with 3 possibilities at each step, proceeds until the 15th step. The subject may remark as time goes on that he is putting together things that fit increasingly less well; reassure him that this is usual, that he will end up with one big group again at the end.

(ix) Remember always to note the subject's reasons at each step.

(x) The subject can decide to change his mind about the tree at any step, and can reorganise the clustering from any breaking point. This may simply mean changing the most recent action, but if he decides to change something several steps back this may mean reorganising all the succeeding brackets.

Note that it is often difficult to avoid making judgements of relative similarity, and this should not be avoided if the subject finds it a useful general criterion.

The hierarchical clustering task was the favourite of many subjects. A wide range of bases for similarity were mentioned. Only rarely did subjects express dissatisfaction at being forced to link large clusters at the last steps, using concepts with a higher level of generality, and judgements of relative rather than absolute similarity were common from the early stages. Subjects were usually reluctant to reorganise their tree from several steps back and preferred to settle for their original choice rather than go through the task again.

Data exist in both raw forms (bracketed hierarchical structure, merged with verbal comments), and as lower-triangular ultra-metric distance matrices (DHA106AD), at the SSRC Archive. Programs were written to implement the distance measures between trees detailed in Boorman and Olivier (1973).

Sentence-frame Substitution Data

In this task, the subject is presented with a list of 25 occupational titles, and 15 sentence frames. Each title is to be fitted into each of the 15 sentence frames forming a set of 375 statements. For each statement the subject is to tell how often it holds true: always, usually, seldom or never.

The same 25 occupational titles (label 45) are printed on sheets bearing the alternative answers. The titles are always in the same order. Sentence frames are typed on flash-cards to be handed out to the subject one by one, always in the same order. As a card is handed out, instructions as printed on the answer sheets, are as shown in Table U.1.4.2.

An introduction could be: 'Here are 15 sheets all showing the same 25 occupational titles. We also have 15 sentence frames on these cards. We would like you to fit each of these titles into the sentence frames and tell us whether the sentence holds true always, usually, seldom or never. For instance, the first statement is — An architect would have served a trade apprenticeship to get into his job. Is this true always, usually, seldom or never? This is a fairly time-consuming task but if you have any comments or query, I shall be glad to hear them and help you along.'

Interviewers were encouraged to read out the sentence frame as they handed the card over to the subject, and to ensure that the subject used the same interpretation of the sentence frame for each occupational title substituted.

TABLE U.1.4.2   Scheme for sentence-frame substitution data

FOR EACH OF THE FOLLOWING OCCUPATIONS, PLEASE TELL US WHETHER
THIS SENTENCE HOLDS TRUE

ALWAYS	A	
USUALLY	U	
SOMETIMES	S	
NEVER	N	
(Circle answer)		

ARCHITECT	A U S N
MINI AMBULANCE DRIVER	A U S N

etc. . . .

This task was viewed by most as an easy exercise, and few objected to its
length. Occasionally, subjects indicated their preference for a neutral
category. Data exist on file DSA145AD at the SSRC Archive.

6 Data from Unconstrained Sortings: Appendices to Chapter 2 of *Class and Hierarchy*

U.2.1 Selection of Subjects for the Free-sorting Task: Type A: Sorting 32 Occupational Titles (by 71 Subjects)

The selection of subjects for this sorting task was accomplished in two ways: by sampling professional registers (especially for subjects in quadrants A and B)

By allocating subjects obtained by the 'combing' procedure in order to produce approximately equal numbers in each quadrant. The numbers and occupations are as follows:

QUADRANT A (*n*=21)			**QUADRANT B** (*n*=18)		
No.	*Occupation*	*Code**	*No.*	*Occupation*	*Code*
4	Church of Scotland Ministers	A	1	Business manager	BM
12	Scottish episcopalian Priests	C	2	Qualified actuaries	F
2	Doctors	D	4	Chartered accountants	G
1	Social worker	SW		Farmer	S
1	Sales manager (oil company)	S		Principal of revenue department (CS)	S
1	Comprehensive school teacher	Y		Higher executive officer (CS)	Y
				Actuary, asst. general manager (insurance company)	S
				Insurance manager (bank)	S
				Assistant pensions secretary (insurance company)	Y
				Quantity surveyor (partner)	S

U.2.1 *continued*

Forest geneticist	S
Chartered surveyor	S
Managing director (investment firm)	S

QUADRANT C (n=15)		QUADRANT D (n=17)	
2 Male psychiatric nurses	K	4 Printers	K
Salesman (electrical engineering)	Y	Engineering inspector	S
Salesman (protective clothing)	Y	Bank clerk	Y
Salesman (part-time)	Y	Post Office clerk	Y
Sales manager for car dealer	Y	Service manager (garage)	Y
Sales agent for publishers (self-employed)	Y	Contracts manager	Y
		Industrial photographer	Y
		Radio mechanic	Y
		Fork truck driver	Y
(2†) Retail advisor	Y	Fitter-welder (foreman)	
Personal assistant to manager	Y	Plant fitter	Y
Boutique manager	Y	Fitter's mate	Y
Grocer (self-employed)	Y	Heating engineer	Y
Sub-postmaster	Y	Heating engineer (chargehand)	Y
Master jeweller	Y		
Police inspector	Y		

*Subjects' code identifier in file DFA108AD (on file at the SSRC Survey Archive, University of Essex)
†This subject did *two* sortings, which are treated as separate sortings

U.2.2 Selection of Subjects for the Free-sorting Task: Types B and C

TYPE B: Sorting 50 occupational descriptions (by 66 subjects)
TYPE C: Double sorting (descriptions followed by insertion of titles) (Denoted by asterisk*) (by 44 of these 66 subjects)

The selection of subjects was accomplished in the same way as in Type A (See T.5.1 and Chapter 2)

QUADRANT A (n_b=18, n_c=18)

No.	Occupation	Code[1]
8	*Doctors (including 5 general practitioners 2 psychiatrists, gynaecologist)	D
10	*Social workers	SW

QUADRANT B (n_b=3, n_c=2)

No.	Occupation	Code
2	*Business managers	BM
	Architectural assistant	Y

QUADRANT C (n_b=7, n_c=4)

Occupation	Code
*Salesman (SE)[2]	Y
Boutique manager	Y
*Junk shop owner	Y
Clerical supervisor	Y
*Male psychiatric nurse	Y
Window cleaner (SE)	Y
*Painter-decorator (SE)	Y

QUADRANT D (n_b=38, n_c=20)

No.	Occupation	Code
3	Heating engineers	Y
	Jobbing heating engineers	Y
	Machine tool engineer	Y
	*Television engineer	Y
	Electronic engineer	Y
	*Electronic engineer	Y
	*Telephone engineer	Y
	Quality control engineer	Y
	Maintenance engineer	Y
	*Service engineer	Y
	*Post Office engineer	Y
	*Maintenance electrician	Y
	*P.O. telephone technician	Y
	*Laboratory technician	Y
	Architectural technician	
	Foreman coachbuilder	Y
	Civil aircraft fitter	Y
	Plant fitter	Y
	Foreman fitter-welder	Y
	*Welder	Y
	*Precision sheet metal worker	Y
2	*Joiners	Y
	Technical clerk	Y
	Wages clerk	Y
	*Comparer of deeds	Y
	Printer designer (SE)	Y
	*Compositor	Y
	Partner, printing firm	Y
	*Draughtsman	Y
	*Service manager (garage)	Y
	*Traffic controller (brewery)	Y

U.2.2 *continued*

*Fireman		Y
Fork-truck driver		Y
*Gardener		Y
*Interior decorator		Y

[1] Subject's code identifier in file DFA136AD (type B) or DFA139AD (type C).
[2] Self-employed (so described).

U.2.3 Interviewer's Report on sorting of 32 occupational titles by a qualified actuary

From the beginning he mentioned that he could classify them in many different ways 'according to the length of time taken to qualify, whether the job was dangerous or not, whether it was confined to a particular sex or not, whether it requires brainwork as opposed to physical skills, even according to what type of economic position they are in: primary producers, distribution, services etc. . . .'. But his 'first instinct' was to classify them between 'white-collar workers and non-white-collar workers, *those requiring intellectual effort predominantly as distinct from those requiring skill'*. This led him to a 4-way grouping of (1) unskilled, (2) semi-skilled and (3) skilled, semi-professionals and professionals, (4) indeterminate. It is by splitting up these original groups and changing 3 or 4 titles around that he came up with the final 9 groups. Before ending the interview, he was still arguing about other possible ways of classifying them and reviewed some of the changes he would have to make to the groups if he changed the basis of classification. He toyed with the idea of classifying them according to the earnings they ought to get (little dissertation throwing in Adam Smith for good measure), according to how much their average salary actually is, in terms of security of job, according to the aptitude they require, possibly how scarce people with a particular aptitude are, which relates to the question of pay. However, he rationalised his final choice as follows: 'I have categorised them by the nature of skill and training. It is the thing that appeals to me because it is the thing that ought to be closest to the earnings that they get.'
Final groupings: In order of 'What I think is roughly the intellectual content of the job'.
1. TD, BSL, UMO *'Jobs requiring very little intellectual content, very little training, but requiring reasonable fitness and strength.'*
'Occupations in which almost minimal training is required, very little contact with people as such, that is, social attitudes are not particularly important for the particular job they are doing. One has to be pretty fit. It is largely physical work. The job is pretty simple. One could earn a lot of money,

largely through overtime, but it is rather erratic. This group would have the least security.'

2. BC, PO, BM 'None of these occupations required a great deal of learning except the basics: reading and arithmetic. Not too physically demanding, they could be regarded as healthy jobs. But a certain amount of responsibility is required for all of these: they probably all handle money; the postman is responsible for his mail. They are somewhat close to group 3 as regards the element of skill but somewhat lower grade in terms of education. Like group 3, they must have a fairly limited range of possible earnings.' To sum up, *'these jobs require very little training but there is a minimal amount of education required. They are relatively unskilled jobs.'*

3. AD, TDR, RED 'Not much education is required but some training. Responsibility must enter into these 3 jobs. They are responsible for lives. Recklessness would be dangerous. In all of these, there is a discipline (meeting a schedule, avoiding accidents). They must have a fairly limited range of possible earnings. *These jobs do not require a great deal of education either, about the same as 2, but the jobs require a responsibility in that lives could be at stake. There must be a certain commitment to the job.'*

4. MPN, BCK, LT, C, GM, RCK, PL 'These are semi-skilled jobs. It might take a few years to learn the skill but once a person has learnt his trade, the range of knowledge . . . [does not vary a lot]. They are predominantly manual rather than intellectual skills. Trades in other words. Although the bank clerk is a white-collar worker, he is in a relatively junior position which can be filled by someone with a few O-levels. It is possible they make a lot of money but normally there are enormous differences between the earnings of different people in this category. To sum up — *They are semi-skilled trade, technician types. They must have a reasonable amount of education, not even necessarily up to Highers, but some skill which would normally take 2-3 years to acquire. The Bank Clerk is using his brain (instead of his skill) all the time, but at a fairly low level.'*

5. PM 'The Policeman has to be regarded in a slightly different light [from group 4]. His work carries a responsibility of a sort of professional nature . [Assuming a Constable or Sergeant.] Nowadays, he requires a bit more education than people in group 4. He may use both his brain and his skill in certain cases. He's got that other element of responsibility and even danger which must categorise him separately. He's got to have the attributes of character, responsibility, danger, commitment but with a higher level of intellectual ability and training than group 4.'

6. SW, CPR, PST 'Most Social Workers and most Computer Programmers are not University graduates although some are. Teachers don't have to be graduates but there are plenty of them who are. Any of these people could have had the same intensity of training as those professionals (in groups 8, 9). To sum up: *They have to have a minimal educational requirement of something like 2 Highers. In most cases, a fair percentage of people could be graduates.* That's about the only thing that brings them together. In no way am I saying

that one of these people could necessarily do what the other one does!'
7. JN, SMG, A, PHT 'These occupations are too ill-defined. All these people require training but the degree of training and the degree of skill can vary enormously so that it's very hard to classify. Sales Managers and Actors have to have certain attributes of personality. A Photographer as an Actor can be considered as an artist. Sales Manager is like an actor in the sense that nothing succeeds like success. Same for a journalist. Journalist is somewhat of an artist. There is an art in writing. These people can earn almost anything, at least as much as group 4 but could earn a lot more. To sum up — *People who don't have to have a very high education but normally they will certainly have to have a linguistic ability, and for complete success in their job they have to have a flair, something they cannot be trained for.'*
8. SST, CA, GEO, CE, ST 'For someone to call himself any one of these, he has had to go through 4 or 5 years professional training with very rigid standards. He has a professional qualification. They cannot practise without that training and qualification. All these jobs require a certain amount of commitment. In most cases it is possible for any one of these to be one of the others. (A Chartered Accountant could become a Secondary School Teacher etc. . . .) They are in somewhat the same range of income although a Chartered Accountant or Civil Engineer could reach much higher incomes.'
9. AP, ES, MOR 'They all need 4 or 5 years' training again but they also have to have something else as well, which unless they've got it, they are no good at it. But an Airline Pilot and an Eye Surgeon have a physical skill or reflex action, also an element of responsibility in that lives depend on their skill. No amount of intellectual ability is going to make them a good one. These three are not similar in terms of income but a Minister of Religion would never take it up without a vocation.'

U.2.4 Characteristics of Individual Sortings: Frequency distributions

A Number of Groups

	32 Occupational titles		50 Occupational descriptions	
Number of groups	Overall	NS*	Overall	NS*
1	0	0	0	0
2	3	3	0	3
3	4	5	6	7
4	5	7	9	18
5	15	17	9	18
6	5	10	10	13

U.2.4 *continued*

Number of groups	32 Occupational titles		50 Occupational descriptions	
	Overall	*NS**	*Overall*	*NS**
7	10	9	10	2
8	12	11	4	3
9	5	5	3	1
10	6	4	3	1
11	4		4	
12	1		2	
13	1		0	
14			2	
15 or over			4†	
Total (*n*)	71	71	66	66
Mean	.6.78	6.06	7.77	4.90
S.D.	2.60	2.07	4.96	1.57

*Non-singleton groups (i.e. excluding 'group' containing one element)
†containing 18, 23, 24, 29 groups respectively

Compare Miller (1969, p.170):	*n*	= 48 (nouns)
	range	= 6 to 26
	mean	= 14.3 groups
	S.D.	= 5.0 groups

B Size of the largest group

	Sorting type	
Size of largest group	*A: 32* Occupational titles	*B: 50* Occupational descriptions
Less than 4	0	0
4 – 6	16	0
7 – 9	26	2
10 – 12	16	9
13 – 15	8	20
16 – 18	2	16
19 – 21	3	7
22 – 24		5

Size of largest group	A:32 Occupational titles	B:50 Occupational description
	Sorting type	
25 – 27		4
28 – 30		3
Total (*n*)	71	66
Mean	9.49	16.54
S.D.	3.66	4.83

C Normalised height measure

Height measure (normalised)	A: 32 Occupational titles	B: 50 Occupational description
	Sorting type	
Less than .05	0	0
.05 – .09	7	3
.10 – .14	20	7
.15 – .19	18	15
.20 – .24	15	16
.25 – .29	2	11
.30 – .34	3	6
.35 – .39	1	5
.40 – .44	2	1
.45 – .49	2	1
.50 – .54	1	1
Total (*n*)	71	67
Mean	.184	.235
S.D.	.101	.194

U.2.5 Measures of Distance between Sortings

1. Boorman and Arabie (1972) classify a number of metrics in terms of 'minimum cost flow' ideas. Each possible partition is viewed as a point in a

graph, and two points are joined by a path or 'edge' if a single move (which is permitted by the rules of the metric concerned) will transform the one partition into the other. A 'distance' between two sortings A and B is the shortest path — or minimum number of links (transformations) — necessary to convert A into B. If the links have a weight attached, representing transport costs, for example, then the problem of defining such distance measures between partitions becomes identical to the scheduling problem of finding the minimum-cost path between two locations.

2. In Arabie and Boorman (1973), they concentrate attention upon twelve permutation-invariant distance measures (pp.156-7) and examine their properties empirically by generating artificial data, which consist of different partitions of a set of a given number of elements. They calculate a number of distance measures, between the partitions (sortings), and scale each of them.

3. Three basic functions (supervaluations) are defined, based upon the height measure and two information-theoretic measures. Additional measures are either normalisations of these functions, or are unrelated to them (e.g. set-move and lattice-move distances together with chi-square and lambda measures of association). It turns out, somewhat surprisingly, that information-theoretic measures are significantly worse adapted to scaling representation than height-based measures, that strong normalisation usually produces lower-stress MDS solutions, and that MDS representations of virtually all these measures *cannot be interpreted at the level of individual points,* but can usually be interpreted in terms of contours around the lumper-splitter axis.

4. The analysis in Chapter 2 of *Class and Hierarchy* is restricted to the height, and minimum set-move measures, and their normalised versions.

U.2.6 Distributions of Pairwise Distances

32 Occupational titles			*50 Occupational descriptions*		
(i) PAIRBONDS	*f*	*Per cent*	*PAIRBONDS*	*f*	*Per cent*
0 — 19	0	—	120 — 149	2	0.1
20 — 39	2	0.1	150 — 179	8	0.4
40 — 59	58	2.3	180 — 209	20	0.9
60 — 79	300	12.1	210 — 239	36	1.7
80 — 99	430	17.4	240 — 259	95	4.4
100 — 119	560	22.5	270 — 299	214	10.0
120 — 139	416	16.7	300 — 329	321	15.0
140 — 159	214	8.6	330 — 359	369	17.2
160 — 179	129	5.2	360 — 389	286	13.3
180 — 199	120	4.8	390 — 419	276	12.9
200 — 219	118	4.7	420 — 449	211	9.8
220 — 239	57	2.3	450 — 479	161	7.5

U.2.6 *continued*

32 Occupational titles			50 Occupational descriptions		
240 — 259	16	0.6	480 — 509	87	4.0
260 — 279	21	0.8	510 — 539	44	2.0
280 — 299	44	1.8	540 — 579	12	0.6
			570 — 599	3	0.1
Total pairs	2485	100.0	Total pairs	2145	100.0

Mean:	126.3		Mean:	366.7	
S.D.	49.6		S.D.	72.8	
Range:	26 — 299 (Possible: 0 — 496)		Range:	133 — 592 (Possible: 0 — 1225)	

(ii) NORMALISED PAIRBONDS*	f	Per cent	NORMALISED PAIRBONDS*	f	Per cent
Less than .40	17	0.7	Less than .40	14	0.7
.40 — .44	36	1.4	.40 — .44	24	1.1
.45 — .49	78	3.1	.45 — .49	74	3.4
.50 — .54	141	5.7	.50 — .54	104	4.8
.55 — .59	238	9.6	.55 — .59	245	11.4
.60 — .64	411	16.5	.60 — .64	383	18.0
.65 — .69	491	19.8	.65 — .69	477	22.2
.70 — .74	524	21.1	.70 — .74	427	'19.9
.75 — .79	328	13.2	.75 — .79	244	11.4
.80 — .84	156	6.3	.80 — .84	112	5.2
.85 — .89	54	2.2	.85 — .89	38	1.8
.90 — .94	11	0.4	.90 — .94	3	0.1
Total pairs	2485	100.0	Total pairs	2145	100.0

Mean:	.674		Mean:	.668	
S.D.	.099		S.D.	.094	
Range:	.189 — .934		Range:	.269 — .938	

*1—NT/1+2: Strong normalisation, based on arithmetic mean.

(iii) APPROX	f	Per cent	APPROX	f	Per cent
1 or 2†	9	0.4	1 or 2†	—	
3, 4	41	1.6	3, 4	11	0.5

U.2.6 *continued*

(iii) APPROX	*f*	*Per cent*	*APPROX*	*f*	*Per cent*
5, 6	143	5.8	5, 6	54	2.5
7, 8	351	14.1	7, 8	121	5.6
9, 10	602	24.2	9, 10	264	12.3
11, 12	590	23.7	11, 12	358	16.7
13, 14	457	18.4	13, 14	354	16.5
15, 16	187	7.5	15, 16	276	12.9
17, 18	69	2.8	17, 18	208	9.7
19, 20	28	1.1	19, 20	169	7.9
21, 22	7	0.3	21, 22	105	4.9
23	1	0.1	23, 24	75	3.5
			25, 26	67	3.1
			27, 28	33	1.5
			29, 30	22	1.0
			31, 32	23	1.1
			33, 34	4	0.2
			(35), 36	1	0.1
Total pairs	2485	100.0	Total pairs	2145	100.0
Mean	10.89		Mean	14.95	
S.D.	3.19		S.D.	5.54	
Range	1 to 23		Range	3 to 36	

†APPROX takes on integer values only

U.2.7 Mean Individual etc. can be seen on page 167 opposite.

U.2.8 Scaling PAIRBONDS Distances between 71 Sortings of 32 occupational titles

1. The 2485 pairwise PAIRBONDS distances were scaled non-metrically by the euclidean distance model (MINISSA-1 algorithm) in 5 through 1 dimensions. $Stress_1$ (*d*-hat) values were:

  5-D   0.0904
  4-D   0.1045
  3-D   0.1303
  2-D   0.1687
  1-D   0.2593

(Compare the $stress_1$ values of around .275 which Arabie and Boorman (1973, pp. 164-5) present for two-dimensional solutions of 60 PAIRBONDS distances between 60 ten lattice partitions.)

U.2.7 Mean Individual Distances by Ocupational Quadrant

32 Occupational titles

	I	II	III	IV
I	PAIRBONDS (N) 128.1 (210) (31.5)† 1−NT/1+2 approx .67 10.9 (.11) (3.5)			
II	130.2 (378) (51.0) .69 11.07 (.10) (3.3)	130.4 (153) (67.8) .68 11.09 (.10) (2.9)		
III	119.5 (315) (35.5) .67 11.08 (.10) (3.4)	118.7 (270) (57.0) .67 10.9 (.10) (3.0)	107.4 (105) (38.8) .66 10.8 (.10) (2.7)	
IV	132.9 (357) (42.0) .68 10.8 (.10) (3.4)	131.9 (306) (59.9) .68 10.9 (.10) (3.0)	121.2 (255) (48.1) .66 10.8 (.10) (3.1)	133.2 (136) (53.3) .65 10.2 (.10) (2.7)

TOTAL: 126.3 (2485 pairs) (49.6)   .67 10.9 (.10) (3.2)   (71 subjects)

50 Occupational descriptions

	I	II	III	IV
I	PAIRBONDS (N) 374.9 (153) (86.1) 1−NT/1+2 approx .69 16.4 (.11) (6.1)			
II	343.7 (54) (82.4) .73 17.7 (109) (5.6)	(*) (3) (*) (*)		
III	379.1 (126) (70.8) .68 15.1 (.08) (5.7)	346.0 (21) (60.6) .72 16.00 (.08) (4.3)	380.1 (21) (63.4) .66 13.2 (.05) (2.1)	
IV	376.2 (684) (81.6) .68 15.5 (.10) (5.9)	335.1 (114) (63.0) .71 16.5 (.09) (5.1)	368.2 (266) (60.4) .65 13.6 (.08) (4.3)	360.4 (703) .65 14.1 (.09) (5.3)

TOTAL: 366.7 (2145 pairs) (72.8)   .67 14.9 (.09) (5.5)   (70 subjects)

*n too small for stable estimates
†standard deviation of distances

1. It is clear that there is a large improvement in fit between one and two dimensions, but only marginal improvement beyond this point. The two-dimensional solution was accepted, and is reproduced in Fig. 2.6 (*Class and Hierarchy*, p. 36). The co-ordinates of the final configuration, together with each subject's height value are:

	Subject no.	'Height'	Coordinates dimension I	II
	1	75	−0.0153	−0.0932
	2	93	−1.1166	−0.0548
	3	115	−0.1437	0.7127
	4	61	−0.3807	−0.0161
	5	164	1.3265	−0.4219
	6	107	−0.9701	0.6386
	7	116	0.6796	−0.2872
	8	189	1.9021	0.1772
	9	95	0.2013	0.2634
('Splitter')	10	33	−0.5628	−0.0776
	11	92	−0.4635	0.4657
	12	164	0.8420	0.9600
	13	54	−0.4754	−0.1322
	14	57	−0.3818	−0.1574
	15	94	−0.9328	−0.3806
	16	109	0.4009	0.4758
	17	157	1.0441	0.8167
	18	77	−0.2655	0.3616
	19	102	0.0018	0.5233
	20	82	−0.3203	0.3114
	21	54	−0.2554	−0.0852
	22	53	−0.3040	0.0838
	23	42	−0.3607	−0.0357
	24	241	2.6475	−0.8662
	25	93	−0.7054	−0.5663
	26	54	−0.2726	−0.1394
	27	84	−0.3923	−0.4027
	28	95	0.0329	−0.5719
	29	64	−0.1508	0.0971
	30	89	0.1538	−0.1679
	31	52	−0.5406	−0.0356
	32	203	0.7896	2.7877
	33	88	−0.6833	0.3972

Table *continued*

	Subject no.	'Height'	Coordinates dimension	
			I	*II*
	34	102	−0.5714	−0.7260
	35	89	0.0913	0.0865
	36	39	−0.3023	−0.0498
	37	71	−0.7563	−0.2349
	38	119	0.5951	0.0455
	39	56	−0.4809	−0.2597
	40	52	−0.2604	0.0944
	41	105	−1.2619	−0.3059
	42	42	−0.2469	−0.0075
	43	49	−0.6215	−0.0811
	44	130	−0.1691	−1.2755
	45	60	−0.3084	−0.0346
	46	49	−0.2924	0.0289
	47	82	−0.0490	0.2424
	48	244	2.5990	−0.5247
	49	84	0.1750	−0.0746
	50	110	0.3395	−0.1017
	51	52	−0.3088	0.0270
	52	103	0.1519	−0.3300
	53	106	0.2193	−0.4564
	54	81	−0.1603	−0.2756
	55	118	−0.2341	0.8436
	56	63	−0.1912	−0.0018
	57	41	−0.3533	0.0474
	58	74	−0.2165	−0.1273
	59	61	−0.4886	−0.1031
	60	45	−0.5740	−0.1134
	61	37	−0.3364	−0.0475
	62	71	−0.0637	0.0845
	63	63	−0.4440	0.0918
	64	98	0.2206	0.1910
	65	213	1.7904	2.0973
('Lumper')	66	256	2.8077	−1.6448
	67	94	−0.1743	−0.6537
	68	129	0.3593	−0.7776
	69	57	−0.3870	−0.1352
	70	97	−0.3504	−0.0688
	71	72	−0.0744	−0.0495

U.2.9 Co-occurrence frequencies between 32 occupational titles

	CA	SST	GM	BM	ST	SW	C	AD	CPR	MOR	PL	MPN	BCK	PST	UMO	PM	CE	PHT	BSL	RCK	AP	A	RED	PO	GEO	SMG	TDH	TDR	ESG	JN	LT
SST	25																														
GM	3	2																													
BM	3	2	9																												
ST	43	29	2	2																											
SW	13	40	6	3	17																										
C	2	1	61	11	3	5																									
AD	2	4	21	21	2	12	19																								
CPR	27	17	8	5	32	19	6	4																							
MOR	26	43	3	2	20	39	64	7	7																						
PL	4	2	58	10	3	6	17	20	25	4																					
MPN	10	22	13	5	9	12	20	11	33	11	13																				
BCK	22	16	10	8	23	26	9	8	21	36	10	10																			
PST	15	54	3	2	47	2	11	22	3	15	22	28	27																		
UMO	1	1	17	39	2	3	16	8	2	3	8	3	3	2																	
PM	6	16	10	12	4	29	22	25	17	17	27	7	8	21	7																
CE	45	27	8	1	34	7	1	1	9	8	12	16	29	16	3	21															
PHT	5	4	16	7	8	17	8	15	26	25	18	6	12	8	7	7	7														
BSL	1	1	15	42	2	1	20	6	15	1	16	5	6	63	14	5	14	3													
RCK	4	2	36	28	2	9	20	13	35	16	35	5	16	18	18	5	18	9	20												
AP	26	14	10	7	15	8	8	22	17	22	7	9	9	4	11	8	9	8	3	7											
A	10	8	7	6	11	12	3	14	15	15	7	9	11	31	9	8	8	28	11	3	10										
RED	5	3	35	12	33	6	33	32	10	4	13	5	11	16	9	9	3	11	35	25	23	10									
PO	2	5	13	40	6	1	6	3	3	26	11	8	12	14	7	3	11	35	18	13	4	8	1								
GEO	37	26	5	0	37	13	24	26	26	5	12	12	11	2	8	10	35	3	5	25	13	6	6	14							
SMG	25	18	3	18	26	3	25	15	1	3	11	14	2	8	8	14	1	22	3	11	25	3	6	3	34						
TDH	2	1	38	35	2	5	18	4	3	11	9	7	57	23	15	8	34	6	1	8	6	17	34	10	3	2					
TDR	2	16	18	38	5	2	14	13	1	26	9	9	26	23	1	8	3	3	30	23	13	32	36	5	18	34	6				
ESG	33	28	3	0	21	20	4	35	4	25	12	5	1	34	15	9	15	1	3	8	10	13	3	2	24	4	10	2			
JN	11	17	9	3	19	19	8	4	13	19	16	12	30	3	14	12	3	30	10	15	39	10	5	34	18	4	2	3	10		
LT	12	8	23	7	10	16	23	35	17	9	21	27	19	8	20	14	14	19	6	38	20	9	18	11	11	18	4	13	8	13	
BC	2	14	14	39	12	33	12	33	2	5	27	15	16	18	15	1	6	4	18	38	4	23	51	5	3	6	2	1	3	3	5

Row label: (CA)   Column label: (BC)

U.2.10 Co-occurrence measures as metrics

Given a matrix of co-occurrences whose entries, s_{jk}, are the frequency with which object j and object k are sorted into the same cell or grouping, and $N = \max(s_{jk})$ referring to the total number of subjects, Miller (1969 pp. 171-4) shows that

$$d_{jk} = N - s_{jk}$$

is a metric. At the individual level, the triangle inequality ($d_{ij} + d_{jk} \geqslant d_{jk}$) must obviously be satisfied, since a subject cannot sort i with j with k without also sorting i with k. Since the sum of metrics is also a metric, the aggregated co-occurrence matrix must also be a metric.

Burton (1972, 1975) shows Miller's distance measure must be corrected slightly to satisfy the positivity axiom of a metric (that $d_{jk} = 0$ if $f_j = k$). When thus corrected, it forms the basis for a family of distance measures, each of which reflects slightly different assumptions about sorting behaviour. The measures all have the form:

$$d_{jk} = N^* - s_{jk}$$

but differ in how N^* and the individual, unaggregated, similarity measure $f_{jk}^{(i)}$ are defined (note that $f_{jk}^{(i)} = s_{jk}$). The measures used for the analysis of the occupational titles and descriptions data are of two types:

Type 1: the individual contribution to the overall similarity has the form

$$s_{jk}^{(i)} = (f_{jk})^\infty$$

In order to satisfy the positivity axiom, $N^* = \max(f_{jk}) + \epsilon, > 0$
The constant, ∞, which differentiates the different measures, is used as a weighting factor to represent different assumptions about sorting behaviour:

($M1$) $\infty = 0$ Here, the similarity is simply the frequency with which pairs of objects are sorted together, and is identical to Miller's measure. Each individual co-occurrence contributes equally to the aggregate co-occurrence, and hence no attention is paid to differential cell-size.

($M2$) $\infty = +1$
($M3$) $\infty = -1$

In these last two instances, the contribution which an individual co-occurrence makes to the overall measure is *weighted* by the size of the cell in which it occurs, and information on the height (or fineness) of a subject's sorting is thus built in before being added to the overall similarity measure.

In $M3$, the smaller the cell size, the greater the contribution to the aggregate similarity. The reasoning behind this measure is that since the smaller cells reflect the finest (most specific) judgements of similarity, the objects which occur there should contribute more substantially to the similarity. The greater the extent to which objects j and k tend to occur only in their own company, the more similar they are.

$M2$ provides the opposite case: the larger the cell in which j and k occur, the higher the similarity. This is an unlikely interpretation of sorting behaviour, but it provides a useful limiting case.

Type 2: (which is an information-theoretic measure akin to the INFOTWO measure of Arabie and Boorman 1973).

$(M4)$ This measure is based upon the information, or 'surprisal value' (Attneave 1959: 6) of cell, a, in a subject i's sorting. Let n_a equal the size of this cell.

Define the *relative size* of cell a as:

$$p_a^{(i)} = \frac{\text{height } (a)}{\text{total height}} = \frac{n_a(n_a - 1)}{N(N - 1)}$$

This expression gives the probability that two objects, j and k, will be found in the *same cell,* a (i.e. the probability that these two objects form a concordant pair). Then the probability that two objects will be found *in different cells,* (i.e. are a discordant pair) is:

$$Q^{(i)} = 1 - p_a^{(i)}$$

The contribution which each pair of objects (j,k) in individual i's sorting make to the overall information is:

$$f_{jk}^{(i)} = -\log_2 (p_a^{(i)}) \text{ if } j \text{ and } k \text{ are in the } same \text{ group}$$

$$= \log_2 Q^{(i)} \text{ if } j \text{ and } k \text{ are in } different \text{ groups and, to satisfy}$$

the positivity axiom, if $j=k$ then

$$f_{jk}^{(i)} = \log_2 \ N!/ (2!(N - 2)!) + \epsilon) \ (\ >0)$$

When normalised (Burton 1972: 60-1), this quantity is distance measure $M4$.

Since surprisal is a negatively accelerated function of the size of the group, we may expect that, like $M3$, this measure will emphasise finer discriminations.

But the principal feature of $M4$ is that explicit account is also taken of pairs in *different* cells. For each such discordant pair, a negative quantity is added to the overall similarity.

In summary:

$M1$: pays no attention to differential discrimination (cell size) (Miller's co-occurrence measure, called F in Burton 1975)

$M2$: big cells make larger contributions to similarity than small cells. It emphasises gross discrimination and tendency towards 'lumpiness' (Burton's G).

*M*3: small cells make larger contributions to similarity than large cells. It emphasises fine discrimination.

*M*4: also emphasises finer discrimination for concordant pairs, but takes account of discordant pairs (Burton's *Z*).

In so far as sociologists have used free-sorting data at all, they have failed to take into account the effects of these factors (see, for example, Kraus, Schild and Hodge 1978).

U.2.11 Occupational titles: MDS analysis of four sorting co-occurrence distance measures

1. Four distance measures defined by Burton (1972, 1975) and discussed in T.3.10 were calculated, and scaled by the non-metric Euclidean distance model, using Roskam's MINISSA algorithm in 5 to 1 dimensions.
2. The stress$_1$ values of the resulting configurations are given below, together with estimated underlying dimensionality according to Spence and Graef's (1973) procedure (see also T.3.10).

	Stress$_1$ Dimensionality						M-Space	
Measure	V	IV	III	II	I	BFD*	EL†	
*M*1 (*F*)	0.0414	0.0659	0.0905	0.1331	0.1955	1	24% (low)	
*M*2 (*G*)	0.0405	0.0596	0.0853	0.1301	0.1913	1	23% (low)	
*M*3	0.0626	0.0914	0.1273	0.1774	0.2614	1	37% (moderate)	
*M*4 (*Z*)	0.0560	0.0829	0.1149	0.1615	0.2341	1	32% (moderate)	

*Best fitting dimensionality (minimising goodness of fit index to simulated data)

†Error level, and qualitative interpretation (see Spence 1973)

3. These stress$_1$ values compare favourably with those reported elsewhere for similar data (Burton 1975, Burton and Romney 1975). The stress$_1$ values (*M*4) for 58 role terms given in the latter go from 0.180 (5 dimensions) to 0.438 (1 dimension). The values given in the former are as follows:

34 Occupations		III-D	II-D	34 Behaviours		III-D	II-D
	*M*1	0.136	0.208		*M*1	0.123	0.160
	*M*2	0.129	0.187		*M*2	0.099	0.141
	*M*4	0.143	0.217		*M*4	0.132	0.177

4. It would appear that *M*2 gives rise to the best fitting MDS solutions, followed by *M*1, *M*4 and *M*3. This suggests that measures which emphasise fine discrimination are more difficult to fit by the Euclidean model. In part, at least, this is because measures such as *M*2 are bound to produce more clustered solutions.

   It also seems that the present data are relatively well fit, even by a one-dimensional solution.

5. *The configuration given in Fig. 2.8 (Class and Hierarchy*, p.43)

Model

Function: Non-metric	Data: *M*3 co-occurrence distances	
Program: MINISSA-1	Subjects: 71	
Dimension: 2		
Fit: Stress$_1$ (d-hat) = 0.1774		

		Dimension	
Occupational titles		1	2
1	CA	−1.2469	−0.0426
2	SST	−1.0959	0.5731
3	GM	0.8118	−0.6401
4	BM	1.1230	0.2709
5	ST	−1.1077	−0.1723
6	SW	−0.5429	0.6870
7	C	0.7622	−0.7154
8	AD	0.6745	0.5612
9	CPR	−0.7297	−0.1307
10	MOR	−1.0017	0.4731
11	PL	0.7258	−0.6975
12	MPN	−0.2166	0.5667
13	BCK	−0.1825	0.3954
14	PST	−0.7561	0.7009
15	UMO	1.3688	0.1700
16	PM	0.0932	0.6668
17	CE	−0.9615	−0.3822
18	PHT	−0.0214	−0.7483
19	BSL	1.4550	0.0236
20	RCK	0.7006	−0.2300
21	AP	−0.5209	−0.3817
22	A	−0.4272	−0.8913
23	RED	0.5688	−0.3333
24	PO	0.9621	0.6213
25	GEO	−1.0491	−0.4403
26	SMG	−0.7152	0.0538

U.2.11 *continued*

Occupational titles		Dimension	
		1	2
27	TDH	1.2768	−0.0054
28	TDR	0.9098	0.2532
29	ESG	−1.3221	0.2247
30	JN	−0.5426	−0.7343
31	LT	−0.1244	−0.0935
32	BC	1.1319	0.3972
	MEAN	−0.0000	0.0000
	SIGMA	0.8746	0.4849

U.2.12 Occupational descriptions and titles: MDS Analysis

1. The four co-occurrence measures (see U.2.10) were calculated for the 44 'type C' sortings of occupational descriptions and occupational titles. The stress$_1$ values were as follows:

Measure	Dimensionality				
	V	IV	III	II	I
$M1$ (F)	0.058	0.072	0.101	0.138	0.218
$M2$ (G)	0.069	0.083	0.108	0.145	0.229
$M3$	0.094	0.115	0.153	0.203	0.302
$M4$ (Z)	0.079	0.097	0.131	0.175	0.268

Note that, compared to the values reported in U.2.11, these scalings give rise to a slightly different order of best-fitted measures; $M1, M2, M4, M3$ (i.e. $M1$ is somewhat better than $M2$ for these data). The actual stress$_1$ values are consistently a little larger than for the 32 occupational titles, which is not surprising in view of the larger number of points (82) and the fact that they are composed of two different types of stimuli.

2. The dimensionality of the solution is not easy to determine, since the Spence-Graef M-SPACE values only exist for up to 35 points.

3. The configuration presented in Fig. 2.8 (*Class and Hierarchy*, p.43) is based upon the Z-measure ($M4$) which was chosen because it produces a well-structured configuration which also markedly resembles the solutions produced from other measures. The technical details are as follows:

Model   *Data M4(Z)* Co-occurrence distance

Function: Non-metric
Program: MINISSA-1   Subjects: 44
Dimension: 2
Fit: $Stress_1$ (d-hat) = 0.1750

| Stimuli | | Dimension | |
A. Occupational descriptions		1	2
1	STRIKE	0.1213	−0.6898
2	HOURS	−0.0461	−0.2775
3	MANAGE	−0.9730	0.4348
4	CLOCK-W	1.0887	0.0125
5	S-EMP	−0.6969	0.7750
6	PHYS	1.2045	0.1645
7	SERVE	−0.5376	−0.8898
8	CLOSED	0.4886	0.7343
9	APPR	0.8033	0.6858
10	IRREG	−0.1311	−0.5934
11	ACAD	−1.1919	0.0736
12	SWITCH	1.1967	−0.2701
13	OTIME1	0.7266	0.0549
14	SONS	−0.4997	0.5464
15	PERKS	−0.6808	0.6285
16	MOST	−0.4278	−0.6182
17	OTIME2	1.0046	0.2996
18	CASUAL	−0.0508	−0.0919
19	TU	0.9961	0.5308
20	DAYOFF	0.8845	−0.1960
21	ANY	1.0098	0.1944
22	WKENDS	−0.0724	−0.3710
23	MEN	0.5616	0.2492
24	PAYWK	1.0686	0.4067
25	CLOCKIN	1.0998	0.2690
26	30	−1.0099	−0.3014
27	PROF	−1.0200	0.0219
28	TRAIN	−0.7719	0.0434
29	HELP	−0.6823	−0.9021
30	BORING	1.4468	−0.1015
31	MONTH	−1.0761	−0.1028
32	MONEY	−0.8437	0.6203
33	STATUS	−1.0893	−0.1498
34	FEES	−0.9762	0.7562
35	MOVE	0.8229	−0.3734

U.2.12 *continued*

| Stimuli | | Dimension | |
A. *Occupational descriptions*		*1*	*2*
36	VARIOUS	0.5023	−0.6631
37	CTY	−0.8506	−0.7939
38	YOUNG	1.1416	−0.0817
39	HOUR	1.1556	0.2188
40	PEOPLE	−0.7742	−0.5753
41	SPEC	−1.1683	0.2676
42	EDUC	−1.2297	0.1951
43	ESSE	0.1046	−0.9320
44	N-TRAIN	1.2893	−0.3982
45	LATER	−1.0578	0.1583
46	YOUNGER	0.7462	−0.9531
47	FIT	1.0122	0.0237
48	SECURE	−0.9593	0.0400
49	EXAM	−1.2297	0.2255
50	SOLIDY	0.5075	0.4428

| Stimuli | | Dimension | |
B. *Occupational titles*		*1*	*2*
51	CA	−1.1225	0.1853
52	SST	−0.7939	−0.4649
53	GM	0.8103	0.5694
54	BM	1.1010	−0.3658
55	S T	−1.2807	0.1457
56	S W	−0.4445	−0.8306
57	C	0.7766	0.6481
58	AD	0.4650	−0.4458
59	CPR	−0.5841	0.1982
60	MOR	−0.9365	−0.5320
61	PL	0.7817	0.6854
62	MPN	−0.4311	−0.7531
63	BCK	−0.0765	0.2503
64	PST	−0.8105	−0.4558
65	UMO	1.3628	−0.1501
66	PM	−0.2053	−0.6518
67	CE	−1.0968	0.3014
68	PHT	−0.0483	0.7599
69	BSL	1.2770	−0.2010
70	RCK	0.7214	0.3501
71	AP	−1.0871	0.0933

U.2.12 *continued*

Stimuli B. Occupational titles		1	2
72	A	−0.2367	0.8196
73	RED	0.4983	0.5639
74	PO	0.8905	−0.4159
75	GEO	−1.2007	0.2255
76	SMG	−0.7344	0.4060
77	TDH	1.2638	−0.0552
78	TDR	0.9790	−0.2319
79	ESG	−1.1269	0.0490
80	JN	−0.6231	0.3195
81	LT	−0.0147	0.4276
82	BC	0.9902	−0.1914
MEAN		−0.0000	0.0000
SIGMA		0.8827	0.4699

7 The Hierarchies Task:
Appendices to Chapter 3 of *Class and Hierarchy*

U.3.1 Hierarchies and Trees

The basic definition of an HCS is given in T.3.6 (q.v.).

The technical terminology in this area is unfortunately far from universal. Usage in this chapter largely follows that of Boorman and Olivier (1973) which is the main technical reference. Commonly used alternatives are given below in parentheses.

(1) A graph $G = (X;R)$ consists of the set X of n nodes (vertices, points) with a binary (0,1) relation (correspondence, mapping) with roots (source, origin) a, if:

 (i) every node, $x_i (\neq a)$ is the terminal mode of a single arc (i.e. every node except the root receives exactly one arc, or has indegree 1)

 (ii) a is not the terminal node of any arc (i.e. the root has indegree 0)

 (iii) G has no circuits (semicycles)

(Note that the hierarchy of constructs inferred from the triadic similarities of subject 6718 (see 3.7) is *not* a tree, since it violates condition (i).)

(2) A rooted tree is termed: a *bare tree* if only the terminal nodes are labelled.

a *ranked tree* if, in addition, the non-terminal nodes are ranked on an ordinal scale.

a *valued tree* if, in addition, the non-terminal nodes are real-valued.

a *binary* (bifurcating) *tree* of every non-terminal node has exactly two 'successors' (i.e. has an outdegree of 2).

(3) A *subtree, rooted in node x_i* is obtained by cutting the tree above x_i. The 'hierarchies' dealt with in this chapter are *binary ranked trees*. Because of the binary property, there are exactly 15 levels to each tree. Each non-terminal node represents a clustering made by the subject, and the rank assigned is the step (or level) at which the consistent subtrees were joined.

U.3.2 Selection of Subjects for the Hierarchies Task (n=93)

Subjects were selected in two ways — by sampling from professional registers
(especially Quadrants A and B), and by allocating subjects obtained from
'combing' procedure to the relevant quadrant (see Chapter 5).
(Data will be found on file DHA106AD at the SSRC Survey Archive,
University of Essex.)

QUADRANT A (n = 31)			**QUADRANT B** (n = 16)		
No.	*Occupation*	*Code*	*No.*	*Occupation*	*Code*
14	Doctors (including 9 general practitioners, 2 psychia-. trists, 2 anaesthetists, 2 gynaecologists	D (and S)	4	Business managers	BM
				Management consultant	S
				Building firm owner	S
			2	Actuaries	S
12	Social workers	SW	2	Chartered accountants	G, S
4	Further Education teachers (including Professor, 3 lecturers)	S		Solicitor	S
			2	Insurance broker	S
			2	Agricultural officers	S
	Comprehensive school principal	S		Architectural assistant	Y
QUADRANT C (n = 9)			**QUADRANT D** (n = 37)		
No.	*Occupation*	*Code*	*No.*	*Occupation*	*Code*
	Car auctioneer	S	13	Engineers (including 3 heating, 2 electronic, 1 machine, 1 machine tool, 1 television, 1 telephone, 1 quality control, 1 maintenance 1 service, 1 Post Office)	Y
2	Salesmen — coffee — toiletries	Y			
	Boutique manager	Y			
	Junkshop owner	Y		Maintenance electrician	Y
	Clerical supervisor	Y	3	Technicians (laboratory, architectural, P.O. telephone)	Y
	Male psychiatric nurse	Y			
	Window-cleaner (SE)	Y			
	Painter-decorator (SE)	Y		Foreman coach builder	Y
				Foreman fitter-welder	Y
			2	Fitters (civil aircraft, plant)	Y
				Welder	Y
				Precision sheet metal worker	Y

U.3.2 *continued*

2	Joiners
	Wages clerk — Y
	Comparer of deeds — Y
	Print designer (SE) — Y
	Compositor — Y
	Partner, printing firm — Y
	Draughtsmen — Y
	Service manager (garage) — Y
	Traffic controller, brewery — Y
	Fireman — Y
	Fork truck driver — Y
	Horticulturist — S
	Interior decorator — Y

U.3.3 Number of Subjects making P,C and J Choices, by step and quadrant membership

		Pairs			By Quadrant: Chainings				Joins				Total P	C	J
Step	A	B	C	D	A	B	C	D	A	B	C	D	P	C	J
2	26	7	8	24	5	9	1	13	0	0	0	0	65	28	0
3	20	15	7	22	10	1	2	15	1	0	0	0	64	28	1
4	19	12	8	24	11	4	0	13	1	0	1	0	63	28	2
5	18	13	5	16	12	3	4	19	1	0	0	2	52	38	3
6	18	9	4	18	13	6	5	16	0	1	0	3	49	40	4
7	11	9	1	20	19	7	8	16	1	0	0	1	41	50	2
8	16	5	2	16	14	11	7	20	1	0	0	1	39	52	2
9	4	4	2	14	24	12	6	21	3	0	1	2	24	63	6
10	7	2	1	9	16	9	6	23	8	5	2	5	19	54	20
11	3	1	1	2	11	4	3	16	17	11	5	19	7	34	52
12	9	0	0	0	5	3	4	8	26	13	5	29	0	20	73
13	1	0	0	0	4	1	2	3	26	15	7	34	1	10	82
14	1	0	0	0	0	0	0	1	30	16	9	36	1	1	91
15	0	0	0	0	0	0	0	1	31	16	9	36	0	1	92

Quadrant:nos.

A:	31
B:	16
C:	9
D:	37
Total	93

U.3.4 Subject Y032: Interviewer's Report

Level	Action	Subject's comments

1. AD and LD — 'Both drive. They have different spheres.'
2. RP and BSL — 'They don't take any specific training.'
3. C and MTO — 'People who work with their hands but more skilled than the other people like AD and LD. They have a technical, manufacturing sort of connection.'
4. PM and CT — 'These are jobs that people go into when they have tried an apprenticeship and are cheesed off with it.'
5. BM to 2 — 'No training.'
6. MPN and MIN — 'They are specialised — they have a specialised category.'
7. SOL and CA — 'I'm not quite sure why I've paired these. They seem to have sort of legal implications.'
8. CST to 6 — 'Specialised.'
9. QA to 7 — 'I don't know the definition of a QA, this is just an enlightened guess.'
10. CSE to 9 — 'They come in same sort of social category i.e. they all have fairly extended university training. They are the type of people who work for a long time. They are poorly paid until they reach a certain stage.'
11. 5 and 1 — 'I started with people who, to my mind, do not need specific training. We must assume that everybody can read and write in the first place. For me, anyone can learn to be a BM in a day or so.'
12. 4 and 11 — 'Next.' After 11 S put PM and CT (4) above it. 'They (PM and CT) need specific training but it's almost as if they take a course, while MTO and C have a bit of training which they've got to have to be able to do the work. They must have a leaning that way.'
13. 3 and 12 — After 12, S then put C and MTO above it, justifying it by saying that 'although CT is considered more important than C, it is an emotional thing with me because I am a person who works with my hands and I have a bent towards people who make or create things.'
14. 10 to 13 — At first S put 8 *and* 13 but changed his mind for 'I have a greater respect for them [group 8] for they are the people with vocation.' Instead he put group 10 next 'because they are the people who spend years and years studying and they have higher pay'.
15. 8 and 14 — 'People who do their job out of love.'

The subject summed up what he had done by explaining that 'that's the way

I would put them into order starting at the very beginning with the blue-collar workers and building right up to the final white-collar workers.'

U.3.5 Distances between hierarchies

1. In Boorman and Olivier's terminology, the hierarchies considered here are binary, (strictly) ranked trees. These properties allow them to be embedded in the space of valued trees.
2. The 'central technical principle' (Jardine and Sibson 1971, p.108), defining the distance measures, m, between two trees, T_1 and T_2, in terms of their constituent partitions, P_1 and P_2 at level is:
$$m_\delta (T,T) = \int_0^\infty \delta\{P_1(\lambda), P_2(\lambda)\} \ d\lambda$$
In this case, it reduces to the discrete 'rank form' measures, r :

$$r_\delta (T_1 \ T_2) = \sum_{d=0}^n \delta\{P_1(\lambda), P_2(\lambda)\}$$

Such measures are shown (pp.40 ff) to have a simple interpretation in terms of a 'tree-move' defined in the space of (valued) trees.
3. A number of partition measures were used, but only results for PAIRBONDS and APPROX are reported here. The PAIRBONDS measure is a simple form of the symmetric distance measure proposed by Flament 1963, among others, and developed in some detail in Boorman 1970, (especially pp.43-58) and in his subsequent work. The APPROX measure has an especially simple structure and interpretation, but only takes on a relatively small number of integer values.
4. The basic subject data is stored in the form of individual lower-half dissimilarity matrices

Δ^k, whose entry δ_{ij}^k gives the level at which occupations i and j were merged in subject k's hierarchy.
These data are on file at the SSRC Survey Archive as DHA106AD.

The calculations of the inter-subject hierarchy distance measures were made by an adaptation of the Free-sorting Partition-metric program (FAIDPCS) used for the analysis of the data in Chapter 2 (of *Class and Hierarchy*).

U.3.6 Scaling of Distances between Individual Hierarchies

A. Scaling
   Subjects: 93 individuals described in U.3.2.
   Data:　The subject's hierarchies were transformed into lower-triangular dissimilarity matrices, whose entries contained the lowest level at which a pair of occupational titles are joined. Inter-individual

distances were then calculated according to the basic r tree-distance measures (see U.3.5) of Boorman and Olivier (1973), based on the 'height' (PAIRBONDS), minimum set move (APPROX) and minimum lattice move (T12MINUS) partition distances.

Model: The inter-individual matrices were analysed in terms of the non-metric Euclidean distance model, by the MINISSA program (Roskam 1975), in five to one dimensions.

Fit: The stress$_1$ (d) values were as follows:

Measure	Dimensionality				
	1	*2*	*3*	*4*	*5*
PAIRBONDS	0.382	0.244	0.179	0.142	0.117
APPROX	0.440	0.286	0.214	0.163	0.132

These values are rather higher than those obtained for the corresponding partition measures (see U.2.8). In the absence of comparable simulated distributions, a pragmatic rule was used: the lowest 'acceptable' dimensionality in which an increase of one dimension does not substantially decrease stress or increase interpretability is regarded as the appropriate one. With these values, two dimensions is accepted in the case of both measures.

B. Final Configuration

The final configuration for the PAIRBONDS distances (presented in Fig. 2.6) is given below. The order of subjects is the same as in DHA106AD, on file at the SSRC Data Archive, University of Essex.

Subject	Q*	I	II	Subject	Q*	I	II
1	B	−0.1075	−0.8264	47	A	0.5189	0.4092
2	B	−0.5203	−0.6362	48	A	−0.5963	0.5186
3	B	−0.2196	−0.1923	49	C	−1.1954	0.1097
4	A	0.4642	0.5596	50	D	0.1556	0.0699
5	A	1.0548	−1.1915	51	D	0.9822	−0.1571
6	A	1.0164	−0.7346	52	D	0.4994	1.4859
7	A	−0.8495	0.5627	53	D	−1.2196	−0.9117
8	A	−0.0341	0.1222	54	C	−0.8606	0.3176
9	A	0.0664	−1.4920	55	C	−0.6057	−0.3963

U.3.6 *continued*

Subject	Q*	I	II	Subject	Q*	I	II
10	A	−0.4937	−0.9032	(Y089)56	C	1.5686	1.3609
11	A	−1.7371	0.4776	57	D	0.5603	−0.2959
12	A	1.3341	−0.8113	58	D	−0.3852	0.2802
13	A	−0.1484	−0.7752	59	D	−1.0393	0.8673
14	A	−0.4686	−1.3166	60	D	1.0180	−0.4092
15	B	0.2075	−1.0282	61	D	−1.2888	0.5538
16	B	−0.4869	0.0022	62	D	−0.5054	0.5760
17	A	−1.2792	−0.3681	63	D	−1.0481	0.0304
18	B	−0.9400	−0.4672	64	B	0.7601	−0.5645
19	B	−0.4783	−0.2921	65	D	0.7113	0.0901
20	B	−0.5022	0.7389	66	D	−0.5508	1.1827
21	B	0.4012	−0.1622	67	D	−0.3018	0.2395
22	B	−0.9191	−0.4380	68	D	1.1227	0.4124
23	A	1.4263	0.3808	69	D	−0.5860	−0.5108
24	A	0.3243	0.2122	70	C	0.2865	1.2316
25	A	0.4451	0.3934	71	D	0.0484	−0.6899
26	A	0.1852	0.1363	72	D	−1.6160	−0.4253
27	B	−0.0630	−0.0690	73	D	0.5525	0.9810
28	B	−0.8436	−0.0027	74	D	−0.3987	0.0311
29	A	0.2576	−0.3091	75	D	0.6005	−0.8612
30	B	−0.0538	0.5462	76	C	−0.2411	1.1433
31	B	−0.2851	−0.4154	77	D	0.5332	−0.5896
32	A	−0.4223	−0.1405	78	D	0.5615	0.7390
33	C	0.2254	−0.8006	79	D	−0.2572	0.7386
34	B	0.5307	−0.4889	80	D	−0.2193	0.9991
190)35	D	−0.3085	−0.2665	81	D	−0.7853	1.4900
36	A	−0.0893	0.3745	82	D	0.2285	−0.3692
37	A	0.0862	0.5683	83	D	0.8210	0.9519
✓O2)38	A	−0.7155	−1.4489	84	D	−0.0721	−0.4260
39	A	1.2841	−0.4547	(Y346)85	C	−0.2023	−0.0929
40	A	0.4737	−0.0102	86	D	1.2771	−0.0805
41	A	0.4450	−0.6378	87	D	−0.3265	−0.7465
42	A	−0.5106	0.1634	88	D	0.6453	−0.1850
43	A	0.3026	−0.6965	89	D	0.2766	0.3376
44	A	0.2498	0.2976	90	C	0.4973	0.8468
45	A	−0.0901	0.0161	91	D	0.9313	0.7448
46	A	−1.0090	1.1555	92	D	0.4566	−1.1048
				93	D	1.4827	0.7461

*Quadrant allocation of subject

U.3.7 Analysis of Variance in Quadrant locations

1. Location of quadrant centroids (2-space)

Measure

Quadrant	PAIRBONDS	APPROX
A	$(-0.13, 0.01)$	$(0.05, -0.16)$
B	$(-0.23, -0.31)$	$(-0.22, -0.27)$
C	$(0.06, 0.10)$	$(-0.06, 0.41)$
D	$(0.19, 0.10)$	$(0.07, 0.15)$
Total:	$(0,0)$	$(0,0)$

2. *Dispersion (s.d.) in centroid locations*

Quadrant	PAIRBONDS	APPROX
A	$(0.96, 0.62)$	$(0.76, 0.69)$
B	$(0.62, 0.36)$	$(0.51, 0.46)$
C	$(0.28, 0.89)$	$(0.83, 0.77)$
D	$(0.65, 0.74)$	$(0.78, 0.69)$
Total	$(0.74, 0.66)$	$(0.74, 0.67)$

3. MANOVA hypotheses: H_1 – Equality of dispersions
H_2 – Overall discrimination $(df1 = 6, df2 = 176)$

Hypotheses (F-value)

	PAIRBONDS	APPROX
H_1 $(df1 = 9, df2 = 7488)$	3.18*	1.22
H_2 $(df1 = 6, df2 = 176)$	1.56	1.90†

*$p < .01$
†$p < .05$

U.3.8 Aggregate Ultrametric distances (Hierarchies Data: File DHA106AD)

1. Averaged ultrametric distances (upper figure)   2. Standard deviations of distances (lower figure)

	MIN (1)	CST (2)	QA (3)	CA (4)	MPN (5)	AD (6)	RSL (7)	MTO (8)	SOL (9)	CSE (10)	CT (11)	PM (12)	C (13)	LD (14)	RP (15)	BM (16)
1. (MIN)																
2. CST	7.31 (3.90)															
3. QA	10.22 (3.81)	10.37 (3.61)														
4. CA	10.33 (3.81)	10.51 (3.54)	5.38 (7.84)													
5. MPN	10.37 (4.49)	10.84 (4.17)	13.00 (2.69)	12.85 (2.99)												
6. AD	12.58 (3.56)	12.65 (3.56)	13.98 (2.00)	13.93 (1.98)	8.90 (4.95)											
7. BSL	14.50 (1.91)	14.67 (1.14)	14.82 (0.50)	14.75 (0.69)	14.15 (1.32)	12.95 (2.84)										
8. MTO	14.39 (1.37)	14.20 (1.83)	14.36 (1.47)	14.35 (1.29)	13.32 (2.22)	12.97 (2.44)	10.45 (3.91)									
9. SOL	9.61 (4.17)	10.27 (3.59)	7.01 (4.23)	6.61 (7.47)	13.06 (6.37)	13.91 (1.90)	14.71 (0.72)	14.25 (1.52)								
10. CSE	10.68 (3.40)	10.26 (3.65)	8.15 (3.74)	7.64 (4.15)	12.98 (2.44)	13.70 (2.46)	14.77 (0.69)	14.27 (1.74)	8.44 (4.12)							
11. CT	13.52 (2.40)	13.54 (2.72)	13.34 (2.90)	13.26 (2.94)	13.07 (2.51)	11.85 (3.98)	12.84 (2.39)	12.55 (2.88)	13.49 (2.57)	13.48 (2.72)						
12. PM	11.18 (3.98)	11.05 (4.35)	13.31 (2.24)	13.29 (2.47)	9.16 (4.39)	8.69 (4.99)	14.00 (1.90)	13.32 (2.47)	12.84 (3.05)	12.49 (3.41)	12.93 (2.85)					
13. C	14.28 (1.57)	14.06 (2.03)	14.23 (1.76)	14.20 (1.62)	12.88 (2.89)	12.98 (2.47)	10.46 (4.45)	6.14 (3.77)	14.08 (1.96)	14.16 (1.93)	12.33 (3.17)	13.08 (2.75)				
14. LD	14.50 (1.31)	14.56 (1.08)	14.66 (0.81)	14.58 (0.96)	13.67 (2.11)	11.04 (4.62)	9.68 (3.88)	10.68 (3.59)	14.53 (0.97)	14.67 (0.85)	11.13 (3.77)	13.48 (2.51)	10.93 (3.73)			
15. RP	14.48 (1.82)	14.63 (1.34)	14.63 (0.83)	14.61 (1.01)	13.67 (2.49)	12.15 (3.82)	7.42 (4.41)	11.86 (2.84)	14.63 (0.89)	14.63 (1.00)	12.49 (2.91)	13.83 (1.97)	12.39 (2.57)	9.85 (4.02)		
16. BM	14.19 (2.26)	14.45 (1.64)	14.47 (1.29)	14.41 (1.36)	13.56 (2.29)	12.43 (3.35)	9.67 (4.24)	12.26 (2.83)	14.44 (1.30)	14.44 (1.35)	11.11 (3.78)	13.42 (2.51)	12.60 (2.85)	11.16 (3.40)	8.83 (4.32)	

U.3.9 Comparison of Aggregate (Mean) Similarities and Hierarchies Data

1. The mean similarities between the LABL06 set of occupational titles
   are given in T.3.8, and the mean ultrametric distances of the hierarchies
   data are given in U.3.8.
2. The two sets of data are plotted against each other in Figure U.3.1 below
       As is usual with such distance (like) data, both distributions are highly
   skewed towards the large distances/small similarities, and there is a slight
   tendency towards non-linearity at this extreme. None the less, the two sets
   are very highly linearly correlated ($r = -0.953$).
3. The regressions are also highly similar, and are both superimposed on the
   plot of Fig. U.3.1.
       Predicting Y from X : $Y = 10.337 - 0.572X$
                   X from Y : $X = 17.542 - 1.586Y$
   As can be seen, the (Ambulance Driver, Lorry Driver) point is most
   discrepant; the two occupations judged far more alike, on average, in the
   similarities than in the hierarchies task.
4. The linear relationship and the degree of fit differ to some extent among
   the occupations being judged.

	Occupational title	*Slope (Y on X)*	*Fit (r^2)*
1.	Church of Scotland Minister	−0.55	0.95
2.	Comprehensive School Teacher	−0.55	0.94
3.	Qualified Actuary	−0.57	0.98
4.	Chartered Accountant	−0.58	0.97
5.	Male Psychiatric Nurse	−0.55	0.95
6.	Ambulance Driver	−0.65	*0.75*
7.	Building Site Labourer	−0.61	0.93
8.	Machine Tool Operator	−0.49	0.97
9.	Country Solicitor	−0.57	0.94
10.	Civil Servant (Executive)	−0.65	0.98
11.	Commercial Traveller	−0.53	0.55
12.	Policeman	−0.45	0.85
13.	Carpenter	−0.50	0.92
14.	Lorry Driver	−0.76	0.87
15.	Railway Porter	−0.57	0.91
16.	Barman	−0.45	0.91

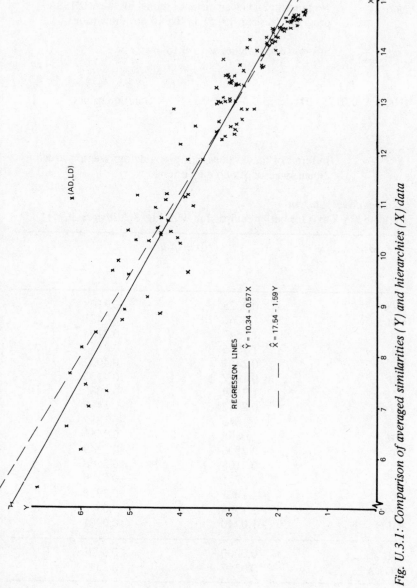

REGRESSION LINES

$\hat{Y} = 10.34 - 0.57X$

$\hat{X} = 17.54 - 1.59Y$

x (AD,LD)

Fig. U.3.1: Comparison of averaged similarities (Y) and hierarchies (X) data

U.3.10 Scaling of aggregate hierarchies data

Subjects: 93 individuals described in U.3.2.
Data: Mean, ultrametric distances defining subjects' hierarchies
                 (summed from file DHA106AD)
Model: Non-metric Euclidean distance model by the MINISSA
                 program (Roskam 1975), in five to one dimensions

Fit: Stress$_1$ (d-hat) values were as follows:

1	2	3	4	5	
0.008	0.017	0.035	0.073	0.111	Solution values

In terms of these values, this probably represents a 'true' dimensionality of two dimensions

2-Dimensional solution
(reflected in *X* axis for better comparison with Fig. 3.2, *Images,* p.75)

Occupation	Dimension	
	1	*2*
MIN	0.9225	0.3108
CST	1.0066	0.3481
QA	1.1547	−0.3103
CA	1.1065	0.3556
MPN	0.2482	0.4032
AD	−0.1997	0.4100
BSL	−1.3689	−0.0085
MTO	−0.8742	−0.5498
SOL	1.1048	−0.1889
CSE	1.0865	−0.2556
CT	−0.2906	−0.2948
PM	0.2108	0.5568
C	−0.7751	−0.5279
LD	−1.1081	0.3628
RP	−1.1998	0.0998
BM	−1.0240	−0.0001
MEAN	−0.0000	−0.0000
SIGMA	0.9357	0.3528

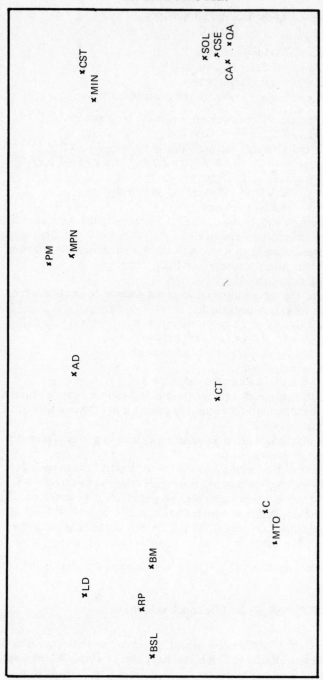

Fig. U.3.2: 2-D Scaling of aggregate hierarchies data

U.3.11 The sum of metrics and ultrametrics

(a) If d is a metric, then:

(i) $d(x,y) \geqslant 0$ (non-negativity)

(ii) $d(x,y) = 0$ if $A = B$ (identity)

(iii) $d(x,y) = d(y,x)$ (symmetry)

and (iv) $d(x,y) \leqslant d(x,y) + d(y,z)$ (triangle inequality)

Given two metrics d_1 and d_2, let $d = d_1 + d_2$. Is d also a metric?

(i) $d(x,y) = d_1(x,y) + d_2(x,y) \geqslant 0$

(ii) $d(x,y) = d_1(x,y) + d_2(x,y)$ iff $d_1(x,y) = d_2(x,y) = 0$

(iii) $d(x,y) = d_1(x,y) + d_2(x,y) = d_1(y,x) + d_2(y,x) = d(y,x)$

(iv) $d(x,z) = d_1(x,z) + d_2(x,z)$
$$\leqslant d_1(x,y) + d_1(y,z) + d_2(x,y) + d_2(y,z)$$
$$= d(x,y) + d(y,z)$$

Therefore $d = d_1 + d_2$ is also a metric. Consequently the summative aggregation of metrics is a metric.

(b) Now consider an ultrametric. A metric d is an ultrametric if it obeys the stronger 'ultrametric inequality' condition:

(iv*) $d(x,z) \leqslant \max (d(x,y), d(y,z))$

The fact that the sum of ultrametrics is not necessarily an ultrametric can be seen by a counter-example.

Suppose $d_1(x,y) = 2; d_1(x,z) = 1; d_1(y,z) = 2$

and $d_2(x,y) = 2; d_2(x,z) = 2; d_2(y,z) = 1$

Clearly d_1 and d_2 are ultrametrics. Once again,

Let $d = d_1 + d_2$, then

$$d(x,y) = 4; d(x,z) = 3; d(y,z) = 3$$

Now d obeys the triangle equality (iv) and is therefore a metric, but it does *not* obey the ultrametric or inequality since it is not the case that $d(x,y) \leqslant \max (d(x,z), d(y,z))$.

It may be, of course, that some ultrametrics may sum to an ultrametric, but this will not, in general, be so.

In the case of the hierarchies data, the ultrametric inequality holds remarkably well for the summed (averaged) data, and this is reflected in the fact that up to the seventh level the Connectedness and Diameter HCS solutions are identical, and, apart from slight differences in the level at which occupations are merged, they differ only in the location of the Commercial Traveller title.

APMC is indebted to Mr M.J. Prentice for his help in producing this appendix.

U.3.12 Full Specification of Occupational Themes

Notes

(1)   The content of themes differ slightly from branch to branch of the aggregate hierarchy. This is especially true of Theme 4 (Job Content).

(2) Each theme is specified by a set of terms (word-senses) together with their relevant contexts. These contexts sometimes serve to eliminate irrelevant homographs, and are used at other times to indicate a cluster of uses (e.g. application to people, or to jobs). Occasionally it is necessary to keep inflected forms separate (e.g. EDUCATE as a job-skill, and hence Theme 4, versus EDUCATED, as a Qualifications theme 2).

(3) Key term entries are prefaced by the frequency with which the term appears (in this sense) in the corpus of HA constructs. Entries are immediately followed by a 'tag-list', which gives the specification of this word-sense in terms of the syntactic and semantic categories of the Edinburgh version of the Harvard IV-3 Dictionary (Kelly and Stone 1975; Coxon and Trappes-Lomax 1977). (Each of the tags is explained in U.4.13.)

The COCOA system (Berry-Rogghe and Crawford 1973) was used to generate Key Word in Context and related listings, on which the theme context construction is based.

Theme 1: Status

(33) STATUS (= STATUS 1: NOUN. ECON. POLIT. THINK. EVALU. MEANS. POWER)
    same —, similar —, common —
    lowly —, higher —, skilled —
    job —
    — in life, — in society
    — thing
    — of

(14) PROFESSION(S) (NOUN.MASS.COLL.ECON.ECON*)
    medical —, legal —, business —, caring —,
    type of —, class of —, sort of —
    chosen —
    — of selling

(38) PROFESSIONALS (not tagged specifically in individual form, = PROFESSION)
    lower —, business —,

(92) PROFESSIONAL (MODIF. EVAL. ECON.ECON*)
(human reference)   higher —, non —
                   — man/men, — people, — chap, — helpers
                   — group(s), — occupations, — jobs, — body/ies, — class
(non-human   —scale
reference)   — training, — qualification, — standards,
              — practice, — service, — aspect, — advice

(52) WORKER(S) (NOUN. HUMAN. ECON. ECON*)
    ordinary —,

skilled —, manual —,
industrial —, shopfloor —,
public —, white-collar —, collar-and-tie —, blue-collar —
weekly-paid —
(110) CLASS(ES) (not directly tagged; composites appear in ECON
and ECON*)
social —
same —, similar —, own —
higher —, upper —, upper-middle —, middle-middle —, lower —
professional —, wealthy —, working —
status —, to-supper —,
— background, — conscious
— terms, — wise
— of people
(Other)
(8) (social/) positions
(8) (social/) scale
(8) (social) standing
(8) looked up to

Theme 2: Qualifications and Training

(63) QUALIFICATION(S) (= QUALIFY 2)
(quant) degree of —
(amount) no —, basic —, high —
(comp) same —, more —, less —
(type) academic —, university —, educational —, paper —,
professional —, special —, formal —, entry
(verbal) require —, need —
(40) QUALIFY/IED (- QUALIF2: SUPV. COMN. QUALIF.)
highly — academically —, university
— type, — people, — individual, — man
— by exam, — by degree
(2) TRAIN (= TRAIN3: SUPV. THINK. EVALU. DOCTR. ACAD)
(19) TRAINED (TRAIN4: MODIF. VIRTUE. THINK. EVALU)
all —
specifically —, well —, university —
— manual workers, — middle class, — professional
(159) TRAINING (= TRAIN3)
(quant) amount of — degree of —, type of
(amount) no —, minimum of —, bit of —, little
not (terribly) much —, certain amount of —, some —, fair degree of —,
good bit of —, lot of —, much —, very high degree of —; very much —,
prolonged —, lengthy —, many years —, extensive —, very long —
(comp) similar —, same —, longer —, lesser —, more —, most —,
(further —)

(type) specialised –, specific –, formal –, intensive demanding job –,
   on-the-job –, practical –, specialist –, occupational –, professional –,
   academic –, college –
(verbal) need –, require)

(55) EDUCATION (= NOUN. THINK. EVALU. DOCTR. ACAD)
   good –, fair –, more –, proper –, further –, formal –, specialised –,
   University –
   level of –, type of –, standard of –

(23) EDUCATIONAL (MODIF. PSTV2. THINK. EVALU. DOCTR. ACAD)
   – attainment, – level, – requirements
   –background,, – qualification, – standards

(37) UNIVERSITY (NOUN. PLACE. POLIT. SOCIAL. ACAD)
   – graduate(s), – type person,
   –qualification(s), – qualified, – education, – requirements, – training,
   –trained, – degrees, – level
   been to –, go to –, study in –
Other: degree, career, expertise, attainment

Theme 2: (Skill)

(59) SKILL (= SKILL1: NOUN. ECON. VIRTUE. PSTV.* THINK. EVALU)
   (grant) amount of –, degree of –, level of –, range of –, order of –,
      kind of –
   (amount) no –, bit of –, little –, element of –, some –, lot of –
   (type) practical –, technical –, inborn –
   (verbal) requires –, have –

(39) SKILLS (= SKILL1)
   (quant) ranging in –
   (amount) no –, low –, some –, vast –
   (comp) similar –
   (type) specialist –, physical –, professional –, untrained –, manual –,
      main –, taught –, social –, basic –, special –
   (verbal) involve –, using –

(90) SKILLED (= SKILL2-ED: MODIF. EVAL. VIRTUE. PSTV.* THINK.
EVALU)
   (amount) hardly –, not terribly –, not particularly –, not so –, fairly –,
      moderately –, pretty –, comparatively –, highly –, very
   (comp) less –, as –, more –
   (modif) –man/men, – people, –group, – professionals, – worker,
      – operator, – craftsmen, – jobs, – occupations, – industry, – trades,
      – work, – status

(24) SEMI-SKILLED (= SKILL2)
   (modif) – chaps, – workers, – working class – jobs, – manual

(56) UNSKILLED (= SKILL2)
   (amount) totally –, rather –, relatively –, almost –
   (comp) most –

(modif) —man/men, — people, — labour, — working class, — jobs,
—occupations

Theme 3: Remuneration
(42) SALARY/IES/IED (= NOUN. ECON. THINK. EVALU. MEANS. ECON*)
comparable —, same —, alike in —, more —, high — range of —, difference
in —
— range, — bracket, — scale(s), — level
(22) INCOME (- INCOME1: NOUN. COM. ECON. COMN FORM.
ECON*)
same —, similar —, same type of —, varying —, low —, differences in —
— bracket, — level, — group
(18) WAGE(S) (= WAGE1: NOUN. ECON. THINK. EVALU. MEANS. ECON*)
same —, similar —, high —, poor —,
— earner, — earning, — packet, — bracket
(15) PAY (= PAY2: NOUN. COM. ECON. ECON.* COMNOBJ)
low(er) —, high(er) —, same —
(35) MONEY (= NOUN. COM. ECON. ECON.* COMNOBJ)
same —, lot of —, high —, not much —, big —, more —
earn/ing —, make/making —, care about —, go for —, want —, in it for —,
working for —
— wise
(14) EARN (= EARN1: SUPV. WORK. EXCH. ECON.* STRNG1. ACTV1.
ACH. COMPLT)
— less, — more, — same money
— money
    EARNER (NOUN. HUMAN. ECON.* STRNG1)
wage —, big —
(3) FEES (NOUN. ECON. ECON*)
exorbitant —, lower —
other standard of living, financial reward, commercial success

Theme 4: Job Content: Financial Dealings
(26) BUSINESS (= BUSINESS1: NOUN. ECON. DOCTR. ECON.* THINK.
EVALU)
same —, different —,
way of —, line of —
do —
— profession/s/als, — affairs, —environment, — capacity
— type
(25) FIGURES (= FIGURE1: NOUN. COM. COMNFORM)
involved in —, manipulation of —, dealings in —, looking at —,
conversant with —, deal with —, work with —
men of —
(5) INSURANCE (NOUN. MEANS. ECON. ECON.* THINK. EVALU)

national −, life −
− area, −risks
(10) MONEY (NOUN. COM. ECON. ECON.* COMNOBJ)
other people's −
deal with −, concerned with −, involved with −
− matters
(13) COMMERCE/COMMERCIAL (NOUN. DOCTR. ECON. ECON* STRNG2. THINK. EVALU)
− figure, − practice
− world, − involvement
− end, − motives
(20) FINANCE/S, FINANCIAL (NOUN. DOCTR. ECON. ECON.* STRNG)
− masters, − affairs
− reward, − choice
−bracket
Others: Statistics, Calculations, Tax, Book-keeping, Economic, Mathematical

Theme 4: Job Content: Legal Dealings
(5) AFFAIRS (= AFFAIR1: NOUN. ACTV. VARY)
financial −, personal −
− of others
(13) LEGAL/LEGALITIES (MODIF. ECON. POLIT. DOCTR. LEGAL. THINK. EVALU)
− practice, − profession, − figure
− framework, − implications, − side

Theme 4: Job Content: (People-Orientation)
(273) PEOPLE (= PEOPLE1: NOUN. HUMAN. COLL. MASS)
(interaction) contact with −, deal with −, concerned with −, to do with −,
    in relationship with −, involved with −, in touch with −, meeting −,
    tell −, talk to −
(influence) handling −, supervision of −, discipline −, guide −, organise −,
    responsible for −
(succurant) help −, assist −, counsel −
(service) serve −, work for −, dedicated to −, look after interests of −,
    look after welfare of −, benefit of −
(affect) get on with −, have to like −, motivated by −, interested in −,
    care about −,
(76) SERVICE(S) (= SERVICE1: NOUN. ECON. ACT. GENRLTY. ECON.* SUBM. PSTV*)
social −, public −, professional −, useful −, inessential −
providing a −, doing a −, giving a−
− people, − occupations, − agencies, − industry − to the community,
    − to the public
− (the) people, − to society

(16) SERVE/SERVING (= SERVE1: SUPV. INTREL. ECON.* SUBM.
— the community, — the public, — the people
(14) SERVANT(S) (= NOUN. HU. ECON. ECON.* SUBM)
public —
(80) (the) PUBLIC (= PUBLIC1: NOUN. COLL. POLIT. PFREQ. MASS)
contact with —, involved with —, deal with —, work with —
serve —, help —, educate —
listen to —, rely on —
— servants, — service, — workers
— good, — duty
(65) SOCIAL (= SOCIAL1: MODIF. POLIT. POLIT.* HUMAN. COLL.
THINK. EVALU. DOCTR)
— service(s), — work, — welfare
— aspect, — concern, — cares
— contact, — sense, — outlook
(47) (the) COMMUNITY (NOUN. MASS. COLL. POLIT. ECON. AFFIL.
PSTV2. STRNG2)
serve/service to —, help —, caring for—, contact with —, involved in —,
deal with —, accountable to —, responsible to —, necessary in —
essential to —, assets to —, loyalty to —

Theme 4: Job Content: (Educative Skills)
(6) EDUCATE (= SUPV. ACAD. POWER. ACTV1. STRNG1. COMN)
to —
— people, — children, — themselves, — the public
(14) TEACHER/S (NOUN. HUMAN. ACAD. POWER)
(8) TEACH (SUPV. COMV. COMN. ACAD. POWER)
— subject, — rules, — no, — something, — the same thing
(37) RESPONSIBILITY (NOUN. ABS. ABS.* VIRTUE. THINK. EVALU.
POWER)
similar —, degree of —, levels of —, more —, modest —,
accept —, have —
sense of —
— for, — type

Theme 4: Job Content: (Manual)
(65) MANUAL (not tagged as such)
purely —, largely —, very —, more or less —
— worker(s), — labourer(s)
— work, — job(s), — type, — labouring, — skills, — dexterity
(12) LABOUR (= LABOR1: NOUN. COLL. ECON. MASS. ECON.*)
unskilled —, manual —, physical —, less paid —, casual —,
white collar —
(18) LABOURER(S) (= LABOR1)
manual —, non-productive —, slave —

(3) LABOURING (= LABOR 1)

    manual —, — jobs

(11) PHYSICAL (= PHYSICAL1: MODIF. BODYIND)

    — skills, — strength, — energy, — effort, — labour, — jobs

Also: menial, muscle, hands

Theme 4: Job Content: (Trades)

(36) TRADE(S) (= TRADE1: NOUN. ECON. PFREQ. THINK. EVALU. DOCTR. ECON.*)

    own —, same —, highest —, better —

    Learn a —

(12) CRAFT(S) (MAN/MEN) (not tagged)

(17) APPRENTICESHIP(S) (not tagged)

    serve an —, do an —, try an —, go through an —

Also: Apprenticed, Time-served

U.3.13 Branch One Themes: Response Patterns

Response Patterns				Frequencies				
Themes							Subtree	
				(i)	*(ii)*	*(iii)*	*(iv)*	*(v)*
1 ST	2 QT	3 RE	4 JC	QA, CA	QA,CA SOL	QA,CA, SOL,CSE	CSM and CST	QA,CA,SOL, CSE,CSM,CST
a +	+	+	+	2	1	0	2	0
b +	+	+	—	2	1	1	1	2
c +	+	—	+	3	0	0	2	0
d +	+	—	—	2	4	4	1	7
e +	—	+	+	0	0	0	0	0
f +	—	+	—	0	1	0	0	0
g +	—	—	+	7	3	3	0	2
h +	—	—	—	3	4	3	1	4
i —	+	+	+	1	0	0	0	0
j —	+	+	—	1	1	2	0	0
k —	+	—	+	5	2	4	7	3
l —	+	—	—	5	3	4	3	3
m —	—	+	+	0	1	0	2	0
n —	—	+	—	1	2	2	0	0
o —	—	—	—	16	3	3	11	1
p —	—	—	—	2	3	0	0	1
				50	29	26	30	23

U.3.13 *continued*

Proportion
Sub-branch

i)	.38	.42	.14	.68
ii)	.48	.41	.24	.34
iii)	.58	.58	.19	.38
iv)	.23	.53	.17	.80
v)	.65	.65	.09	.26
Total:	.42	.50	.16	.53

Themes
(1) ST Status
(2) QT Qualifications
(3) RE Remuneration
(4) JC Job Content:
    (a) Economic dealings (Subtree i,ii,iii)
    (b) Legal dealings (Subtree ii,iii)
    (c) People orientation/Educative skills (Subtree iv)

U.3.14 Branch Two Themes: Response Patterns

Response Patterns *Themes*			*Frequencies* *(i)*	*(ii)*	
PO	CR	EV	AD,PM	AD,PM, MPN	
a +	+	+	3	0	
b +	+	−	4	1	
c +	−	+	5	0	
d +	−	−	13	12	
e −	+	+	0	0	
f −	+	−	0	4	
g −	−	+	2	1	
h −	−	−	0	1	
			27	19	N

Proportion
Sub-branch

i)	.93	.26	.37
ii)	.68	.26	.11
Total:	.83	.26	.26

U.3.14 *continued*

Themes

Job content (i) PO: People-orientation (2): Public service
(ii) CR: Crisis (emergency, danger, accident)
EV: Evaluation (essential, important, useful)

U.3.15 Branch Three Themes: Response Patterns

	Response Patterns	*Themes*			*Frequencies*				
					(i)	*(ii)*	*(iii)*	*(iv)*	*(v)*
	1	*2*	*3*	*4*	*RP,BSL*	*+BM*	*+LD*	*C,MTO*	*(iii)+(v)*
	ST	*QT*	*RE*	*JC*					
a	+	+	+	+	1	0		1	
b	+	+	+	–	0	1			
c	+	+	–	+	0	0			
d	+	+	–	–	4	0			
e	+	–	+	+	0	0			
f	+	–	+	–	0	0			
g	+	–	–	+	1	0		2	
h	+	–	–	–	2	0			
i	–	+	+	+	1	1		2	1
j	–	+	+	–	1	2		1	
k	–	+	–	+	9	3	1	21	4
l	–	+	–	–	13	11	3	12	2
m	–	–	+	+	1	0		1	
n	–	–	+	–	1	1		2	
o	–	–	–	+	3	0	2	14	
p	–	–	–	–	2	7	2	1	
					39	26	8	58	7

Proportions *Sub-branch*					
i)	.21	.74	.13	.44	
ii)	.04	.69	.20	.15	
iii)	*	*	*	*	(too small for analysis)
iv)	.07	.66	.12	.72	
v)	*	*	*	*	(too small for analysis)
Total:	.11	.70	.14	.15	

U.3.16 Strategies in Hierarchy Construction

In forming a hierarchy, three basic choices are open to a subject:
  pairing (P) to join two hitherto unconnected single occupations
  chaining (C) to join a single occupation to an already existing pair (or larger subtree)
  joining (J) to connect two previously formed pairs or subtrees
Every subject must begin by pairing two occupations when constructing his subjective hierarchy. At step 2 he may either create a new pair or begin to 'chain' by adding a single occupation, but he obviously cannot, as yet, join the subtrees. From the third to the penultimate (14th) step however, each of the three options are open and he may now choose between them freely, subject to a few single constraints. (On the final step no new unconnected pair can be formed, so only joining or chaining are possible.)

The sequence of choices which a person makes in constructing his hierarchy we shall term his 'choice strategy' and it will be denoted by a string of 15 letters, where each position (step) contains the letter symbol of the choice made. For instance, the choice strategy of the aircraft fitter outlined in Fig. 3.2 (*Class and Hierarchy*, p.61) can be denoted as:

$$PPPPCPPPCJJJJJJ$$

He began by forming four distinct pairs, then he joined the Solicitor to the (Accountant – Actuary– pair at step 5. He then formed another three new pairs, and after chaining Policeman to the (Ambulance – and Lorry-driver) pair he made his first 'join' step 10, concatenating the 'narrow-minded' (Teacher, Civil servant) pair with the 'professional interest group' (Accountant, Actuary, Solicitor) to form 'the professional men'. Since none of the original 16 occupations were now left unmerged, each of the subsequent steps consist of joining subtrees.

A sequence such as this is common: to begin by forming distinct pairs, alternating between chaining and forming new pairs in the middle section, and finishing up by joining together already-formed clusters. But it is by no means the only one, and far more sequences are possible than appear empirically (or indeed could appear, given the numbers involved). The number of *possible* sequences well exceeds two million, and it is by no means a trivial combinatorial task to enumerate them. Nonetheless, as Coombs (1964:154) comments, if 'nature' constrains the sequences which do occur, then the data are of interest beyond mere description. Examination even of the first few steps in the choice process indicates that such constraining factors are at work. The first few steps are strongly biased towards the formation of pairs, and even if a person adds a single occupation, he usually reverts to forming new pairs immediately afterwards.

On the other hand, the joining of pairs rarely occurs in the earlier stages of hierarchy construction. The process is summarised in diagrammatic form in Fig. U.3.4.

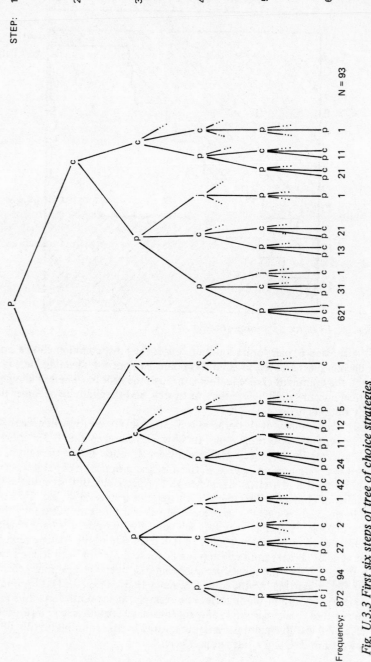

Fig. U.3.3 *First six steps of tree of choice strategies*

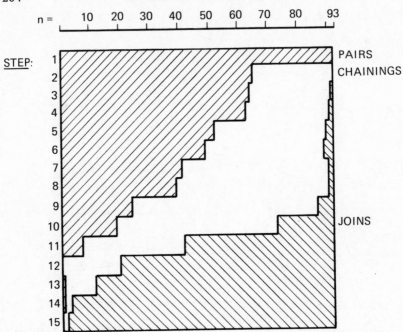

Fig. U3.4 Choice of joining-strategy, by step

After step 6, pair-formation is no longer the most common choice, and it becomes less and less so from this point. By contrast, chaining increases to be the dominant choice half-way through the process, whereas joining scarcely occurs at all before the fourth step, and then rapidly becomes the only option chosen.

The consistency of this process is illustrated very clearly when these data are represented as a trilinear plot (see Fig. U.3.5 and section U.3.3 above).

Each step in the process of hierarchy construction can be thought of as a point in a 3-dimensional space, defined by the proportion of subjects choosing to form PAIRS, CHAININGS and JOINS respectively. But because the total number of choices is the same at each step this means the points all lie on a 2-dimensional triangle in this space. The trilinear plot simply exploits this fact, making it possible to locate each point by triangular (or barycentric) coordinates (see Mosteller 1968:114 ff.). Each side of the triangle represents one type of choice, and each step can be located by grid lines drawn from these sides. Thus, the point corresponding to a step where pairings, chainings and joinings are made with equal frequency (0.33, 0.33, 0.33) is located at the (bary-) centre of the triangle. For example, at the ninth step, 24 subjects (26 per cent) make pairs, 63 (68 per cent) make chainings, and 6 (6 per cent) make joinings: this point is therefore located by the coordinates (26, 68, 6) drawn from P, C and J sides respectively.

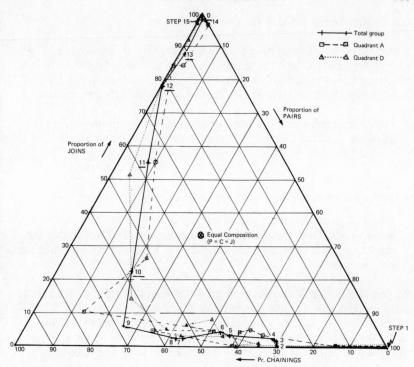

Fig. U3.5: Differences in choice strategy in constructing hierarchies

When the points which represent each step are joined up, the resulting line forms a representation of the overall choice sequence used to form occupational hierarchies. The process must begin at the right-hand base of the triangle (100,0,0) of course, since everyone must begin by choosing a pair. But the shape of the line shows very clearly that the early stages consist virtually entirely of growth in the number of chainings, but after step 9 the direction is abruptly changed. From here on the number of joins dramatically increases, and it is virtually the only option chosen in the last four steps.

In Fig. U.3.5 the lines corresponding to the choices of Quadrant A and Quadrant C subjects are also drawn in (the number of subjects in the other two quadrants is too small for reliable separate analysis; see U.3.3). The lines for each Quadrant are very similar to the overall pattern, and differ only in showing a less stable progression, and in the tendency towards an even more marked shift away from chaining in the middle stages on the part of the Quadrant A subjects. In any event, occupational membership does not seem to affect the hierarchy-construction process in any significant manner.

U.3.17 High Status and Low Income: The Minister

A number of sociologists (Wilson 1966:82 *et seq*, Towler and Coxon 1979) have commented on the unusual conjunction of high status with low income which occurs in the case of the clergy. Many of the professional respondents in this study also draw attention to this fact, often for different reasons:

> I think Ministers are in a peculiar position in society for they are very intelligent, and have more status than financial rewards such as the teacher has.
>
> (Social worker)

A consultant anaesthetist goes further in his ascription of status:

> I think of them [Ministers and Teachers] as being of similar social backgrounds. The level of education is similar, too. This is probably the main criterion for putting them togehter. . . . I equate them very much with my own position.

But the Minister's role also elicits unparalleled disapprobation on the part of other professionals, as these two examples illustrate.
1. One subject, himself an assistant principal in a comprehensive school, makes the following comments in allocating the Church of Scotland Minister to a group consisting of the Railway Porter and Building Site Labourer:

> We can very well get along without Ministers . . . obviously there's no immediate connection between the type of jobs and it may seem a peculiar sort of grouping. The only reason why I would put them together is, I think, it [CSM] is almost a *non-job* (emphasis in original).

At a later stage, he put the Comprehensive School Teacher with the Country Solicitor, Qualified Actuary and Chartered Accountant, saying as he did so:

> Perhaps I'm more biased than I thought I was, but I think a teacher's job is very much underrated in its importance to society.

2. A general practitioner, before putting the Ambulance Driver with the Lorry Driver, said:

> Although Ministers have their calling, I have come to reappraise this —
> they disseminate guilt, and give guilt to people who would not otherwise
> have had guilt. I have to try and rid people of guilt . . . They [Ministers] are
> doing the community a disservice and deserve low remuneration. We can
> do without all Ministers and all Priests and all Rabbis who are of the old
> way of thinking . . . I put a Lorry Driver higher up than him — one crash
> of a lorry driver on an icy road can kill a family of people.

He went on to comment that both Policemen and Comprehensive School Teacher were:

> underpaid chaps . . . we won't get more till we pay them more.

He then returned to the Church of Scotland Minister, bracketing him with a Commercial Traveller:

> . . . because they're both touts — one for religion, one for a private company.

What is significant, of course, is that these comments are made by people who are in precisely the occupations generally thought of as being most similar to the Minister. Of all the occupational titles we consider, the Minister evoked the most varied range of responses; the present examples are merely instances of the differences which occur. (Substantial and socially patterned differences in the evaluation of the Minister have also been referred to in T3.1 above).

8 Content Analysis of Interview Protocols: Appendices to Chapter 4 of *Class and Hierarchy*

U.4.1 Official and Full Transcript of Subject S027's HA Interview

A Official Transcript Report

(Time taken: 25 minutes)

Step	Action	Comment
1	CA and SOL	Professional but not necessarily professionals who need to have a university education.
2	BSL and RP	Unskilled, don't need any particular training.
3	BM and CT	Involved in personal relationships, may have some social skills but still rather untrained people.
4	C and MTO	Both skilled manual workers.
5	CST and CSM	Very similar jobs, probably in qualification and training, also in the nature of the job in that it's in contact with the community or part of the community.
6	CSE to 1	He is a professional too, similar educational background.
7	LD to 4	It's a skilled job and a manual job with some training required.
8	AD and MPN	An AD has the sort of skills for dealing with accidents etc . . . that an MPN might have.
9	QA to 1	With the professionals. It's a desk-job, a white-collar job.
10	P to 5	Policeman also goes around meeting people (as CSM and CST) although he doesn't have the same academic training.
11	7 and 2	Unskilled and skilled manual workers at one extreme.
12	9 and 10	The professionals who sit at desks and the professionals who don't sit at desks but have contacts with the community in which they live.
13	3 and 11	Relatively low skills — no, not true — relatively low

academic attainment, also in a sense a low responsibility rating in relation to the society in which they
live.

| 14 | 8 and 12 | Because all the people have responsibilities in relation to the community other people in group 13 do not have. |

(Subject found the task very hard.)

B Full Transcript

Note

(1) The interviewer's speech is represented throughout in italic, and the
subject's in ordinary type (note that interruptions also follow this convention).
(2) Paralinguistic phenomena are noted in curly brackets { . . . } : Short
silences, pauses and elision are noted by: +, and longer pauses by { p } .
Other phenomena are:

{ 1 } : laughs
{ t } : speaking together indistinguishably.
{ i } interrupted by other speaker
{ *l* } laughs
{ ? } editional querying of sense.

Hesitations are represented by: um, er, mmm,
Agreement by: hm, hm.

Counter	Speaker	Verbal comment	Action
001	Int.	*What I'd like you to do in the first place is pick a pair of two titles which you think go naturally together.*	
	Subj.	You mean in, in respect to their hierarchy?	
	I	*In respect of whatever you like, um, two titles that go naturally together, and then tell me why you think they go together.*	
	S	Oh I see {p}	
005		I suppose 'Chartered Accountant' and 'Solicitor' are y'know two that occur to me first of all + (*Yes*) + They are <u>professions + um + but not necessarily professions that one + needs to have a + university education</u>, I believe, I think you can { t } + { t } Do you want me to carry on like this? (*Yes*) pairing them?	1) CA & SOL
	I	*Eventually you have to clarify all of them in one or another, but, er*	

Counter	Speaker	Verbal comment	Action
	S	I see, but you want to carry on pairing (*No*) Oh, or not? (*OK*)	
	I	*You're making up this one pair*	
	S	Well that's {i}	
	I	*That's your decision, right, in the second place you've got two choices, you can either make up another pair or you can add one title to this group if you think it goes* (I see, yeh) {t}	
	S	{t} Now will you, do you want me to pair them all eventually or not, because, I mean	
010	I	*OK, in your second, at that second stage you can make up another pair or add one title to this group* (Oh, I see) *but by the time you've got two or three groups you have the extra choice of merging the two of the groups you've already made up +* (OK) *and what we finish up with is two groups to be merged, large groups + {p} + mmm +*	
	S	Well, I've stuck the Building Site Labourer and the Railway Porter together + because they seem to me to be unskilled + (*hm, hm*)	2) BSL & RP
	I	*I mean, if it helps if you can sort of think aloud as much as you can* (Oh I see, I can) *and tell* {t} (Oh right, OK) *y'know* (OK) *all the various reasons why you think* (yes, um) *they should go together* (yes, um) +	
015	S	That seems to me to be, they seem to me to be <u>unskilled and don't need any particular training</u> for that + um + I suppose the Barman and the Commercial Traveller in a sense don't need any + well, Commercial Traveller might need to be trained but the Barman might + but on the other hand they are the people who +	3) BM & CT

Counter	Speaker	Verbal comment	Action

involved in face to face {1} relationships and therefore might need + to
have perhaps more social skills and
er + sorry, as unskilled, or rather
untrained people (*mm*) + mm. I suppose
I am to a certain extent, um, condi-
tioned by, er + slight familiarity with
social classes, y'know er categories
+ um + but that doesn't matter {1}

	I	*Well, we're very interested in all your personal*	
		values (Yes, well you know, I mean	
		having) *That's what we want to find out*	
	S	+ having, having to do in planning,	
		having something to do with data of that	
		sort, I'm sort of, I'm *aware* of it, so	
		y'know + I think it's probably fitting	
		into my, into the way of my decisions	4) C & MTO
		+ um, I think Carpenters and Machine	
		Tool operators seem to me to be	
		similar in that they are both skilled	
020		manual workers + um + {t} {p}	
	I	*Remember, he{l}? can add one title on to*	
		one of these groups (yes) *if you wish.*	
	S	If I want to, right + um + I can only add	
		one to them, I can't more than one	
		(One) One at a time *(or you can merge*	
		two groups) I can merge two groups, right	
		+ um, I would say the Church of Scotland	
		minister and the Comprehensive	5) CSM & CST
		School Teacher seem to me to be very	
		similar um jobs + um + probably in	
		qualification um, + training, also in the	
		nature of the job, in that it's + um,	
		contact with the, with the community,	
		or with part of the community + um	6) CSE 1
		+ I think I'll put Civil Servant, Executive	
		grade, in this first group that I have,	
		the Solicitor and Chartered Accountant	
025		+ um, in that he + in a sense, I suppose,	
		is a professional worker + shall I put it?	
	I	*Yes, no he'll go right on top, um {t} + um,*	

U.4.1 *continued*

Counter	Speaker	Verbal comment	Action
		sorry I wasn't quite listening, I was *playing with my cards + you said that* *they* {t} +	
	S	Well, I felt that it probably had a *similar, er, educational background in* *the sense of professional* + I'm not a member of {?} + that Civil servants are professions telephone rings, break in transcription	
030		Um I'm not sure what a Qualified Actuary is + (*Oh yes*) Hold on, I didn't see that + um, it's a sort of lawyer isn't it? It's a Scottish thing (*well strictly speaking I'm not*) you're not { 1 } *supposed to help you)* + a sort of notary, isn't it? (+ *own definition*) {t} Oh no it's not, it's a person who deals with insurance, isn't it? + (*Yes*) sort of life expectancies, that sort of thing + that's interesting + I wouldn't rate him with, with the professions + he's pretty good, but he's not as, kind of qualified, as these I should imagine + or as highly trained + I'm not sure quite where I would put him + so I think I'll leave him for a bit.	
035		Ambulance Driver and Lorry Driver + um + they're both drivers − the Ambulance Driver I would imagine, has more skills than the Lorry Driver + presumably they have to deal in a sort of first aid + I'll put the Lorry Driver, I think in this category + with the Machine Tool Operator and the Carpenter +	7) LD 4
	I	*What do they have in common, er,* *these two?*	
	S	Um + well, <u>it's a skilled, er job + of</u> <u>some sort, it's a manual job + in the</u> <u>skilled line, it's got some sort of</u> <u>training,</u> it's, um + I've put the	

U.4.1 *continued*

Counter	Speaker	Verbal comment	Action

<table>
<tbody>
<tr><td>040</td><td></td><td>Psychiatric Nurse and the Ambulance Driver together, um, just because I would imagine that the Ambulance Driver and the {i} <u>having this skill would have the sort of skill in having to deal with accidents and so on, that the Male Psychiatric Nurse might help</u> + (*um*) + shall I just put that? (*Yes* {t} *that's the 8th decision*) + which leaves me with the Policeman and the Qualified Actuary + now + {p} um, I really find it very difficult to classify these two in relation to the other groups, but I've got + um + I would think I would + tend to put the Policeman into the Male Psychiatric Nurse + category and the Ambulance Driver.</td><td>8) AD & MPN</td></tr>
</tbody>
</table>

045   It's possibly they have more skill and perhaps more responsibility than + these, um, similar skills and responsibilities in some ways, I would imagine as the School Teacher and the Minister + but yet he doesn't have the same sort of + um + academic training that these people have + um + So you know, I find it very difficult to categorise him.

I   *Well, um, may I remind you that the next step, when you've got rid of these last two titles will be to merge groups* (Oh I see) *one by one until you are left with only two groups, so you are going to have to find some other, um common factor.*

S   Yes + um + {t} well in that case, well I think I would probably put the actuary

050   <u>with the professionals in that he, + that his work seems to me to be very similar, sitting at a desk largely, which these other people would be, um, a white-collar job</u> + a policeman + um, I would therefore merge with, with the Minister and the Teacher in that it's, er + a job which   QA   1

10) PM   5

Counter	Speaker	Verbal comment	Action
		involves <u>going out meeting people without</u> <u>even though it doesn't have the academic</u> <u>training</u>	
	I	*Thank you, there we are + six groups, now* *+ at this stage I'd like you to start merging* *groups, taking them one by one* (yes) *and* *again giving the reasons why you think they* *go together more* (right)	
055	S	p um, <u>Well the unskilled and skilled</u> <u>manual workers I would suggest probably go</u> <u>together + um, at one, one extreme;</u> the other extreme I would have pro- fessionals that sit at desks most of the time, these people	
	I	*OK, so, shall we merge these two?* (Yeh) *Unskilled and Skilled manual* *workers + Now then you said the* *next*	11) 7 and 2
	S	Well, I was just trying to rationalise my + I think there would be perhaps a group at the other extreme, this group, <u>who are the professionals, um, who sit</u> <u>at desks, um, and perhaps one would</u> <u>put together with this group the pro-</u>	
060		<u>fessionals who {1} don't sit at desks</u> <u>who, um, move round perhaps in, more</u> <u>in direct contact with + um, the com-</u> <u>munities in which they live</u> *(right)* um + there's these two groups in the middle + {p} Well, um, I think I would put the Barman and the Commercial Traveller into this group, um, <u>on relatively um low</u>	12) 9 and 10
		<u>skills + well, sorry, no, that's not true —</u> <u>a Carpenter doesn't have + quite high</u>	13) 3 and 11
065		<u>manual skills but, say, low, um +</u> <u>·academic, possibly, attainments, um,</u> <u>and also in a sense a low responsibility</u> <u>rating in relation to the society we live,</u> but, um, compared to someone like a policeman who, um, whilst possibly he doesn't have the evident skills that I've	

U.4.1 *continued*

Counter	Speaker	Verbal comment	Action

mentioned before, he does have some
responsibility in relation to the community
he lives in (*hm, hm*) {t} and for that
reason I think that I would put the
Psychiatric Nurse and the Ambulance   14) 8 and 12
Driver in this category as well, um, I
realise there's a contradiction here —
I've got people with professional
qualifications and perhaps academic

070   skills, um, and an ambulance driver,
but the reason I mentioned {i} Policeman
vis a vis the Commercial Traveller
and Barman; it seems to me these people
have <u>responsibilities in relation to the</u>
<u>community which they're working in</u>
<u>that perhaps the Commercial Traveller</u>
<u>and Barman doesn't have.</u>

I   *OK, we're there* {*I*} (Yes) *How did*
you find it?
INTERVIEW PROPER ENDS

S   Very hard {*I*} {t} I mean y'know
all sorts of other things you could do —
I suppose outdoor and indoor jobs as well
+ which, er

I   *Yes, I think when it does get difficult*
is after the first five or six decisions (Yes)

075   *then you're stuck for words I think*
for (Yeh, yeh) *for abstract things* (Yeh)
+ *It's a bit of a trick on our part not telling*
you immediately (yes) *where you are*
going

S   Do you get much variation?

I   *Um, a fair amount, but what's most fascinating*
to me is the variation in the way in
which people explain why (I see) *they're*
categorising in one way or another.
(really?) *They might make up the same*
kind of groups but +

S   different reasons? Interesting, so it's very
important that you have, that people

079   should . . .

U.4.2 List and frequency of the 100 most common words in the HA corpus

Rank	Word	Frequency of Occurrence	Rank	Word	Frequency of Occurrence	Rank	Word	Frequency of Occurrence
1	the	1253	34	or	136	67	know	65
2	is/are/be/was/were	1173	35	at	134	68	MANUAL	65
3	a, an	1062	36	WORK	124	69	SOCIAL	65
4	of	945	37	this	120	70	by	64
5	to	862	38	these	117	71	SERVICE	63
6	and	669	39	would	112	72	about	62
7	they	629	40	can	106	73	sort	62
8	in	624	41	CLASS	105	74	which	61
9	I	439	42	than	105	75	also	60
10	he	399	43	no	102	76	put	59
11	with	355	44	SKILL/S	98	77	well	59
12	JOB/S	328	45	what	95	78	out	58
13	have	299	46	PROFESSIONAL	92	79	EDUCATION	57
14	PEOPLE	286	47	so	92	80	SOCIETY	57
15	that	280	48	there	92	81	really	56
16	both	257	49	could	91	82	UNSKILLED	56
17	but	248	50	one	90	83	need	54
18	it	238	51	SKILLED	89	84	up	54
19	all	231	52	who	89	85	just	53
20	as	220	53	from	88	86	different	50
21	for	219	54	has	88	87	go	50
22	not	208	55	like	86	88	QUALIFICATIONS	50
23	their	171	56	PUBLIC	85	89	quite	49
24	more	166	57	other	83	90	lot	49
25	on	166	58	WORKING	83	91	type	48
26	them	166	59	had	76	92	any	48
27	same	165	60	similar	76	93	kind	48
28	do	162	61	think	75	94	only	48
29	very	160	62	much	73	95	COMMUNITY	47
30	TRAINING	159	63	because	72	96	said	47
31	his	153	64	him	71	97	high	46
32	GROUP	139	65	if	70	98	probably	46
33	you	138	66	get	68	99	together	46
						100	too	46

Note: Occupation names and abbreviations (e.g. BM,CST) are omitted.

U.4.3 Harvard IV-3 (Edinburgh) Dictionary specification

A Tag specification

Notes

1. This appendix documents those entries in the Edinburgh version of the Harvard IV-3 Content Analysis Dictionary which appear on the tag-tally program output. (It excludes, for instance, the tags MODIFY and NOTAG, which do not appear on the tag tally list.)

2. Columns are as follows:

(i) *Tag Tally Entry Reference*

Each 'document' (distinct piece of text) produces 5 pages of tag-tally output. When the entries of each page are numbered sequentially, this provides a useful cross-reference system.

The form is: page no./entry no.

Thus: 4/48 refers to the 48th entry on page 4, namely: FALL (SUPV)

(ii) *Short name*

The short tag name follows the conventional abbreviations of the basic HIV-3 Dictionary. (Underlined tags are those also defined in the Sydney version of HIV-3.)

(iii) *Full name*

This is normally self-explanatory.

(iv) *Part of speech*

Most tags contain words from different syntactic classes (i.e. parts of speech). In the tag-tally list the occurrences in different word-classes are distinguished. The classes follow conventional nomenclature, except for 'SUPV' (Super-verb) which is slightly more general class than verbs.

(v) *No. of entries*

This gives the number of words (strictly, de-inflected word-senses) which are subsumed by the tag concerned. (These are given in the Cross-Sort version of the Dictionary.) The number given is approximate.

(vi) *Status*

The two types of tag (distinguished by their function in disambiguation, and by the stage at whcih they are added in the Edinburgh version) are *Markers* (of Punctuation, Word Form, Sentence Structure, Semantic) and Harvard IV-3 'Content' tags.

(vii) The Harvard IV-3 Dictionary is an hierarchical structure (i.e. some categories or tags are subsets of others), and this is reflected in the indented form of the Tag-Tally list. The subset relationship (if any) is indicated in this column by the immediately superordinate category

Thus: VIRTUE is a subset of EVALU, and

EVALU is a subset of THINK.

Note: The origin of the Tag is also sometimes indicated in this column (e.g. Osgood's EPA dimensions of connotative meaning).

Short name	Tag no.	Full name	Parts of speech	No. of entries	Status	Subcategory of
ABS	78	Abstract	Mostly Nouns	270M	Marker	–
ABS*	175	Abstract*	Nouns	190	Marker	ABS
ACAD	240	Academic	Noun,Supv,Modf	150	H-IV	(Institution)
ACH	81	Achieve	Supv	150M	H-IV	–
ACT	79	Act	Modif, Noun	430M	H-IV	–
ACT1	213	Active-1	Supv,Modif,Noun	530M	Osgood	Activity
ACTV2	214	Active-2	Supv,Modif,Noun	590M	Osgood	Activity
ACTV3	215	Active-3	Supv,Modif,Noun	450M	Osgood	Activity
AFFIL	249	Affiliation	Most all	340M	H-IV	(Leary)
AG	134	Agent	Supv	?M	H-IV (Edin)	AGPAT
AGPAT	141	Agent-Patient	Supv	?M	H-IV (Edin)	–
ANI	61	Animal	Noun	75M	H-IV	–
ART	38	Article	Article, Determiner	3	Marker	DET
BE	39	Be	Supv,Verb	20+	Marker	VERB
BEGIN	187	Begin	Mostly Supv	40	H-IV	CHANGE
BLDG(PT)	85	Building	Nouns	30	H-IV	PLACE
BODY(PT)	62	Bodypart	Nouns,Modif	80	H-IV	–
BODYIND	233	Body-indicator	Most all	230M	H-IV	–
CARD	13	Cardinal	Determiners	40	Marker	NUM
CAUSAL	229	Causal	Most all	60	H-IV	–
CHANGE	186	Change	Supv,Noun,Modif	330M	H-IV	–
COLL	63	Collectivity	Nouns, Modif	190	Marker	–

Short name	Tag no.	Full name	Parts of speech	No. of entries	Status	Subcategory of
COLOR	40	Colour	Modif & few nouns	30	Marker	—
COM	64	Communicate Marker	Nouns	420	Marker	—
COMN	238	Communicate	Supv,Noun,Modif	820	H-IV	—
COMV	84	Communicate Marker	Supv	?M	H-IV	—
COMP	14	Comparatives	Modif, incl. determiner	25	Marker	—
COMPLT	92	Complete	Supv,Noun,Modif	60	H-IV	ACH
CONJ	41	Conjunction				
CONJ1	42	Sentential	Conjunctions	4	Marker	CONJ
CONJ2	43	Clausal	Conjunctions, Determiner	50	Marker	CONJ
DECR	191	Decrease	Supv,noun	45	H-IV	CHANGE
DEF	44	Definite	Pronoun	40	Marker	PRON
DEF1	15	Nominative	Definite Pronouns	10	Marker	DEF
DEF2	60	Objective	Definite Pronouns	8	Marker	DEF
DEF3	45	Reflexive	Definite Pronouns	3	Marker	DEF
DEF4	46	Other	Definite Pronouns	12	Marker	DEF
DEM	47	Demonstrative	Determiners	4	Marker	DET
DEM1	48	'This,that'	Demonstrative determiners	2	Marker	DEM
DEM2	49	'These,those'	Demonstrative determiners	2	Marker	DEM
DET	16	Determiner				
DIM	65	Dimension Marker	Modif	50	Marker	—
DIMN	221	Dimension H-IV	Most all	1200M	H-IV	—
DISORDR	89	Disorder	Supv,Noun,Modif	40M	Dewhirst	—
DIST	66	Distance	Noun	20	Marker	—
DO	17	Do	Supv	6	Marker	—
DOCTR	95	Doctrine	Noun,Modif	200	H-IV	Evalu

Short name	Tag no.	Full name	Parts of speech	No. of entries	Status	Subcategory of
ECON	67	Economic M.	Noun,Modif	500	Marker	—
ECON*	241	Economic H-IV	Noun,Modif,Supv,Prep	480	H-IV	(Institution)
ED	18	'– ed' suffix	Supv	130+	Marker	—
EGOP	136	1st person marker	Pron	200	Marker	FRSTP
EGOP	68	Emotion	Modif,Noun	10+	Marker	—
EMOT	19	'– er'	Comparative Modifiers	10	Marker	—
ER	20	'– est'	Comparative Modifiers	330	Marker	—
EST	50	Evaluate Marker	Modif	1400M	Marker	—
EVAL	98	Evaluate H-IV	Most all	40	H-IV	THINK
EVALU	99	Exchange	Supv	80	H-IV	WORK
EX(CH)	100	Exert	Supv	80	H-IV	MOVE
EXERT	100	Exert	Supv	290	H-IV	MOVE
EXPRS	243	Expressive	Noun,Modif,Supv		H-IV	(Institution)
FAIL	102	Fail	Supv	30	H-IV	ACH
FALL	103	Fall	Supv	40	H-IV	MOVE
FEEL	235	Feel	Modif,Noun,Supv	350M	H-IV	—
FEMALE	69	Female	Noun,Pron,Modif	40	H-IV	HU
FETCH	105	Fetch	Supv	40	H-IV	MOVE
FINISH	192	Finish	Supv,Noun,Modif	60	H-IV	CHANGE
FOOD	107	Food	Noun	80	H-IV	—
FORM	108	Form	Noun,Modif	380	Marker-H-IV	COMN
FREQ	70	Frequency	Modif,Noun	50	Marker-H-IV	TIME
FRSTP	154	1st pers. marker	Pronoun		Marker	

Short name	Tag no.	Full Name	Parts of speech	No. of entries	Status	Subcategory of
GEN	21	Genitive	Determiners	10	Marker	DET
GENRLTY	228	Generality	Noun,Modif,Pron,Conj	230M	H-IV	—
GO	51	Go	Supv, Verb	8	Marker	VERB
GOAL	110	Goal	Noun	50	H-IV	EVALU
HANDELS		Handle-elsewhere	***special housekeeping tag***			
HAV	52	Have	Supv,Verb	4	Marker	VERB
HOSTILE	247	Hostile	Noun,Supv,Modif,Intj	500	H-IV	(Leary)
HU(MAN)	72	Human	Noun	550	Marker	—
IMPLNEG	231	Imply-negative	Most all	230M	H-IV	—
INCR	190	Increase	Supv,Noun,Modif	55	H-IV -	CHANGE
INDEF	53	Indefinite	Pronoun	25	Marker	PRON
INDEFP	57	Indef. pronouns	Pron		Marker	INDEF
ING	22	'– ing' suffix	Supv			
INT	54	Interrogatives	Pron,Modif,Conj	12	Marker	—
INTJ	113	Interjections				
INTREL	114	Interpersonal action	Supv only	360	H-IV	—
IRREL	125	Irrelevance		?M	H-IV (Edin)	—
KIN	73	Kinship Marker	Noun	35	Marker	—
KIN*	234	Kinship H-IV	Noun, Modif, Supv	50	H-IV	—
KNOW	199	Know	Noun,Supv,Modif	390	H-IV	THINK

Short name	Tag no.	Full name	Parts of speech	No. of entries	Status	Subcategory of
LABOR	117	Labour	Supv	130M	H-IV	WORK
LAND	118	Land	Noun	55	H-IV	—
LEGAL	243	Legal	Supv,Noun,Modif	160	H-IV	(Institution)
LINK	55	Linking	Verb,Supv	7	Marker	VERB
LY	23	Adverb				
MAKE	120	Make	Supv	50	H-IVM	WORK
MALE	74	Male	Noun,Pron,Modif	70	H-IV	HU
MASS	121	Mass	Noun	40	H-IVM	COLL
MEANS	237	Means	Noun,Modif,Prep,Supv	280	H-IV	EVALU
MILIT	244	Military	Noun,Modif,Supv	100	H-IV	(Institution)
MOD	24	Modal verb	Verb,supv	25	Marker	VERB
MODIF	25	Modifier				—
MOVE	193	Move	Supv,Noun,Modif	450	H-IVM	—
NAME	75	Name	Noun	90	H-IV	—
NATURE	232	Nature	Noun,Supv,Modif	200	H-IV	—
NEED	197	Need	Supv,Noun,Modif	40	H-IV	—
NEG	26	Negation	Supv (contractions), Adv	7	Marker	—
NGTV*	129	Negative	Modif,Noun	560	H-IV	—
NGTV1	205	Negative-1	Most all	280M	Osgood	Evaluation
NGTV2	206	Negative-2	Noun,Modif,Supv	500M	Osgood	Evaluation
NGTV3	207	Negative-3	Noun,Modif,Supv,Intj	460M	Osgood	Evaluation
NONADLT	130	Non-Adult	Noun,Modif	25	H-IV	HU

Short name	Tag no.	Full name	Parts of speech	No. of entries	Status	Subcategory of
NOUN	131	Noun				
NUMB	27	Number	Determiner	50	Marker	DET
OBJ	132	Objects	Noun,Modif	680	H-IV	—
ORD	28	Ordinal	Determiner	20+	Marker	—
ORDER	88	Order	Noun,Modif	35M	Dewhirst	NUMB
ORG	133	Organization	Noun	120	H-IV	—
OVRST	225	Overstate	Most all	450	Dewhirst	COLL
PASSIVE	179	Passive	Supv	5	H-IV	—
PAT	135	Patient	Supv	?M	H-IV (Edin)	AGPAT
PERV	198	Perceive	Supv,Noun,Modif	140	H-IV	—
PERSIST	189	Persist	Supv,Noun,Modif	70	H-IV	CHANGE
(PFREQ		Predominate-Frequency ***Special tag to help breaklock routine; sense accounts for over 85% of frequencies***)				
PLACE	76	Place	Modif,Noun,Pron	400	Marker & H-IV	—
POLIT	77	Political M	Noun,Modif	530	Marker	—
POLIT*	245	Political H-IV	Noun,Modif,Supv	250	H-IV	(Institution)
POS	56	Position	Noun,Modif	40	Marker	—
POWER	248	Power	Noun,Modif,Supv,Prep	500	H-IV	(Leary)
PRE1	58	Count	Determiner,Prearticle	30	Marker!	PRE
PRE2	59	Mixed	Determiner,Prearticle	15	Marker!	PRE
PRON	30	Pronoun				
PSTV*	139	Positive	Mostly Modif,Noun	490	H-IV	—

Short name	Tag no.	Full name	Parts of speech	No. of entries	Status	Subcategory of
PSTV1	202	Positive-1	Noun,Modif,Supv	330	Osgood	Evaluation
PSTV2	203	Positive-2	Noun,Modif,Supv,Intj	450	Osgood	Evaluation
PSTV3	204	Positive-3	Modif,Noun,Supv	330	Osgood	Evaluation
PSV1	217	Passive-1	Noun,Supv,Modif	150M	Osgood	Activity
PSV2	218	Passive-2	Noun,Supv,Modif	310M	Osgood	Activity
PSV3	219	Passive-3	Noun,Supv,Modif	410M	Osgood	Activity
QUAL	196	Quality	Modif,Noun,Supv	230	H-IV	—
QUALIF	227	Qualify	Most all	250M	Dewhirst	—
QUAN	224	Quantity	Modif,Noun,Prep,Pron	260	H-IV	—
RACE	239	Race	Noun,Modif	20	H-IV	—
REGION	144	Region	Noun,Modif	100	H-IV	—
REL	230	Relation	Most all, incl prep, conj	140	H-IV	—
RELEV	125	Relevance		?M	H-IV (Edin)	
RELIG	246	Religion	Noun,Modif,Supv	100	H-IV	(Institution)
RLTV	106	Relatives	Marker			
RISE	147	Rise	Supv,one Noun	30	H-IV	MOVE
RITUAL	148	Ritual	Nouns	120	H-IV	ACT
ROOM	86	Room	Nouns	25	H-IV	PLACE
ROUTE	150	Route	Nouns	30	H-IV	PLACE
S	31	s-ending	Noun,Pron,Determiner	50+	Marker	—
SAY	151	Say-tell	Supv	15	H-IV	COMN

Short name	Tag no.	Full name	Parts of speech	No. of entries	Status	Subcategory of
SCNDP	152	2nd person	Pronoun, determiner	4	H-IV	—
SEA	153	Sea	Noun	15M	H-IV	—
SKY	155	Sky	Noun	25	H-IV	—
SOCIAL	156	Social-place	Noun	130	H-IV	PLACE
SOLVE	157	Solve	Supv	80	H-IV	THINK
SPACE	223	Space	Noun,Modif,Prep	310	H-IV	DIMN
STASIS	138	Stasis		?M	H-IV (Edin)	
STAY	194	Stay	Supv,few Modif	70	H-IV	MOVE
STRNG1	208	Strong-1	Supv,Noun,Modif,Pron	450	Osgood	Strength
STRNG2	209	Strong-2	Supv,Noun,Modif	800	Osgood	Strength
STRNG3	210	Strong-3	Supv,Noun,Modif,other	570	Osgood	Strength
SUBM	201	Submission	Noun,Supv,Modif	200	H-IV	(Leary)
SUPV	32	Super-verb				
SURF	161	Surface	Modif,Noun,Supv	90	H-IV	QUAL
TANG	162	Tangible	Modif,Noun,Supv	140M	H-IV	QUAL
THINK	236	Think	Most all	1950M	H-IV	—
THRDP	164	Third person	Pronoun, Determiner	20	H-IV	—
TIME	35	Time Marker	Noun,Modif	80	Marker	
TIME*	222	Time H-IV	Noun,Modif,Prep	330	H-IV	DIMN
TO	34	To	Sense one of to (infinitive)	1	Marker	VERB
TOOL	166	Tool	Noun,Modif	300	H-IV	OBJ
TRAVL	196	Travel	Supv,Noun,Modif	150	H-IV	MOVE
TRY	168	Try	Supv	60	H-IV	ACH

Short name	Tag no.	Full name	Parts of speech	No. of entries	Status	Subcategory of
UNDRST	226	Understate	Most all	200'	Dewhirst	—
USE	169	Use	Supv	30	H-IV	WORK
VARY	188	Vary	Supv,Noun,Modif	50	H-IV	CHANGE
VB	35	Become link	Verb,Supv	5	Marker	—
VEH	171	Vehicle	Noun	40	H-IV	OBJ
VERB	36	Verb				
VICE	172	Vice	Noun,Modif	280	H-IV	EVALU
VIRTUE	173	Virtue	Noun,Modif	450	H-IV	EVALU
WEAK1	211	Weak-1	Noun,Supv,Modif	140	Osgood	Strength
WEAK2	212	Weak-2	Noun,Modif,Supv	220	Osgood	Strength
WEAK3	213	Weak-3	Supv,Noun,Modif,Pron	250	Osgood	Strength
WORK	174	Work	Supv	260	H-IV	—

B Tag numbering

1	26	51	76	101	126	151	176	201	226
2	NEG 27	GO 52	PLACE 77	DETPRE 102	127	SAY 152	177	SUBM 202	UNDRST 227
3	NUMB 28	HAV 53	POLIT 78	FAIL 103	128	SCNDP 153	178	POS1 203	228
4	ORD 29	INDEF 54	ABS 79	FALL 104	129	SEA 154	179	POS2 204	GENLTY 229
COMMA 5	PREP 30	INT(WH—) 55	ACT 80	DETPRON 105	NGIV 130	FRSTP 155	180	POS3 205	CAUSAL 230
DASH— 6	PRON 31	LINK 56	81	FETCH 106	NON ADLT 131	SKY 156	181	NEG1 206	REL 231
7	S(Plur) 32	POS 57	ACH 82	RELTV 107	NOUN 132	SOC 157	182	NEG2 207	IMPLNEG 232
8	SUPV 33	INDEFP 58	83	FOOD 108	OBJ 133	SOLVE 158	183	NEG3 208	NATURE 233
PERIOD 9	TIME 34	PRE1 59	84	FORM 109	ORG 134	159	184	STRNG1 209	BODY 234
PUNC 10	TO 35	PRE2 60	COMV 85	110	AG 135	160	185	STRNG2 210	KIN 235
QC? 11	VB 36	DEF2 61	BDG 86	GOAL 111	PAT 136	161	186	STRNG3 211	FEEL 236
QUOTE 12	VERB 37	ANI 62	ROOM 87	112	EGOP 137	SURF 162	CHANGE 187	WEAK1 212	THINK 237
ROOT 13	38	BODY 63	88	113	138	TANG 163	BEGIN 188	WEAK2 213	MEANS 238

B Tag numbering Cont.

CARD 14	ART 39	COLL 64	ORDER 89	INTJ 114	STASIS 139	164	VARY 189	WEAK3 214	COMN 239
COMP 15	BE 40	COM 65	DISORDR 90	INTRL 115	PSTV 140	THRDP 165	PERSIST 190	ACTV1 215	RACE 240
DEF1 16	COLD2 41	DIM 66	91	116	INTREFL 141	166	INCR 191	ACTV2 216	ACAD 241
DET 17	CONJ 42	DIST 67	92	117	AGPAT 142	TOOL 167	DECR 192	ACTV3 217	ECON 242
DO 18	CONJ/BUT 43	ECON 68	COMPLT 93	LABOR 118	143	168	FINISH 193	PSV1 218	EXPRS 243
ED 19	CONJ2 44	EMOT 69	APOST1 94	LAND 119	144	TRY 169	MOVE 194	PSV2 219	LEGAL 244
ER 20	DEF 45	FEMALE 70	95	120	REGION 145	USE 170	STAY 195	PSV3 220	MILIT 245
EST 21	DEF3 46	FREQ 71	DOCTR 96	MAKE 121	146	171	TRAVL 196	221	POLIT 246
POSS 22	DEF4 47	72	97	MASS 122	147	VEH 172	QUAL 197	DIMN 222	RELIG 247
ING 23	DEM 48	HU 73	98	DIFF 123	RISE 148	VICE 173	NEED 198	TIME 223	HOSTILE 248
LY 24	DEM1 49	KIN 74	EVALU 99	SPEC 124	RITUAL 149	VIRTUE 174	PERCV 199	SPACE 224	POWER 249
MOD 25	DEM2 50	MALE 75	EXCH 100	IRREL 125	150	WORK 175	KNOW 200	QUANT 225	AFFIL 250
MODIF	EVAL	NAME	EXERT	RELEV	RATE	ABS		OVRST	

U.4.4 Tag-Tally list entries

I	II	III	IV
Punctuation markers			
1	PUNC	9	PUNCTUATION
2	PER	8	PERIOD
3	Q	10	QUESTION MARK
4	COMMA	4	COMMA
5	DASH	5	DASH
6	QUOTE	11	QUOTATION MARKS
7	APOST	93	APOSTROPHE
Word form markers			
8	ROOT	12	WORD ROOT ONLY, NO:
9	ING	22	ING SUFFIX
10	S	31	S OR OTHER PLURAL
11	ED	18	ED OR OTHER PAST TENSE
12	LY	23	LY OR OTHER ADVERB
13	COMP	14	COMPARATIVES
14	ER	19	'ER', 'MORE'
15	EST	20	'EST', 'MUST'
Markers of sentence structure (i)			
16	PREP	29	PREPOSITIONS
17	CONJ	41	CONJUNCTIONS
18	CONJ1	42	AND,BUT,OR
19	CONJ2	43	THE OTHERS
20	INTJ	113	INTERJECTIONS
21	NOUN	131	NOUNS
22	NAME	75	PROPER NAMES
23	MODIF	25	ADJECTIVES
Markers of sentence structure (ii)			
24	SUPV	32	SUPERVERB: ALL VERBS
25	VERB	36	AUXILIARY VERBS
26	BE	39	BEING
27	LINK	55	LINKING
28	VB	35	BECOMING
29	HAV	52	HAVING
30	MOD	24	MODAL (MAY,MUST,...)
31	GO	51	GOING TO
32	DO	17	DO
33	TO	34	INFINITIVE
34	PASSIVE	179	PASSIVE VERBS
35	NEG	26	NEGATIVE VERBS

U.4.4 *continued*

I	II	III	IV

Document counts

a TOTAL DOCUMENTS
b TOTAL SENTENCES
c TOTAL TOKENS
d TOTAL WORDS
e TOTAL PUNCTUATION
f TOTAL LEFTOVERS

Column headings: I: Page number and serial position on page
II: Short tag name
III: Tag number (n.b. 'R' signifies that the tag is repeated.
Thus 3/1 NOUN appears in this position as a MARKER TAC
but has already occurred on 1/21.
IV: Full tag name

Markers of reference: pronouns and determiners

1	DET	16	DETERMINERS
2	DETPRE	101	PRECEDING A NOUN
3	DETPRON	104	REFERRING TO A NOUN
4	PRON	30	PRONOUNS
5	DEF	44	DEFINITE REFERENCE
6	DEF1	15	PERSONAL PRONOUN NOMINATIVE
7	DEF2	60	PERSONAL PRONOUN OBJECTIVE
8	DEF3	45	PERSONAL PRONOUN REFLEXIVE
9	DEF4	46	TOTALITY/IDENTITY (ALL, EACH, . . .)
10	INDEF	53	INDEFINITE REFERENCE
11	INDEFP	57	PRONOUNS (SOMEONE, . . .)
12	PRE1	58	DETERMINERS:' COUNT NOUNS ONLY
13	PRE2	59	DETERMINERS: COUNT AND/OR MASS
14	ART	38	ARTICLE (A,AN,THE)
15	GEN	21	POSSESSIVES
16	DEM	47	DEMONSTRATIVES
17	DEM1	48	THIS,THESE
18	DEM2	49	THAT,THOSE
19	NUMB	27	NUMBERS
20	CARD	13	CARDINAL
21	ORD	28	ORDINAL
22	RELTV	106	RELATIVES (WHO, WHICH, . . .)
23	+ GEN		WHOSE
24	INT	54	WH– QUESTION WORDS (WHO?,. . .)
25	+ GEN		WHOSE?
26	+ LY		HOW? WHERE? WHY? WHEN?

Markers of 'person'

27	FRSTP	154	FIRST PERSON
28	EGOP	136	I,ME,MY,...
29	SCNDP	152	SECOND PERSON
30	THRDP	164	THIRD PERSON

Semantic markers

31	ANI	61	ANIMAL
32	HU	72	HUMAN
33	MALE	74	MALE
34	FEMALE	69	FEMALE
35	KIN	73	KINSHIP
36	COLL	63	COLLECTIVE NOUNS
37	ABS	78	ABSTRACT NOUNS
38	ABS*	175	'ISM' AND 'NESS'
39	TIME	33	TIME MARKER
40	DIST	66	DISTANCE
41	PLACE	76	PLACE
42	BODY	62	BODYPART
43	POLIT	77	POLITICAL MARKER
44	ECON	67	ECONOMIC MARKER
45	COLOR	40	COLOR
46	COM	64	COMMUNICATION (NOUNS)
47	COMV	84	COMMUNICATION (VERBS)
48	EMOT	68	EMOTIVE
49	FREQ	70	FREQUENCY
50	EVAL	50	EVALUATE MARKER
51	DIM	65	DIMENSION MARKER
52	POS	56	SERIAL POSITION
53	INTRLFL	140	INTERPERSONAL-FEELING (VERBS)
54	AGPAT	141	AGENT-PATIENT (VERBS)

Marker tags

1	131%	NOUN (M) &
2	25R	MODIFIER (M)
3	72R	HUMAN (M)
4	73R	KINSHIP (M)
5	74R	MALE (M)
6	69	FEMALE (M)
7	130	NON-ADULT
8	61R	ANIMAL (M)
9	239	RACE
10	+72,63	HUMAN,GROUP
11	−72,63	ABSTRACT OTHER
12	76	PLACE (M)
13	144	REGION

U.4.4 *continued*

14	150	ROUTE
15	85	BUILDING
16	86	ROOM
17	156	GATHERING (SOCIAL)
18	118	LAND
19	153	SEA
20	155	SKY
21	132	OBJECT
22	171	VEHICLE
23	166	TOOL
24	108	FORM
25	79	ACT (EVENT)
26	148	RITUAL
27	75R	NAME (M)
28	63R	COLLECTIVE (NOUN) (M)
29	133	ORGANISATION
30	121	MASS
31	78R	ABSTRACT (NOUN) (M)
32	175R	'ISM' AND 'NESS' (M)
33	33R	TIME (M)
34	66R	DISTANCE (M)
35	139	PSTV*
36	139	NGTV*
37	221	DIMENSION
38	+16	DETERMINER
39	+29	PREPOSITION
40	+32	SUPV
41	+131	NOUN
42	+25	MODIF
43	222	TIME
44	+16	DETERMINER
45	+29	PREPOSITION
46	+131,25	NOUN,MODIF
47	223	SPACE
48	+29	PREPOSITION
49	+131	NOUN
50	+25	MODIF
51	224	QUANTITY
52	+16	DETERMINER
53	+131	NOUN
54	+25	MODIF
55	196	QUALITY
56	+32	SUPV
57	162	TANGIBLE

U.4.4 *continued*

58	161	SURFACE
59	27 R	NUMBER (M)
60	70R	FREQUENCY (M)
61	56R	SERIAL POSITION (M)
62	40R	COLOR (M)

(Institutions)

63	240	ACADEMIC
64	+32	SUPV
65	−32	NOUN,MODIF
66	+72,63	ROLE,GROUP
67	+132	ARTIFACT
68	+76	PLACE
69	241	ECONOMIC
70	+32	SUPV
71	−32	NOUN,MODIF
72	+72,63	ROLE,GROUP
73	+132	ARTIFACT
74	+76	PLACE
75	242	EXPRESSIVE
76	+32	SUPV
77	−32	NOUN,MODIF
78	+72,63	ROLE,GROUP
79	+132	ARTIFACT
80	+76	PLACE
81	243	LEGAL
82	+32	SUPV
83	−32	NOUN,MODIF
84	+72,63	ROLE,GROUP
85	+132	ARTIFACT
86	+76	PLACE
87	244	MILITARY
88	+32	SUPV
89	−32	NOUN,MODIF
90	+72,63	ROLE,GROUP
91	+132	ARTIFACT
92	+76	PLACE
93	245	POLITICAL
94	+32	SUPV
95	−32	NOUN,MODIF
96	+72,63	ROLE,GROUP
97	+132	ARTIFACT
98	+76	PLACE
99	246	RELIGIOUS

U.4.4 *continued*

100	+32	SUPV
101	−32	NOUN,MODIF
102	+72,63	ROLE,GROUP
103	+132	ARTIFACT
104	+76	PLACE
105	232	NATURE
106	+32	SUPV
107	−32	NOUN,MODIF
108	+132	OBJECT
109	62R	BODYPART (NOUN) (M)
110	233	BODY CONNOTE
111	+32	SUPV
112	−32	NOUN,MODIF
113	107	FOOD
114	234	KINSHIP REF.
115	+72	ROLE
116	−72	EVENT OR STATE

Content tags (Psychological States)

1	197	NEED
2	+32	SUPV
3	−32	NOUN,MODIF
4	235	FEEL
5	+55	'FEEL','FELT' (LINKING)
6	+32−55	OTHER SUPV
7	−32	NOUN,MODIF
8	+139	POSITIVE (PSTV*)
9	+129	NEGATIVE (NGTV*)
10	198	PERCEIVE
11	+32	SUPV
12	−32	NOUN,MODIF
13	236	THINK (CONNOTE)
14	+32	SUPV
15	+29	PREP
16	−32,29	OTHER
17	157	SOLVE
18	199	KNOW
19	+32	SUPV
20	−32	NOUN,MODIF
21	98	EVALUATE
22	237	MEANS
23	+29	PREP

U.4.4 *continued*

24	−29	NOUN,MODIF
25	110	GOAL (NOUN)
26	95	DOCTRINE (NOUN)
27	173	VIRTUE
28	172	VICE

(Natural Processes)

29	186	CHANGE
30	+32	SUPV
31	−32	NOUN,MODIF
32	187	BEGIN
33	+32	SUPV
34	188	VARY
35	+32	SUPV
36	189	PERSIST
37	+32	SUPV
38	190	INCREASE
39	+32	SUPV
40	191	DECREASE
41	+32	SUPV
42	192	FINISH
43	+32	SUPV
44	193	MOVE
45	+32	SUPV
46	−32	NOUN,MODIF
47	147	RISE
48	103	FALL (SUPV)
49	194	STAY
50	+32	SUPV
51	195	TRAVEL
52	+32	SUPV
53	−32	NOUN,MODIF
54	105	FETCH (SUPV)
55	100	EXERT (SUPV)
56	88	ORDER
57	89	DISORDER
58	81	ACHIEVE (SUPV)
59	168	TRY
60	92	COMPLETE
61	102	FAIL
62	174	WORK (SUPV)
63	120	MAKE
64	117	LABOUR
65	169	USE

U.4.4 *continued*

66	99	EXCHANGE
67	238	COMMUNICATE
68	151	'SAY', 'TELL'
69	+32−151	OTHER SUPV
70	+132	OBJECT
71	+108	FORM
72	114	INTERPERSONAL ACTION
73	225	OVERSTATE
74	+16	DETERMINER
75	+41,113	CONJ,INTERJ
76	+30	PRONOUN
77	+32	SUPV
78	+131,25	NOUN,MODIF
79	226	UNDERSTATE
80	+16	DETERMINER
81	+30	PRONOUN
82	+32	SUPV
83	+131,25	NOUN,MODIF
84	227	QUALIFY
85	+41,29	CONJ,PREP
86	+32	SUPV
87	+131,25	NOUN,MODIF
88	228	GENERALITY
89	+16	DETERMINER
90	+30	PRONOUN
91	229	CAUSAL
92	+41,29	CONJ,PREP
93	230	RELATION
94	+29	PREP
95	+32	SUPV
96	231	IMPLY-NEGATION
97	+30	PRONOUN
98	+32	SUPV
99	26	NEGATION (M)

(Interpersonal axes)

100	249	AFFILIATION
101	+154	FRSTP
102	+32	SUPV
103	−32,154	NOUN,MODIF
104	247	HOSTILE
105	+29	PREP
106	+32	SUPV
107	−29,32	NOUN,MODIF

U.4.4 *continued*

108	248	POWER
109	+29	PREP
110	+32	SUPV
111	−29,32	NOUN,MODIF
112	201	SUBMISSION
113	+32	SUPV
114	−32	NOUN,MODIF

Osgood dimensions

1	***	POSITIVE (TOTAL)
2	***	(WEIGHTED)
3	*+32	SUPV
4	202	INTENSITY 1
5	203	2
6	204	3
7	***	NEGATIVE (TOTAL)
8	***	(WEIGHTED)
9	*+32	SUPV
10	205	INTENSITY 1
11	206	2
12	207	3
13	***	STRONG (TOTAL)
14	***	(WEIGHTED)
15	*+32	SUPV
16	208	INTENSITY 1
17	209	2
18	210	3
19	***	WEAK (TOTAL)
20	***	(WEIGHTED)
21	*+32	SUPV
22	211	INTENSITY 1
23	212	2
24	213	3
25	***	ACTIVE (TOTAL)
26	***	(WEIGHTED)
27	*+32	SUPV
28	214	INTENSITY 1
29	215	2
30	216	3
31	***	PASSIVE (TOTAL)
32	***	(WEIGHTED)
33	*+32	SUPV
34	217	INTENSITY 1

U.4.4 *continued*

35	218	2
36	219	3
37	***	TOTAL POSITIVE-NEGATIVE
38	***	TOTAL STRONG-WEAK
39	***	TOTAL ACTIVE-PASSIVE

Edinburgh tags

40	122	DIFFUSENESS
41	123	SPECIFICITY
42	124	IRRELEVANCE
43	125	RELEVANCE
44	140	INTERPL-FEELING VERBS (M)
45	141	AGENT-PATIENT VERBS (M)
46	134	AGENT
47	135	PATIENT
48	138	STASIS

U.4.5 First and Second-Order Content Tags

First order categories: these are the basic analytic categories, organised into a fully hierarchical structure. Hence, if a word-sense is mapped to a lower level category, it must also occur in all higher level categories. There are 75 first order categories in the Edinburgh version of Harvard IV-3, and they comprise the *Behaviour, Concrete Objects, Psychological States, Natural Processes* and *Dimension* headings in U.4.4.

Second order categories: these provide further psychological or sociological specification of words and idioms which principally derive from specific theoretical approaches within the social sciences, such as Osgood's 'Evaluation/Potency/Activity' theory of connotative meaning (Osgood 1965) and Murray's theory of motivational drives (Murray *et al.* 1938). There are 37 second-order categories in the Edinburgh version, described under the headings of *Institutions, Interpersonal Axes, Osgood Dimensions, Ascribed Status* and the stylistic tags (Understate, Overstate, Imply negative) in U.4.4.

U.4.6 Summary data on verbal transcripts, by level

Level/stage	Sentences	Tokens	Words	Leftover words N	Leftover words % words
1	161	2119	1810	92	5.1
2	167	2280	1959	134	6.8
3	177	2531	2198	146	6.6
4	170	2340	2023	133	6.6
5	168	2493	2170	126	5.8
Stage I	843	11763	10160	631	6.2
6	196	2729	2377	138	5.8
7	183	2514	2160	136	6.3
8	170	2672	2309	154	6.7
9	166	2318	2013	150	7.5
10	171	2459	2104	133	6.3
Stage II	886	12692	10963	711	6.5
11	172	2807	2199	135	6.1
12	141	2094	1826	131	7.2
13	154	2357	2020	128	6.3
14	135	2298	1972	102	5.2
15	34	465	408	26	6.4
Stage III	636	10021	8425	522	6.2
Total	2365	34476	29548	1864	6.3

U.4.7 Contrastive comparison between texts and within occupational judgement material (HACONS) (based upon Tag-Tally output from Inquirer III)

Note: entries are shown if the differences between *corpora* exceed 1%, or if the differences *within* phases of the occupational data exceed 0.2%

Tag no.	Description	Percentage/word					
		HACONS text			Comparative texts		
		P	C	J	TOTAL (HACONS)	COAL	HTOGOD
A. Markers of sentence structure (i)							
29	PREPOSITIONS	10.6	10.5	11.0			
41	CONJUNCTIONS	6.8	6.9	7.9			
42	AND,BUT,OR	3.2	3.3	3.9			
43	THE OTHERS						
113	INTERJECTIONS						
131	NOUNS	19.6	18.4	18.7	18.9	13.6	15.8
75	PROPER NAMES						
25	ADJECTIVES	8.9	8.1	7.3	8.2	2.7	6.4
Markers of sentence structure (ii)							
32	SUPERVERB: ALL VERBS	20.9	22.2	20.6	21.3	24.7	20.6
36	AUXILIARY VERBS	13.1	13.8	12.7			
39	BEING	5.5	5.2	5.2			
55	LINKING						
35	BECOMING						
52	HAVING	2.4	2.6	2.3			
24	MODAL (MAY,MUST,....)	2.0	2.4	2.1			
51	GOING TO						
17	DO						
34	INFINITIVE	1.7	2.0	1.8			
179	PASSIVE VERBS						
26	NEGATIVE VERBS						

Tag no.	Description	HACONS test			Percentage/word	Comparative texts	
		P	C	J	TOTAL (HACONS)	COAL	HTOGOD
B. Markers of reference: pronouns and determiners							
16	DETERMINERS						
101	PRECEDING A NOUN						
104	REFERRING TO A NOUN	2.2	2.2	2.6	2.3	1.1	1.5
30	PRONOUNS	7.7	8.6	8.1	8.1	8.3	6.8
44	DEFINITE REFERENCE	5.3	5.6	5.3	5.4	5.1	3.8
15	PERSONAL PRONOUN NOMINATIVE						
60	PERSONAL PRONOUN OBJECTIVE						
45	PERSONAL PRONOUN REFLEXIVE						
46	TOTALITY/IDENTITY(ALL,EACH,...)	3.8	2.9	2.6	3.1	0.6	0.9
53	INDEFINITE REFERENCE						
57	PRONOUNS (SOMEONE,...)						
58	DETERMINERS: COUNT NOUNS ONLY	2.3	1.3	0.9	1.5	0.3	0.7
59	DETERMINERS: COUNT AND/OR MASS	2.9	3.2	3.6	3.2	0.1	1.5
38	ARTICLE (A,AN,THE)	2.4	2.1	1.9			
21	POSSESSIVES						
C. Markers of 'person'							
154	FIRST PERSON	1.4	1.7	1.6	1.6	3.6	3.6
136	I,ME,MY,...	1.1	1.5	1.3	1.4	1.4	2.8
152	SECOND PERSON	0.5	0.5	0.4	0.5	1.2	1.3
164	THIRD PERSON	5.5	6.1	5.5	5.7	3.2	2.9

Tag no.	Description	Percentage/word					
		HACONS text			Comparative texts		
		P	C	J	TOTAL (HACONS)	COAL	HTOGOD
D. Semantic markers							
61	ANIMAL	3.0	3.1	2.7			
72	HUMAN	1.4	2.5	1.4			
74	MALE						
69	FEMALE						
73	KINSHIP	2.9	2.9	4.1			
63	COLLECTIVE NOUNS				3.2	0.5	0.7
78	ABSTRACT NOUNS				2.6	4.3	3.1
175	'ISM' AND 'NESS'				2.2	1.0	2.3
33	TIME MARKER				0.4	2.4	0.8
66	DISTANCE						
76	PLACE						
62	BODYPART						
77	POLITICAL MARKER				2.1	0.8	1.1
67	ECONOMIC MARKER	6.2	5.3	5.3	5.6	1.4	0.7
40	COLOUR						
64	COMMUNICATION (NOUNS)						
84	COMMUNICATION (VERBS)				0.7	2.9	1.9
68	EMOTIVE						
70	FREQUENCY						
50	EVALUATE MARKER				2.5	0.9	2.0

| Tag no. | Description | HACONS text | | | Percentage/word | | |
| | | | | | TOTAL (HACONS) | Comparative texts | |
		P	C	J		COAL	HTOGOD
	D. Semantic markers (continued)						
65	DIMENSION MARKER	0.8	1.0	0.7			
56	SERIAL POSITION						
140	INTERPERSONAL-FEELING (VERBS)						
141	AGENT-PATIENT (VERBS)						
	E. Psychological states						
197	NEED				1.0	0.3	0.4
235	FEEL				(0.6)		
198	PERCEIVE				(0.4)		
236	THINK	15.9	14.3	14.2	14.8	7.3	10.6
157	SOLVE				(0.3)		
199	KNOW	4.4	4.2	3.9	4.2	2.5	3.4
98	EVALUATE	10.2	8.8	9.3	9.5	3.5	6.3
237	MEANS	3.6	2.8	2.8	3.1	1.5	1.5
110	GOAL				(0.2)		
95	DOCTRINE				2.4		
173	VIRTUE	2.7	2.5	3.0	2.7	0.2	1.0
172	VICE	0.6	0.6	1.1	(0.8)	1.0	2.6
	F. Behaviour						
81	ACHIEVE				(0.3)		

Tag no.	Description	HACONS text			Percentage/word TOTAL (HACONS)	Comparative texts	
		P	C	J		COAL	HTOGOD
F. Behaviour (*continued*)							
174	WORK	2.5	2.1	1.9	2.2	2.5	0.8
120	MAKE				(0.9)		
117	LABOR				(0.5)		
169	USE				(0.2)		
99	EXCHANGE				(0.3)		
238	COMM	2.2	2.1	1.8	2.0	4.6	3.9
114	INTREL	1.1	1.2	1.1	(1.2)		
G. Institutional							
240	ACADEMIC	5.5	4.8	4.8	2.0	0.1	0.8
241	ECONOMIC				5.1	1.4	0.7
242	EXPRESSIVE				(0.2)		
243	LEGAL				(0.4)		
244	MILITARY				(—)		
245	POLITICAL				(0.2)		
246	RELIGIOUS				0.2		2.5
H. Style/categories							
227	QUALIFY	2.5	2.9	3.4	(2.6)		
228	GENERALITY				2.9	1.7	2.4
229	CAUSE				(0.6)		

Tag no. Description	HACONS text			Percentage/word TOTAL (HACONS)	Comparative texts	
	P	D	J		COAL	HTOGOD
H. Style/categories (continued)						
230 RELATION	3.5	2.7	2.5	2.9	0.5	1.1
231 IMPLY-NEGATIVE				(0.7)		
225 OVERSTATE	3.5	4.0	4.5	4.0	2.6	3.9
226 UNDERSTATE				2.0	1.0	1.2
I. Interpersonal axes						
249 AFFILIATION				1.2	1.4	2.2
247 HOSTILITY				0.3	*1.5*	0.6
248 POWER				2.0	1.4	2.6
201 SUBMISSION				(0.8)		
J. Osgood's semantic differential						
Evaluation: POSITIVE				(1.5)		
NEGATIVE				(0.6)		
Power: STRONG				(2.6)		
WEAK				(0.4)		
Activity: ACTIVE				2.4	0.3	2.1
PASSIVE				0.8	0.1	1.8
NO. OF WORDS					2083	11734
NO. OF SENTENCES					107	552
NO. OF LEFTOVER WORDS					111	584

U.4.8 Sympathetic circularity sequences (S.C. sequences)

This graphic phrase (so named in Bernstein 1971, Ch. 6) describes

> sequences such as 'I mean', 'I think' and terminal sequences such as
> 'isn't it', 'you know', 'ain't it', 'wouldn't he' etc. The terminal sequences . . .
> are called sympathetic circularity sequences (ibid. 96-7).

Bernstein continues:

> They are used much more frequently by the working class groups.

In our edited protocols, most of the SC sequences were stripped by the
interviewers in making their selected written account (see U.3.1). None the
less, they are sufficiently noteworthy to be included from time to time, and
survive in a number of transcripts — all of them referring to subjects of
'working-class' occupations.

(a) Isn't it
(Does not survive in this form; it is fairly uncommon as a Scots idiom.)

(b) You know
   Eleven uses survive, from nine subjects, of which all but one (a boutique
manager) are quadrant D subjects.
Examples
> Both [BM and CT] take a lot of abuse from the public, and must have a
> quick answer for everybody. The Traveller especially is two-faced, *you
> know,* yes sir, no sir. (Aircraft Fitter)

> Just the working, normal, everyday job, *you know* . . . manual. (TV
> Engineer)

> Bus and lorry drivers often go into ambulances because they get more
> money or they like to feel that they do their bit . . . they graduate to it,
> *you know,* step up.

(c) Wouldn't he etc.
   (No survivals)

(d) Ken (Lowland Scots idiom for 'y'know')
   Six uses survive, all for one subject (Machine engineer).
   [PM and CST] have a lot to do with society, *ken.*

> Two large groups are joined at level 13. These were together 'only in
> relation to the social scale, . . . *ken,* as folks think about them'.

U.4.9 Identification of Bernstein's Grammatical Elements and Inquirer Tags (see Tables 4.4 to 4.7)

1. *Use of adjectives:* Word frequencies of MODIF tag by Quadrant documents.
2. *Uncommon conjunctions:* Word frequencies of CONJ2 (Conjunctions excluding AND, BUT and OR).
3. *Passive verbs:* Word frequencies of PASSIVE.
4. *'I':* Isolated by the cross-tabulation of EGOP (first person singular) and DEFI (nominative case) frequencies, provided in Tag Tally List under Markers of Reference.

Ratio measures

   (i) *using personal pronouns*
   Frequencies of personal pronouns calculated by summing FRSTP, SCNDP and THRDP for DEF1 (nominative) only.

   (ii) *using total words*
   The relevant counts are:

Quadrant	A:	10872
	B:	4741
	C:	2126
	D:	8632

Total	26371

Note: interviewer comments and glosses are removed from these protocols.

5. *Ratio: 'I'/PP:* (EGOP.DEF1) as fraction of PP.
6. *Ratio: 'I'/Words*
7. *Use of 'You':* Cross-tabulation of SCNDP.DEF1.
8. *Use of 'They':* Cross-tabulation of THRDP.DEF1.
9. *Ratio:* 'You' and 'They' as fraction of PP.
10. *Ratio:* 'You' and 'They' as fraction of words.
11. *Ratio:* 'Of' as fraction of 'of', 'in', 'into'; identified from concordances of text using COCOA.
12. *'I think':* Identified by concordance (COCOA) KWIC on NEWOUT disambiguated (but not content-tagged) file from (Edinburgh) Inquirer IV. Strictly, THINK1 ('hold as an opinion, suppose, believe, consider') should isolate the correct 'semantic uncertainty' usage. Unfortunately it was not very good at doing so.

Note: Chi-square expected values are calculated from the total sample proportions, reinflated by the size of the two quadrant groups. Significance levels should obviously be treated with caution.

U.4.10 Transcript of SO49's hierarchies task

Subject: SO42

Counter	Speaker	Verbal comment	Action
	Inter-viewer	Right, I have here 16 occupational titles *(yeh)* which I'd like you to look at, and you'll need a little bit of space (*yeh, sure*)	
	Subject	You can pull this out if you want it incidentally I + (*er*) turned my desk round to save power as far as possible but y'know I have the light on (*I see, um +*)	
	I	What I'm going to ask you to do is to group them. In the first instance, um, make up one pair of two titles which you think go naturally together. Now /l/ this, we say "go naturally together" because we intentionally want to leave it + vague, and we'd like you to define your own criteria for putting them together (*I see, just two?*) Just two in the first place (*mm*) and er + I'd like you to sort of talk aloud and let me know the reasons why you picked those two	
005	S	Yeh, well I'll need er + mm /l/ +	
	I	Um,um, if you'd like, if you'd (*yeh?*) like to know what the exercise is about	
	S	No, it's all, well it's up to you; if you don't want to tell me I don't want (*yeh*) to know, y'know? (*It's alright*) mm it's er, it's a bit harder than the usual intelligence test matching-up, isn't it?	
	I	/l/ well there's no right or wrong answers you know (*No,no,*) /tg/ what's interesting is that (*no,no*) just the way that (*well, I*) you structured it [?].	
	S	Well I, well, I find it very difficult um + yes, yes, very well chosen list um + I	
010		would picked out, I think, Chartered Accountant and the Civil Service, servant executive grade	1. CA,CSE

Counter	Speaker	Verbal comment	Action
	I	Right + um, could you tell me the reasons why you think these two go together?	
	S	Well, um, it seemed to me that the, the work was, was very similar between those two in that they're both, they both need a good bit of training, they both have to know something about er management structures, they have to know about looking at figures and making decisions from them + y'know I could, I know a chartered accountant, I know an executive grade civil servant and I would say that er /l/ they're fairly similar. I also know Church of Scotland Ministers, so this [?] the others on your list, I think in general	
015	I	Yes, um, yes, it's nice to have some (*yeh*) way of getting to know the profession and you may remember that these are labels for the whole professions so try not to get /too (*oh, no,no*) tied personal, y'know, but [?] /tg/ oh no, no,y'know I	
	(S)	mean, no, no, but er, but I'm saying I know most of them, roughly, I think (*yeh*) and I can see a direct parallel there (*right*) whereas I don't see for instance any, any on the list which would, could remotely really relate to a Church of Scotland Minister. (*well*) so, you know (*in er*) it's just an illustration I think, it	
	I	OK, well in the second instance, um, I'd like you either to make up another pair, (*yeh*) that go together or add one title to this group + [?] (*yeh, uh*) and gradually I'm going to be asking you to use them all up in that way (*yeh, I see*) for varying reasons, y'know, in the end they might not have very much in common but /l/ (*yeh*) +	
020	S	Yes, it's very difficult + [telephone rings . . .] yeh, uh, let me put together Barman and Railway Porter (*right*) and if you want some reasons (*yes please*) it's because I think that both of them	2. BM and RP

Counter	Speaker	Verbal comment	Action

could, wouldn't be worried too much
if, um, they had to get another job;
I don't think they would be terribly
committed to being either a Barman
or a Railway Porter, they'd find something else to do they'd like to do just as
025   much if they had to leave for instance
+ in other words I think they probably d
drifted into it rather than er chose it
$/l/$+ um, another pair or, er?

I   At this point, yes, either another pair or
adding (*yeh*) one title on to the (*yeh*)
groups that already exist or the other
logical alternatives (*yeh*) till we start
merging (*yes*) some of the groups that
you have made

S   I think I should perhaps merge the   3. AD and MPN
Ambulance Driver and the Male
Psychiatric Nurse + (*yes*) and the reasons
for that I think would be that they're,
they're both jobs where I think the
people very often are welfare-driven,
they're not terribly well-paid; usually
the people that do it tend to have
some, some commitment +, probably +
they'd try to go higher in the medical
030   profession if they'd had the chance or
the training (*hm,hm*) + Carpenter and   4. C and MTO
Machine Tool Operator + I'd say often
quite similar because they have the
draughtsman's appraoch, + they enjoy
er doing, in general doing + a, a good
piece of work + specially if they can do
individual, + the trouble with many
Machine Tool Operators they'd like to do
individual $/l/$ machining and they have to
do mass production, but in general, they're
035   people with that kind of approach +
Um, + I think, in a way if I was grouping
+ if I'm allowed to group for any type
of similarity then I would say that probably
a Solicitor with a country practice and a

Counter	Speaker	Verbal comment	Action
		Qualified Actuary both, both have a common characteristic in that they're well, very well trained and yet tend to work in a, in a solitary way, in other words an Actuary tends to just be working very often on his own producing actuarial figures for the insurance company and, er, a solicitor in a country practice is really completely his	5. SOL and QA
040		own boss /t/ (*hm,hm*) I would say that they're people who, who've decided that they want to be their own boss, do their own thing, and not get involved in groups working with other people +	
	I	OK, now (*mm*) you remember that you also (*yeh*) have the choice of adding one title (*yeh*) to the existing groups or merging two groups before you add a title	
	S	Yeh, that's fine, but + it's easier said than done (. . . *alternative*) /l/	
	I	give you a little bit of choice /l/	
	S	Well, I think perhaps I suppose if you could add the Building Site Labourer if you take my arguments as valid, add the Building Site Labourer to the Barman and the Railway Porter because, again, they could go and do something which involved a different job and, er, not be, not be too + too er worried about it + (*yeh*)	6. BSL to 2
	045	Now then, let's have a look at these others + I think very often a Comprehensive School Teacher could earn more by doing something else, so therefore I would perhaps put them in with the Ambulance Driver and the Male Psychiatric Nurse as the, someone who even though they wouldn't admit it has an inner feeling that they ought to help the community +	7. CST to 3
	I	Which is, er, also in common to all the others	
	S	Yeh, which was, I think was the sort of thought I had about it, it's educational rather than medical + and if you accept	

Counter	Speaker	Verbal comment	Action
		that as a heading then I suppose that at the top of the list you should put a properly motivated Church of Scotland Minister /l/ (*Right*)	8. CSM to 7
050	I	I think so, yes, I think that that category is turning into the people who are not entirely money motivated (*right*) +	
	S	Now + of course that group is turning imperceptibly into public services /l/ so, possibly I'd add the Policeman to that list in a looser way; in that, at any rate in Britain, not possibly in America, in Britain Policemen are, tend to be motivated, often for the public good, + in other countries possibly /tg/ put in just as, er I mean one can see how that group's developing. Now I think I'm left with two that I nearly put together earlier, because, er + I do think that these two do go together in a way as a group because, er, they always want to be moving on to something new + which is a very easy mood to get into in life, you just keep y'know + in general you've, you've slightly fewer responsibilities if you keep moving on than if you stay in the same place and make something of it. So I think I would accept that as a separate group and, um + if you force me to do any more merging	9. PM to 8
055			10. LD and CT
	I	Yes, er, I'd like you to merge groups one by one until you're left with only two (*I see, well*) and again, give me reasons for it (*yeh*) each time	
	S	Well, well then + the next way I would start grouping them is by looking at, I think in, the ones that are left, er, those that sort of care and those that don't. So I think that you could put — well, you may want to do it in your own way, but I think I would therefore say,	
060		er, ignoring the pecking order /l/ for the	

Counter	Speaker	Verbal comment	Action
		time being so to speak, that these people are all trained, and probably have a sense of responsibility, don't need to have. Some do, I've met very conscientious railway porters /l/ but er in general they don't have to be as responsible, those two, as those three (*OK*) If you want to put those together	
	I	Well in the rule of the game there you'll have to do it one at a time, so let's put this	
	S	Well, then, put those two, those there (*Yes*) and say that in general (*this is 10 and 6*) yeh, that er, (*yes*) that — and I've grouped those on the basis that they don't have to worry too much, whereas the other three groups have	11. 10 and 6
065	I	Now if you could do that at, in, at each stage, (*each stage*) add groups	
	S	I would join those two first (*OK*) +	12. 1 and 5
	I	Um, any particular reason why these two come first?	
	S	Um, just higher training, that's all, higher training, but, um, and then, then I'd put these Carpenter and the Machine Tool Operator with them because, again, they care very much about what they do and they stay in one place and accept a commitment there and get on with the job (c) +	13. 4 to 12
	I	Er, we're still left with three groups	
	S	Yeh, well, I'll put them together in a moment (*Right*) + So if you force me to get down to two groups I would put those with those, because in general	
070		/c/ these people accept, should do, if they're doing the job properly, should accept responsibility to a higher, to a highest, highest level, and I think that although people often *do* at this, at this level, the group here, nevertheless in general they can just sort of flit away to another job, or er some /t/ They may not do when	14. 13 and 9

Counter	Speaker	Verbal comment	Action
		they're older because they get locked in, but in general they don't have to be responsible for commitments from day to remote day + that will be my er final break-up +	
	I	Right, well thank you very much — we're	
075		there! I must say I've enjoyed that . . .	

Added signs

/tg/	both speak together
/l/	laughs
/c/	coughs, clears throat
/t/	voice tails off
[?]	inaudible or possible mishearing
+	pause

U.4.11 Class terminology usage: descriptive characteristics

A Subjects making (at least one) class reference

Quadrants:	People-orientation	Non-people-orientation
Higher education	29% (33%)	6% (17%)
Lower education	10% (10%)	58% (40%)

Cell entries:

$N\%$ = percentage of subjects using class terminology in quadrant x

$(M\%)$ = percentage of subjects in quadrant x)

B Frequency of mention

Number of class references in HA task	Per cent
0	65
1	17
2	1
3	3
4	4
5	1
6	3
7 or over	5
	99% ($N = 94$)

C Number of references (106)

(i) *by level*

Level	Per cent
General comment (0)	6.6
1 or 2	17.0
3 or 4	12.3
5 or 6	13.2
7 or 8	8.5
9 or 10	10.4
11 or 12	15.1
13 or 14	17.0
	100.1%

No. of references = 106

(ii) *by construction strategy and Quadrant*

Strategy	Quadrants A and B	C and D
Pairing	9	17
Chaining	1	20
Joining	9	25
Total	19	62 $N = 81$ (references)

U.4.12 Occupations cited as belonging to Middle and Working Classes

	Occupational title	Middle class	Working class
		Proportion Identifying Occupation as	
1.	Church of Scotland Minister	0.55	0
2.	Comprehensive School Teacher	0.70	0.05
3.	Qualified Actuary	0.75	0
4.	Chartered Accountant	0.90	0
5.	Male Psychiatric Nurse	0.35	0.21
6.	Ambulance Driver	0.20	0.37
7.	Building Site Labourer	0	0.84
8.	Machine Tool Operator	0.05	0.89
9.	Country Solicitor	0.85	0
10.	Civil Servant (Executive)	0.60	0
11.	Commercial Traveller	0.20	0.58
12.	Policeman	0.25	0.32
13.	Carpenter	0.05	0.74
14.	Lorry Driver	0.05	0.74
15.	Railway Porter	0	0.95
16.	Barman	0.10	0.74
	Based on:	$n_1 = 20$	$n_2 = 19$

(Total identifying occupation(s) as belonging to either Middle or Working Class is 29.)

U.4.13 High-level differentiation and approbation

Approbation and disapprobation are best captured in the Harvard IV-3 Dictionary by the tags: VIRTUE, VICE and strength of feeling by the tag OVRST (overstate). Such instances are underlined in the following four examples:

(1) Chartered Accountant

(Level 12) 'This group { SOL, CST, MIN, QA, SOL } requires a greater degree of *skill* and education, a sense of being members of a profession, and this second group { LD, PM, MTO, C } is a *skilled* group and perform necessary *functions*. They both are necessary in a *civilised* community'.
(all VIRTUE tags)
The contrast implied is to the group { RP, BSL } who
'perform − if not an *essential* − certainly a *useful* service'.

(2) Professor

(Level 13) 'Although they { C, MTO } have less training [than CA, CSE, SOL, QA, whom they now join] they care very much about what they do. They have accepted a *commitment*. They have a sense of *responsibility*'. –

compared, that is, to the group { BM, RP, BSL, LD, CT } who do not, and who are described as being unstable in their job.

(3) Fork-truck Driver

(Level 14) He had three groups:
　　　　Professionals: { QA, CA, SOL, MIN, CST } ,
　　　　Services occupations: { POL, AD, CSE, BM, BSL, RP } and
　　　　'those in industrial production' { MPN (an admitted exception), C, MTO, CT, LD }
　　　　'If you took out any one of these groups, you'd diminish the effectiveness of the others. Though any broad division on class terms is out – this is a one-class society.'
After some cogitation, he joined the Service occupations to the Professionals, describing them as:
　　　　'service in the business side of things' as opposed to the
Production groups, who gave
　　　　'service of a practical nature',
adding, after a pause:
　　　　'It's all theory or practice, I suppose.'
As the interviewer comments,
　　　　'I felt Lukács turn in his grave.'

(4) Medical Laboratory Technician

(Level 13) He joined the group { BSL, CT, BM, RP } , whom he described as
　　　　'Just *unskilled* men out to get the bread – only think in terms of money',
　　　　to the group {C, MTO} , and described the new group as
　　　　'semi-skilled working class'.
He went on:
　　　　'May be big earners, some of them, but they spend all their money on horses and booze.'
At the next step he joined the 'vocational jobs' {CST, PM, MIN, MPN, LD, AD} to 'the qualified lot' {SOL, CSE, CA, QA|} .
　　　　'Compared to the other lot',
he says
　　　　'all of them are highly *conscientious.'*

U.4.14 'Models of Class': A detailed example of theme applicability

Subject SO49's data form the basis of the following analysis. A full transcription of his hierarchies task is given in U.4.10 above, and various parts of the local environment of theme applications are portrayed in Figure U.4.1 below.

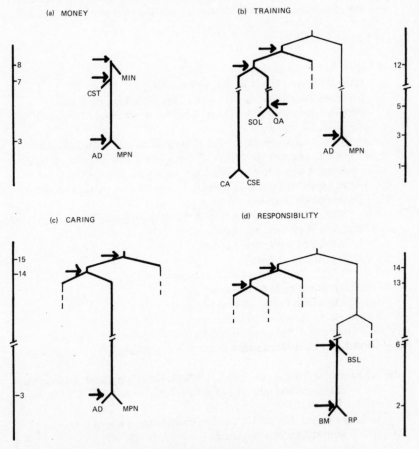

Fig. U4.1: Local Structure of Theme Applicability
note: arrows [ ] denote points at which a theme is mentioned or implied.

A brief reading of the transcript may initially persuade the reader that this man's data provide strong support for the Affluent Worker position that 'money models' strongly dominate 'prestige' or 'power' models (Goldthorpe *et al.* 1969:147 ff., and he does not invoke any 'power' terminology, other than to talk of Actuaries and Solicitors being 'their own boss'. His only explicit reference to a 'prestige' component occurs in the generalising stage (level 10), after he has separated the sheep ('those that sort of care') and the goats ('those that don't') and it consists of a simple allusion:

> but I think I would therefore say, er, *ignoring the pecking order* [laughs] for the time being so to speak . . . (060, emphasis added, such counter-references to the transcript in U.4.10 are approximate.

But he returns several times to 'money' themes:

(*a*) *Money* (see Fig. U.4.2)

(pairing)   the Ambulance Driver and the Male Nurse are 'not terribly well-paid' (029)

(chaining) a Comprehensive School Teacher 'could earn more by doing something else' (045)

(chaining, but beginning to generalise)

'I think that that category is turning into people who are not entirely money-motivated' (050)

(An implicit contrast with the Accountant, Civil Servant, Solicitor, Actuary *and* with Carpenter, Machine Tool Operator.)

But does his image really approximate the 'money model'? It is significant, first, that references to money occur, as he himself recognises, only locally in one branch. Moreover, even a casual reading indicates that other themes outside the Affluent Worker (and other commonly used) lists are for him far more salient, and are by no means peculiar to this subject. What themes?

(*b*) *Training:* (see Fig. U.4.1b)

is a theme which occurs at several points in the structure. At the most specific level, it is used to characterise Accountants and Civil Servants, Solicitors and Actuaries, and to account for the reason why Ambulance Drivers and Male Nurses have not moved up the medical profession (030).

In the generalising stage (levels 12), 'higher training' is used to describe the professional branch:

((CA,CSE) (SOL,QA)) (level 12)

and the implied contrast is with the lower responsibility group:

(((BM,RP) BSL) (LD,CT)) (level 10, see 061)

(*c*) *'Caring'* (see Fig. U.4.1c)

This is a distinction of some importance to the subject. It is used as the most general differentiating characteristic at level 15, when he contrasts the two major groups:

'those who care':

((((CA,CSE) (SOL,QA)) (C,MTO)) ((((AD,MPN) CST) MIN) PM))

(LHS at level 15)

with *'those who don't':*
(((BM,RP) BSL) (LD,CT)) (RHS at level 15)
In addition, a caring theme ('welfare-driven') is cited as a reason for
joining the Ambulance Driver and Male Psychiatric Nurse at level 3
(029) in contrast to 'those who don't care' (RHS at level 15) where,
he implies, they would normally fit — fit, that is, in terms of the
'pecking order', which he has chosen to ignore, but which he
equally recognised.

In slightly different form, the 'caring' theme appears as the distinction
between 'Working with people' and 'Working with things', hailed by John
Robinson in his review of measures of occupational characteristics (1969:
402) as

one of the most fruitful of the frequently used distinctions used in this
volume

and forming, of course, the major distinguishing category of the US
Department of Labor's definitive *Dictionary of Occupational Titles.*
It is not frequently encountered as a component in sociological accounts.

(d) Responsibility and Commitment (see Fig. U.4.1d)
A further salient contrast is the one he draws between jobs including
responsibility, commitment and stability of employment, as opposed
to those where the jobholders show little or no signs of responsibility
or commitment, but rather a marked propensity for work instability
(see 057, 062, 068 and 070).

The groups being compared are basically: the low responsibility,
unstable groups:
((BM,RP) BSL), versus the rest:

'Both of them [Barman and Porter] wouldn't be worried too much
if, um, they had to get another job. I don't think they would be
terribly committed to being either a Barman or a Railway Porter;
they'd find something else to do they'd like to do just as much if
they had to leave for instance . . .' (023)

By contrast, the Ambulance Driver and the Nurse

'do tend to have some commitment . . . probably . . . they'd try
to go higher in the medical profession' (029)

and, unlike their less trained fellows, the Carpenter and Tool Operator
are put with the professionals (not so called)

'because, again, they care very much about what they do and they stay in one place and accept a commitment there, and get on with the job.' (068)

Apart from his tendency to locate employment instability in the person rather than the job structure (he is after all not a social scientist), his description corresponds surprisingly well to the differences used to distinguish primary and secondary labour market jobs (Doeringer and Piore 1971, Gordon 1972). We have had cause to comment before (Coxon and Jones 1975:184) that analysts of social mobility have been surprisingly tardy to recognise the importance and consequences of precisely this distinction.

Is this man's 'image' a power model, a prestige model or a money model? The point does not need labouring; it is not so much the presence or absence (or even the relative preponderance) of particular 'types' which is significant in understanding images of society, but rather how such themes are located in subjective structures and how they are brought out in different situations. The advantage of the hierarchies task is that it provides giving us information about the level(s) of generality at which such themes occur, the occupations which they cover (that is, their range of applicability), and those occupations with which they are in semantic contrast.

9 Sentence-frame Data: Appendices to Chapter 5 of *Class and Hierarchy*

U.5.1 Parametric mapping of aggregate data on occupational titles

Parametric mapping is a type of scaling that treats both the data and the solution as being metric. Thus it differs from quasi-non-metric scaling methods such as MINISSA, where only rank order comparisons are made among the data elements. There are other metric scaling methods. For example, INDSCAL is most frequently used in its metric version. Like other metric scaling methods, parametric mapping (PARAMAP) takes a set of distances between stimulus points as data, and seeks to find a corresponding set of distances in a 'solution space' of low dimensionality. Most other scaling methods try to find a solution space such that the inter-point distances in the data are as close as possible to a linear or monotonic function of the corresponding distances, or dissimilarities in the solution. PARAMAP is different. It tries to find a solution space such that the function by which distances in the 'data space' can be predicted from corresponding distances in the solution space is as continuous, or 'smooth' as possible. The function relating distances in the data to distances in the solution need not be monotonic, so long as it is 'smooth'. As with other scaling methods, an iterative 'steepest descent' algorithm finds stimulus coordinates in a solution space of given dimensionality. These stimulus coordinates serve to generate Euclidean distances in the solution space, and these are found so as to minimise an index of departure from continuity or 'smoothness', of the function relating distances between pairs of points in the data space to corresponding distances in the solution space. This index is called *kappa*, and (in the simplest and standard form) it is defined by the formula:

$$Kappa = \frac{\sum_i \sum_j \left(\dfrac{d_{ij}{}^2}{D_{ij}{}^2} \cdot \dfrac{1}{D_{ij}^2} \right)}{\left(\sum_i \sum_j \dfrac{1}{D_{ij}^2} \right)}$$

where the d_{ij} are distances in the data space and the D_{ij} are distances in the solution space. (See Shepard and Carroll 1966 and Kruskal and Carroll 1969 for more general versions of the formula.)

The essential component of this index is the ratio of squared distances in the data space to corresponding squared distances in the solution space. It is of extreme importance that this ratio is *weighted* by the reciprocal of the square of the distance in the solution space. The weighted ratios are summed over all the $\frac{1}{2}N(N-1)$ pairs of stimuli, and the total sum is divided by a normalising factor.

In the limiting case, where all distances in the solution space are just the same as corresponding distances in the data space, the value of *kappa* would obviously be unity. It is also clear from simple inspection of the weighting section of the formula, that pairs of points between which the fitted (solution) distances are large will have relatively little influence on the *kappa* badness-of-fit value. Contrariwise, those pairs of points that are placed near to each other in the solution space will have a relatively large influence upon *kappa,* and therefore, upon the partial derivatives of *kappa* with respect to changes in the stimulus configuration for the solution space.

The sense in which *kappa* can be viewed as an index of departure from continuity can be seen if we consider the behaviour of the above formula when the solution space is one-dimensional. In that event, the stimulus points will be arranged along a straight line, and if there are N points, then $N-1$ pairs of points will be adjacent to one another. If the N points are evenly distributed along the straight line in the solution space, then these $N-1$ pairs of points will be the smallest distances. The concept of a smooth relationship (when distances in the data space are viewed as a function of distances in the solution space) implies that small values of D_{ij} will generate correspondingly small values of d_{ij}, so that the ratio of d_{ij}^2 to D_{ij}^2 will be about the same, for all values of i and j (so long as D_{ij} is small). Shepard and Carroll give an example where they use y to refer to distances in the data space (d_{ij}) and x to refer to distances in the solution space (D_{ij}).

If we say that the y values seem to change in a continuous manner as we move along the underlying x continuum, we are essentially saying that the change in y as we move from one x value to the next tends to be small compared to the change in y generally associated with larger jumps in x. (p. 579)

The Shepard and Carroll formula given above is concerned with comparisons between d_{ij}^2 and D_{ij}^2 for all pairwise distances, and not merely for the distances between points that would be adjacent to one another in a one-dimensional solution space. The crucial role of the weighting part of the formula (the reciprocal of the square of D_{ij}) is that it forces *kappa* to concentrate its attention upon pairs of points which are neighbours in the solution space. The further apart are two points, k and l in the solution space, the less it matters what is the correspondence between D_{kl} and d_{kl}.

We used parametric mapping in Chapter 5 of *Class and Hierarchy*. Our collection of sentence-frame data from sociology students, about the relationships between 20 occupational titles and 50 sentence frames, had led to a data matrix in which the percentage of 'Always' judgements for each combination of sentence frame and occupational title made up the entries of a matrix with 50 rows and 20 columns. The data were thus aggregated over subjects, and they were also metric. Euclidean distances were calculated between all pairs of the 20 occupational titles, using the 50 sentence frames as a 50-dimensional space. These distances constituted the d_{ij} for the analysis. PARAMAP generated a random 'first guess' at the configuration of the 20 occupational titles in a two-dimensional solution space, generated solution distances, D_{ij} from this, checked the degree of continuity of the relationship between d_{ij} and D_{ij} over all i and j, and proceeded to make modifications to the solution space, in such a way as to make the relationship between d_{ij} and D_{ij} as smooth as possible. PARAMAP is known to be sensitive to 'local minima'. Even with error-free data, the steepest descent algorithm may fail to find the solution with the lowest possible value of *kappa*. Several analyses were carried out, each having a different random starting configuration, and the results from the analysis having the smallest value of *kappa* are reported in Table U.5.1.1. The figure which corresponds to this table was shown as Figure 5.2 in *Class and Hierarchy,* and we remarked then on the similarity between this configuration and the cognitive map derived from INDSCAL analysis of quite a different kind of data (see Chapter 3 of *Images,* and T.3.15 in this book). A more formal kind of comparison is made in the next technical appendix (U.5.2).

TABLE U.5.1.1 Parametric mapping analysis of '% always' data from 20 occupational titles on 50 sentence frames (sociology students)

Three different analyses were carried out, different random starters being used in each run. This was to allow for the possibility of local minima.

Run	Starter	Final kappa after 30 iterations
1	37901	1.0968
2	11135	1.1137
3	17355	1.0985

The Two-Dimensional Configuration of the Twenty Occupational Titles
(from run 1) — matrix normalised and rotated to principal axes.

	Dimensions	
	I	*II*
Church of Scotland Minister	+200	+143
Barman	−194	−109
Business Manager (10 to 99 hands)	+061	−110
Carpenter	−068	+029
Civil Servant (Executive Grade)	+134	−069
Commercial Traveller	−057	−102
Solicitor (Country Practice)	+246	−040
Male Psychiatric Nurse	+036	+139
Jobbing Master Builder	−070	+021
Lorry Driver	−197	+003
Policeman	+023	+097
Railway Porter	−202	+071
Works Manager (Industrial)	+038	−100
Comprehensive School Teacher	+327	+067
Qualified Actuary	+215	−045
Ambulance Driver	−091	+129
Building Site Labourer	−234	+046
Machine Tool Operator	−246	+088
Newsagent and Tobacconist (One-man Shop)	−134	−207
Chartered Accountant	+214	−049

A scatterplot of the relationships between distances in the 2-D solution
space (D_{ij}) and distances in the data (d_{ij}) is shown as Figure U.5.1. A plot of
this kind is sometimes called Shepard diagram (see Green and Rao 1972).

The relationship between corresponding distances is very close, so long
as we are talking about comparatively small distances (the left-hand half of the
Shepard diagram). Where large distances are concerned the relationship
between corresponding distances is rather loose. This is just what we should
expect from our analysis of the formula for the badness-of-fit function,
kappa. The parametric mapping analysis, whose aim was to maximise the
smoothness of the function relating distances in the solution space to
corresponding distances in the data, seems to have behaved as if it was
maximising the degree to which distances in the data were a monotone
function of distances in the solution, but only for small solution distances.
(This is called 'locally monotone scaling', and is discussed in Chapter 3 of
Images, under the heading of 'occupational sequence'.)

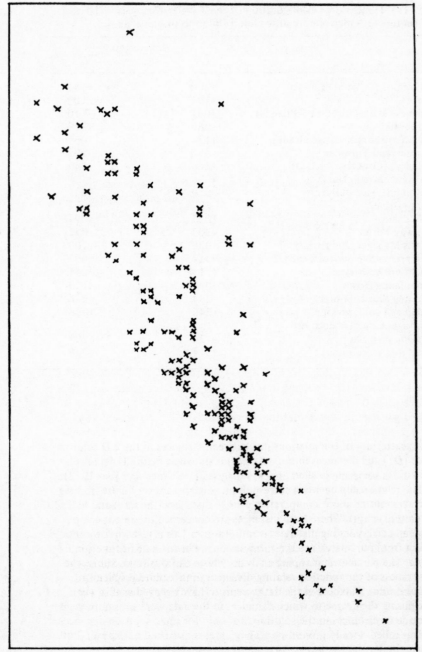

Distances in 2-D Solution Space

Distances in Data Space

Fig. U.5.1 Shepard diagram from parametric mapping analysis

U.5.2 Comparison of cognitive maps obtained from sentence-frame data by parametric mapping and by individual differences scaling

Different methods of data analysis can lead to separate estimates of cognitive or evaluative maps of occupations. In an ideal world, a researcher's conclusions would not depend on his choice of technique for data collection and analysis. In practice, it is wise to check one's results for 'method artefacts'.

In Chapter 5 of *Class and Hierarchy* we showed that sentence-frame data can be looked at in a variety of ways. Two methods of analysis resulted in cognitive maps of the same set of 20 occupational titles. One method ('parametric mapping') is explained in appendix U.5.1, and the other, ('individual differences scaling') is explained in the first section of U.5.7. Naturally enough we wish to know the extent to which the same 'true' cognitive map manifests itself in the two results. One intuitively reasonable method for comparing cognitive maps is to find the correlation between pairwise distances in the two maps. We chose another method: individual differences scaling of the pairwise distances from the two cognitive maps. The results were in the usual INDSCAL format, with weights on the two dimensions, and a goodness-of-fit correlation between observed and fitted values being given for each pseudo-subject. (The term 'pseudo-subject' is used when a set of distances input to INDSCAL arises from some source other than an individual subject.) The goodness-of-fit correlations were quite high, 0.982 for the cognitive map derived from parametric mapping, and 0.943 for the map derived from INDSCAL with sentence-frame data. Here the similarity ended, since the patterns of weights were completely different. The parametric mapping cognitive map weighted the two dimensions about equally (0.68 and 0.71), while the INDSCAL-derived cognitive map essentially weighted only the first dimension (the weights were 0.942 and 0.030).

It is worth mentioning that the use of INDSCAL to carry out a 'congruence' analysis of the kind discussed above can be potentially misleading. The reason for this is that the INDSCAL algorithm estimates both the sets of individual subject-weights *and* the coordinates of the occupational titles in a 'group' cognitive map. Since the estimation procedure is iterative, it is not guaranteed to find the minimum of the error function (see T.3.12). The analysis reported here above, was the best-fitting of four attempts, each with a different random starting configuration for the 'group' cognitive map.

A rather different method of using INDSCAL to carry out congruence analysis is to find some 'group' cognitive map in which one has some confidence, and to take that as 'fixed'. In that case, the INDSCAL subject weights can be estimated by ordinary least squares, and no problems of 'local minima' arise. The set of 20 occupations for which cognitive maps were found by parametric mapping and by individual differences scaling with sentence frame-data contained the standard set of 16 occupations and four others. These extra four were discarded and interpoint distances were only computed for the standard set of 16. Another congruence analysis was then carried out, but this time using the two-dimensional cognitive map of T.3.15 or a fixed configuration (see also T.4.2). Both cognitive maps had low weights on the second dimension of the fixed reference configuration. (See Chapter 3 of *Images* for interpretation of these dimensions.) The weights on the first dimension were much larger, being 0.679 for parametric mapping and 0.874 for individual differences scaling of sentence frames, so that the ratios of weights on dimension one to weights on dimension two were 3.2 to 1 and 3.7 to 1 respectively. The goodness-of-fit correlation was lower for the parametric mapping pseudo-subject than for the individual differences scaling pseudo-subject (0.716 and 0.910 respectively).

Two conclusions emerge from this analysis.

(*a*) The parametric mapping and individual differences scaling methods for analysing the same set of sentence-frame data yield results which are broadly similar in having one dimension which is like the first dimension of the cognitive map of T.3.15.

(*b*) The cognitive map from parametric mapping analysis contains a dimension which is shared neither by the fixed cognitive map of T.3.15 nor by that from the individual differences scaling of sentence-frame data.

U.5.3 Selection of Subjects for the Sentence-Frame Task (*n*=52)

Quadrant A (*n*=7)			Quadrant B (*n*=17)		
2	Anaesthetists	S	2	Actuaries	S
1	Obstetrician	S	1	Solicitor	S
3	Further education teachers	S	1	Higher executive officer (C.S.)	Y
1	Sales manager for large company	S	1	Chief agricultural officer (C.S.)	S
			1	Farmer	S
			1	Principal of revenue department (C.S.)	S
			1	Forestry Commission asst. conservator (C.S.)	S
			1	Management consultant	S
			1	Insurance broker	S
			1	Insurance manager (bank)	S
			1	Assistant pensions secretary (insurance company)	Y
			1	Building firm owner	S
			1	Quantity surveyor (partner)	S
			1	Forest geneticist	S
			1	Chartered surveyor	S
			1	Managing director (investment firm)	S

Quadrant C (*n*=13)

1	Salesman (electrical engineering)	Y
1	Salesman (protective clothing)	Y
1	Salesman (part-time)	Y
1	Sales manager for car dealer	Y
1	Car auctioneer	S
1	Sales representative	Y
1	Clerical supervisor	Y
1	Retail advisor	Y
1	Personnel assistant to manager	Y
1	Boutique manager	Y
1	Sub-postmaster	Y
1	Master jeweller	Y
1	Police inspector	Y

Quadrant D (*n*=16)

1	Engineering inspector	S
1	Bank clerk	Y
1	Post office clerk	Y
1	Service manager (garage)	Y
1	Contracts manager	Y
1	Industrial photographer	Y
1	Radio mechanic	Y
1	Fork truck driver	Y
1	Fitter-welder (foreman)	Y
1	Plant fitter	Y
1	Fitter's mate	Y
1	Heating engineer	Y
1	Heating engineer (chargehand)	Y
1	Machine engineer	Y
1	Technical clerk	Y
1	Interior decorator	Y

U.5.4 Analyses by Quadrants: Two-way Analyses of Variance

These analyses are referred to in Chapter 5 of *Class and Hierarchy*. A total of 52 Edinburgh men were interviewed with the sentence-frame task, and their resulting data were summarised by the INDSCAL model as discussed in appendix U.5.7 of this book. The weights which INDSCAL estimates for each subject can be used as scores for subsequent analysis, and so also can the goodness-of-fit correlations between data and fitted values that are estimated for each subject. In addition to these summary measures, we have taken the total number of minutes the subject took to get through the sentence-frames task, and the mean and standard deviation of the set of gamma coefficients generated from each subject's sentence-frame data.

These analyses of variance take as independent variables the dichotomous classifications of subjects into High Education or Low Education, and High People-orientation or Low People-orientation. Two-way analyses of variance were carried out for seven variables, as reported in Table U.5.4.1. Most of the *F*-ratios are non-significant, and, in particular, none of the interaction terms was significant. The Educational Requirements classification was definitely related to the weights on the first of the two dimensions of the 2-D INDSCAL solution. Strictly speaking, we should have accepted our own arguments in Chapter 3 of *Images* (as well as those of MacCallum 1977) and reported the analysis of *ratios* of INDSCAL weights on the two dimensions. An analysis of a logarithmic transformation of this ratio of weights has in fact been carried out, and it yields *F*-ratios of 8.9 and 2.9 for the Educational Requirements and the People-orientation factors respectively.

TABLE U.5.4.1   Analyses by quadrants: two-way analyses of variance

Characteristics of interviewees on measures derived from the sentence-frame task	*(a)* For 'educational requirements'	*(b)* For 'People-orientation'
	F-Values for Main Effects, (at 1 and 48 d.f.)	
(a) INDSCAL solution: weights on dimension I	8.85†	3.06 n.s.
(b) INDSCAL solution: weights on dimension II	7.13*	4.51*
(c) INDSCAL Solution in one dimension: correlations	6.91*	0.94 n.s.
(d) INDSCAL Solution in two dimensions: correlations	1.28 n.s.	0.48 n.s.
(e) Minutes taken for the interview	0.19 n.s.	0.00 n.s.
(f) Mean of absolute gamma coefficients	0.80 n.s.	0.07 n.s.
(g) Spread (std. dev.) of the gamma coefficients	1.20 n.s.	0.04 n.s.
Fisher Z Transformations		
(c) INDSCAL Solution in one dimension: correlations	6.89*	0.94 n.s.
(d) INDSCAL Solution in two dimensions: correlations	0.53 n.s.	0.77 n.s.
(f) Mean of absolute gamma coefficients	0.79 n.s.	0.07 n.s.

Note: At 1 and 48 d.f., critical values for F are 7.20 and 4.04 for the 1% and 5% levels. Standard (default) options in the SPSS Anova programme were used for the 1% (*) and 5% (†) levels.

† means significant at 1% Level.
* means significant at 5% Level.

U.5.5 Tabular Presentations of Several 15-element Belief Systems

The seven tabular presentations of belief systems in this appendix underlie Figures 5.7 to 5.13 in Chapter 5 of *Class and Hierarchy*.

A key to the meanings of the elements in the cells of the tables follows:

IMPL   if a row property implies a column property IMPL is entered in the cell.

SUPR   if a row property is implied by a column property, SUPR is entered in the cell.

EXCL   if the row property excludes the column property, EXCL is entered in the cell.

NEG   if the negation of the row property implies the column property, NEG is entered in the cell.

IDENT   if the row and column properties are treated identically by the subject, IDENT is entered in the cell.

OPP   if the row property is treated precisely oppositely to the way the column property is treated, then OPP is entered in the cell.

The row and column properties are the modified set of occupational descriptions as shown in Table U.1.4.

TABLE U.5.5.1   The 15-element belief system for subject S220

| | 1 | 2 | 3 | 4 | 5 | 6 | 7 | 8 | 9 | 10 | 11 | 12 | 13 | 14 | 15 |
	TRA	EDQ	OVT	STU	STA	PBW	CLK	PRO	PUB	BOR	LAB	OWN	SEC	FEE	CLA
TRA 1		SUPR			SUPR	NEG		SUPR				SUPR	SUPR	SUPR	
EDQ 2	IMPL		EXCL		SUPR	EXCL	EXCL			EXCL	EXCL		IMPL	SUPR	EXCL
OVT 3		EXCL			EXCL	IMPL	EXCL				IMPL	EXCL		EXCL	IMPL
STU 4															
STA 5	IMPL	IMPL	EXCL			EXCL	EXCL	IMPL		EXCL	EXCL		IMPL	IMPL	EXCL
PBW 6	NEG	EXCL	SUPR				SUPR	EXCL		SUPR			EXCL	IMPL	IMPL
CLK 7		EXCL				IMPL		EXCL			IMPL		EXCL	EXCL	SUPR
PRO 8	IMPL		EXCL		SUPR	EXCL	EXCL		EXCL	EXCL	EXCL	EXCL	IMPL	IMPL	EXCL
PUB 9										EXCL					
BOR 10		EXCL			EXCL	IMPL		EXCL			IMPL	EXCL	EXCL	EXCL	IMPL
LAB 11		EXCL	SUPR		EXCL		SUPR	EXCL		EXCL					
OWN 12	IMPL		EXCL		SUPR			SUPR		EXCL			IMPL	SUPR	EXCL
SEC 13	IMPL	SUPR			SUPR	EXCL	EXCL	SUPR		EXCL	EXCL	SUPR			
FEE 14	IMPL	SUPR	EXCL		EXCL	IMPL	EXCL			EXCL	EXCL		IMPL		EXCL
CLA 15		EXCL	SUPR		EXCL	IMPL	SUPR	EXCL		SUPR		EXCL		EXCL	

TABLE U.5.5.2   The 15-element belief system for subject Y006

	1 TRA	2 EDQ	3 OVT	4 STU	5 STA	6 PBW	7 CLK	8 PRO	9 PUB	10 BOR	11 LAB	12 OWN	13 SEC	14 FEE	15 CLA
1 TRA															
2 EDQ								SUPR							
3 OVT					IMPL			SUPR					NEG		
4 STU		EXCL			EXCL			EXCL					NEG	IMPL	EXCL
5 STA		SUPR						SUPR					NEG	EXCL	SUPR
6 PBW		EXCL			EXCL			EXCL					NEG	IMPL	EXCL
7 CLK		EXCL		SUPR	EXCL			EXCL		EXCL			NEG	EXCL	SUPR
8 PRO		IMPL		EXCL	IMPL					EXCL			NEG	EXCL	EXCL
9 PUB		SUPR	EXCL	EXCL	SUPR	EXCL	SUPR	SUPR		SUPR	EXCL	IMPL	NEG	IMPL	EXCL
10 BOR		EXCL	EXCL	EXCL	EXCL	EXCL	EXCL	EXCL	IMPL		EXCL	IMPL	NEG	SUPR	SUPR
11 LAB		EXCL	EXCL	EXCL	EXCL	EXCL	EXCL	EXCL	EXCL	EXCL		EXCL	NEG	EXCL	SUPR
12 OWN	IMPL	SUPR	EXCL	EXCL	SUPR	IMPL	EXCL	SUPR	IMPL	EXCL	EXCL		NEG	SUPR	EXCL
13 SEC	IMPL	NEG	NEG	NEG	NEG	NEG	EXCL	NEG	IMPL	NEG	EXCL	NEG		NEG	NEG
14 FEE	IMPL	SUPR	EXCL	EXCL	SUPR	EXCL	NEG	SUPR	NEG	EXCL	NEG	IMPL	NEG		EXCL
15 CLA	NEG	EXCL	IMPL	EXCL	EXCL	IMPL	EXCL	EXCL	IMPL	IMPL	IMPL	EXCL	NEG	EXCL	

TABLE U.5.5.3   The 15-element belief system for subject S166

	1 TRA	2 EDQ	3 OVT	4 STU	5 STA	6 PBW	7 CLK	8 PRO	9 PUB	10 BOR	11 LAB	12 OWN	13 SEC	14 FEE	15 CLA
TRA 1		SUPR						SUPR						SUPR	
EDQ 2	IMPL				IMPL			SUPR					IMPL		EXCL
OVT 3											IMPL				EXCL
STU 4															
STA 5		SUPR						SUPR			NEG			EXCL	EXCL
PBW 6															SUPR
CLK 7															EXCL
PRO 8	IMPL				IMPL					SUPR			IMPL	SUPR	SUPR
PUB 9		IMPL													
BOR 10						IMPL								EXCL	
LAB 11			SUPR		NEG		SUPR							EXCL	EXCL
OWN 12														EXCL	
SEC 13		SUPR	EXCL		IMPL	IMPL									
FEE 14	IMPL	EXCL	EXCL		EXCL	EXCL	EXCL	SUPR		EXCL	IMPL				EXCL
CLA 15		EXCL	EXCL		EXCL	IMPL	EXCL	EXCL			IMPL	EXCL		EXCL	

TABLE U.5.5.4   The 15-element belief system for subject Y349

	1 TRA	2 EDQ	3 OVT	4 STU	5 STA	6 PBW	7 CLK	8 PRO	9 PUB	10 BOR	11 LAB	12 OWN	13 SEC	14 FEE	15 CLA
TRA 1													IMPL		NEG
EDQ 2													IMPL		
OVT 3								NEG					NEG		
STU 4						SUPR	SUPR	NEG		IMPL			NEG		IMPL
STA 5								IMPL		NEG	SUPR		IMPL	SUPR	NEG
PBW 6			IMPL				SUPR	NEG	NEG	IMPL			NEG	EXCL	IMPL
CLK 7			IMPL			SUPR		NEG		NEG		EXCL	NEG	EXCL	IMPL
PRO 8			NEG	NEG	SUPR	NEG	NEG		NEG	NEG	SUPR		IMPL	SUPR	NEG
PUB 9													NEG		NEG
BOR 10			NEG	SUPR	NEG	SUPR	EXCL	NEG			NEG		NEG		
LAB 11					IMPL			IMPL		NEG		SUPR	IMPL		
OWN 12							NEG			NEG	SUPR		IMPL		NEG
SEC 13	SUPR	SUPR	NEG	NEG	SUPR	NEG	EXCL	IMPL	NEG	NEG	SUPR	SUPR		SUPR	NEG
FEE 14					IMPL	EXCL	EXCL	IMPL					IMPL		NEG
CLA 15	NEG	SUPR		SUPR	NEG	SUPR	SUPR	NEG	NEG			NEG	NEG	NEG	

A. Data derived from students of sociology

The first study was carried out on 41 lower triangle matrices of similarity coefficients. Each matrix showed the similarity relations between the 20 occupational titles which are shown in full in Table U.1.1 in this book. The similarity coefficients were defined in the following way. Each of the 41 subjects had judged the appropriateness of about 15 sentence frames for the 20 occupational titles. All subjects used the same occupational titles, but each used a different set of between 13 and 16 sentence frames. All the sentence frames used came from the overall set of 50, which are shown as label set 36 in Table U.1.3 in this book. The judgement of appropriateness for any combination of occupation and sentence frame was recorded as 'Always', 'Sometimes', or 'Never'. A crude co-occurrence count was made for each pair of occupational titles, by counting up the number of sentence frames for which they received the same judgement (whatever that might be). A coefficient of similarity was then defined as the number of times the two stimuli were 'sorted together' (by the sentence frames), as a proportion of the number of times they *could* have been sorted together. It will be evident that the sentence-frames task is here treated as a kind of 'context-bound' sorting, each sentence frame providing a context or scenario for judgements of similarity to be made. (See Chapter 6, U.2.10, in this book for a critical discussion of co-occurrence measures as defining similarity coefficients to be used in multi-dimensional scaling.) The pairwise similarity coefficients were formed up into a lower triangle matrix containing the coefficients for all possible pairs of occupational titles. Each of the 41 subjects had a matrix of this kind worked out from the small set of sentence frames he or she had been assigned. Most subjects used a different subset of 15 frames, but one used 13, and another used 16 from the total set of 50 in label set 36.

An individual differences scaling analysis was carried out using the 'metric' version of Carroll's INDSCAL programme, with a randomly generated starting configuration, and a 'simultaneous' solution for the dimension coordinates. The average 'goodness-of-fit' correlation coefficient over the 41 subjects was 0.75 with a solution in four dimensions, 0.71 for a solution in three dimensions and 0.66 for a solution in two dimensions. A plot of the first two dimensions of the three-dimensional solution was given as Figure 5.3 in *Class and Hierarchy*. The coordinates of the 20 occupational titles in that three-dimensional solution are shown as Table U.5.7.1. Informal 'eyeball' comparisons suggest that this representation of the average 'cognitive map' for the 20 occupational titles of label set 15 is broadly similar to the map derived from a parametric mapping analysis of the same data in aggregated form (see Figure 5.3 in *Class and Hierarchy* and Appendix U.5.1 in this book). Furthermore, the standard set of 16 occupational titles (label set 06) which are a proper subset of these 20, occupy much the same relative positions here as they did in the cognitive map derived in Chapter 3 of *Images*. More formal comparisons of this kind are made in appendix U.5.2 in this book, and

they show that the stimulus configuration derived from INDSCAL analysis
of these 20 occupational titles is closely related to the first dimension of
the other solutions, but much less closely related to other of their dimensions.

TABLE U.5.7.1   INDSCAL group space for 20 occupational titles

Occupation	Dimensions		
	I	II	III
MIN	0.166	0.385	−0.115
BM	−0.336	−0.035	−0.106
BMG	0.273	0.000	−0.387
C	−0.089	−0.201	0.204
CSE	0.287	0.100	−0.120
CT	−0.145	−0.033	−0.234
SOL	0.238	0.246	−0.252
MPN	−0.016	0.288	0.208
JMB	0.138	−0.297	0.218
LD	−0.262	−0.276	0.168
PM	−0.010	0.262	0.201
RP	−0.266	−0.229	0.230
WMG	0.306	−0.081	−0.216
CST	0.167	0.347	0.130
QA	0.206	0.133	−0.201
AD	−0.174	0.004	0.297
BSL	−0.303	−0.345	0.219
MTO	−0.244	−0.310	0.248
NT	−0.203	−0.049	−0.338
CA	0.268	0.092	−0.152

Correlations between dimensions
 I, II = +0.55   I, III = −0.48   II, III = −0.31

B. Data derived from a sample of Edinburgh men

The second INDSCAL analysis used a completely different set of sentence
frame data. Furthermore, the mapping was made of the sentence frames
rather than of the occupational titles. Each of 52 subjects judged the same
set of 25 occupational titles in terms of the same set of 15 sentence frames
(shown as Table U.1.4 in this book). Goodman-Kruskal gamma coefficients
were worked out within each subject, for the association between each pair
of sentence frames, over the 25 occupational titles (see Chapter 5 of *Class and
Hierarchy* for further information and an example). Table U.5.7.2 shows
the mean values of these gamma coefficients, averaged over the 52 respondents.
Most of the gammas in this table are quite large in absolute size, though the
signs vary. This reflects our deliberate strategy of selecting 15 sentence

TABLE U.5.5.5 The 15-element belief system for subject S180

		1	2	3	4	5	6	7	8	9	10	11	12	13	14	15
		TRA	EDQ	OVT	STU	STA	PBW	CLK	PRO	PUB	BOR	LAB	OWN	SEC	FEE	CLA
TRA	1															
EDQ	2															
OVT	3														EXCL	
STU	4															
STA	5							EXCL							SUPR	
PBW	6							SUPR					NEG		EXCL	
CLK	7					EXCL	IMPL								EXCL	
PRO	8															
PUB	9												NEG		SUPR	
BOR	10															
LAB	11															
OWN	12						NEG			NEG						
SEC	13															
FEE	14			EXCL		IMPL	EXCL	EXCL		IMPL			IMPL			
CLA	15															

TABLE U.5.5.6   The 15-element belief system for subject Y139

	1 TRA	2 EDQ	3 OVT	4 STU	5 STA	6 PBW	7 CLK	8 PRO	9 PUB	10 BOR	11 LAB	12 OWN	13 SEC	14 FEE	15 CLA
TRA 1															
EDQ 2											EXCL	IMPL	IMPL	IMPL	IMPL
OVT 3													IMPL	IMPL	IMPL
STU 4		EXCL										IMPL	IMPL	IMPL	
STA 5		EXCL		EXCL								IMPL	IMPL		
PBW 6															
CLK 7		EXCL		EXCL	EXCL						IMPL		IMPL	EXCL	EXCL
PRO 8				EXCL	EXCL							SUPR	SUPR		
PUB 9															
BOR 10												NEG	NEG		
LAB 11												NEG	NEG	EXCL	EXCL
OWN 12		SUPR		SUPR	SUPR			SUPR		NEG	NEG		SUPR	SUPR	NEG
SEC 13		SUPR		SUPR	SUPR		SUPR	SUPR		NEG	NEG	SUPR		SUPR	NEG
FEE 14							EXCL				EXCL	SUPR	SUPR		NEG
CLA 15			SUPR				EXCL				EXCL	NEG	NEG	EXCL	

TABLE U.5.7.2 Goodman-Kruskal gamma coefficients between all pairs of 15 sentence frames: mean values averaged over 52 subjects

	TRA	EDQ	OVT	STU	STA	PBW	CLK	PRO	PUB	BOR	LAB	OWN	SEC	FEE
EDQ	0.06													
OVT	0.10	−0.59												
STU	0.16	−0.27	0.69											
STA	0.13	0.79	−0.63	−0.45										
PBW	0.01	−0.76	0.79	0.57	−0.76									
CLK	0.08	−0.59	0.82	0.71	−0.72	0.81								
PRO	0.10	0.79	−0.55	−0.31	0.73	−0.71	−0.66							
PUB	−0.08	0.12	−0.35	−0.46	0.33	−0.34	−0.47	0.18						
BOR	−0.27	−0.50	0.50	0.41	−0.67	0.59	0.58	−0.57	−0.49					
LAB	0.00	−0.60	0.73	0.68	−0.66	0.77	0.79	−0.56	−0.57	−0.49				
OWN	0.17	0.71	−0.64	−0.45	0.77	−0.81	−0.70	0.64	0.28	−0.58	−0.75			
SEC	0.16	0.71	−0.39	−0.24	0.73	−0.62	−0.48	0.69	0.22	−0.49	−0.48	0.66		
FEE	0.12	0.83	−0.69	−0.46	−0.86	0.87	−0.76	0.78	0.27	−0.60	−0.76	0.88	0.77	
CLA	0.03	−0.83	0.73	0.51	−0.81	0.86	0.75	−0.78	−0.28	0.56	0.77	−0.82	−0.70	−0.92

frames which would have strong social class connotations, and it should not be taken as representative of the relationships in some universe of sentence frames.

The group space which was estimated from individual differences scaling of the 52 matrices of gamma coefficients is shown as Table U.5.7.3, and corresponds to Figure 5.4 in *Class and Hierarchy*. This solution is so dominated by the two tight and mutually opposed clusters of higher and lower-class jobs, that it is almost one-dimensional. Our justification for reporting the stimulus configuration for a two-dimensional INDSCAL model is that the data for a small percentage of cases were much better fit by the two-dimensional than by the one-dimensional solution. The dimensions of the two dimensional solution were very highly correlated however and this makes it difficult to make a differential interpretation of the two dimensions.

TABLE U.5.7.3   Two-dimensional coordinates of the 15 sentence frames in the INDSCAL group space

	Sentence frame	Dimensions I	II
1.	TRA	−0.149	+0.294
2.	EDQ	0.215	+0.244
3.	OVT	−0.228	−0.236
4	STU	−0.282	−0.107
5	STA	0.299	+0.276
6	PBW	−0.234	−0.320
7	CLK	−0.268	−0.270
8.	PRO	0.240	+0.233
9.	PUB	0.404	−0.037
10.	BOR	−0.239	−0.313
11.	LAB	−0.267	−0.249
12.	OWN	0.271	+0.270
13.	SEC	0.195	+0.234
14.	FEE	0.269	+0.300
15.	CLA	−0.225	−0.319

Correlation between dimensions = +0.78

10 Postscript and Some Conclusions

In reporting our research we have systematically relegated technical material to the appendixes of this third volume. It has not been an easy rule to follow: we have often debated for a long time before deciding that a particular piece of explanation should be banished to an appendix. In the final analysis we have taken George A. Miller's dictum to heart: that whilst methodology is the bread and butter of the scientist working in a given field, it is usually spinach to those outside. (In the case of sociology, one is tempted to add that it is often unpalatable to those inside the field as well.) But in this brief final chapter, we shall indulge ourselves a little and address those who share our predilections.

We began these volumes by asserting that a methodology appropriate to the research problems we had posed would need to be adequate to the 'complex, messy and apparently intractable complexity of social life' *Images*, p.x), and would be eclectic, adapting the rigour and systematic nature of the formal approach to the fluidity, complexity and constructive nature of the ethnographic tradition (*Class and Hierarchy*, p.xii).

That our methodology has been eclectic few would deny, but in what other ways do we see it as unusual or innovative? We would select two main characteristics:

(1) Taking serious account of the language through which people express their conceptions of social reality, but integrating this with systematic methods of collecting data.

(2) Matching data with appropriate and sensitive models for their analysis, whilst recognising that no single representation can capture all the relevant aspects of the phenomena.

A number of more specific issues also feature centrally in our approach, not least that of 'appropriate aggregation'. Once we had committed ourselves to being sensitive to socially-patterned individual differences, we soon discovered that problems of aggregation (averaging) are intensified as the data become more complex, so that it becomes increasingly difficult to decide upon what the criteria for a good 'overall representation' might be. In the second part of the research we felt very acutely that we were in ill-explored territory. Comparing one rank-ordering to another (the limit of complexity in conventional analysis) is a relatively straightforward procedure, but it is not quite so

283

obvious how to set about comparing a hundred classifications, or hierarchical trees, or substitutions in sentence frames. Indeed, when we began the research we had no definite idea of how to approach the analysis of such data. We did, however, know what sort of information was necessary to study occupational predication, and we were simply prepared to find out (or develop) the appropriate models for analysis. There were other problems. Since we had deliberately encouraged our subjects to talk as much as possible during the task, the analysis of the formal aspects of the data could not proceed independently of their semantic analysis. That proved to be the hardest problem we faced, and in the last resort we have to admit that our solution is far from adequate. By and large we have found that the most useful strategy has been first to study the formal characteristics of the data (for instance, how many occupational classes our subjects formed), then look at the content of the structures (e.g. how similar the content of subjects classes are) and finally examine their semantic significance (e.g. what the classes are called, and what their interrelationships are thought to be).

But the problem of integrating the formal and semantic aspects became so great in analysing the hierarchies data that the two aspects were analysed separately, and only at a later point did we attempt to relate one to the other. The problem proved to be an interesting one, not least because the process of constructing a sorting or a hierarchy is sequentially constrained and is not equifinal (that is, different ways exist of arriving at a given sorting); hence, earlier choices come to limit later choices to a very dramatic degree.[1] Sociologically, such constraints were often recognised by our subjects in the form of repeated requests for the interviewer to restate the 'rules' of the hierarchy-formation: it was the experienced chess players among our subjects who recognised the constraining power of earlier moves most clearly. This, perhaps more than any other single experience, convinced us that data collection of this sort (and probably in other more conventional contexts) is not so much unreliable (in the test-retest sense) as situation- and context-dependent. Data represent, in part, the end-result of the games which people play, and this fact should be recognised in the analysis.

Equally, the attempt to integrate the formal and semantic aspects of our data, using verbal transcripts to interpret the collective representations, drove home the inherent indexicality of such language (see *Images*, pp. 61-2). However else it may be interpreted, a subject doing a Project task is performing a 'practical activity' in Garfinkel's sense: it clearly presupposes a good deal of taken-for-granted information, and the subjects repeatedly allude to 'what everyone knows'. (Indeed, training our interviewers to know when to exhibit 'methodical ignorance' and be lacking in social competence proved to be an important technique for eliciting this information.)

The more demanding and extended tasks, such as hierarchy-construction, permit a good deal of background knowledge and assumptions to surface in the actual talk of the subject. We therefore felt a good deal more secure in comparing our subjects' constructions of their occupational world in the more complex context than in other simpler tasks. But our experience also prompts us to differ radically from these (both ethnomethodologists and positivists) who, whilst granting the indexicality of expressions used in (most) discourse, would maintain that such indexicality is not universal, and that literal, 'scientific', expressions and reasoning are also a reasonable possibility. In this matter we follow Barnes and Law (1976) in arguing for the universality of indexicality that 'human discourse is constitutively indexical' (ibid. p. 235). That is, we presuppose that it is part of the taken-for-granted orientation of practitioners like ourselves as well as of our subjects. We have no desire to claim for our account any privileged methodological status that would make it generically different from that of our subjects. As we have commented elsewhere (Coxon and Jones 1978a), the sociologist has the same freedom as his subject to select whatever features he wishes to describe or explain social phenomena, but the competence and consistency of at least some subjects' accounts serve to remind us that subjects' 'lay' accounts may also be as coherent as a sociologist's 'professional' one. To argue for the universal and irreparable indexicality of occupational discourse may make a virtue of necessity, but it frees us (as Barnes and Law again remind us) to concentrate upon the reasoning and accounting processes involved:

> We can, that is, take it for granted that reasoning and accounting is invariably performed 'for the practical purposes at hand', noting merely that 'practical purposes' can, on occasion, be esoteric, and lie beyond the concern of everyman in the member's society. (ibid., p. 235)

Such freedom carries a cost. We have learnt a good deal from setting the formal data in the verbal context of its production, to such an extent that we should be reluctant ever again to treat such data as self-explanatory — even, and perhaps especially, in the case of our subject who initially disavowed the use of class terminology, and then proceeded to use it liberally when producing his hierarchy.

Perhaps the most hazardous part of the enterprise was the process of comparing accounts and data, and building up to collective representations. Hazardous though it may be, and far removed as it may be from everyman's normal concerns, it is central to the sociologist's task. We are not so foolish as to believe that 'collective representations' consist of simply aggregated individual accounts: conceptions of the occupational structure, like other social constructs, have a history — they are culturally transmitted as an integral part of the stock of concepts and ideas which a socially competent member of society possesses, and they may often serve ideological functions. That granted, sociology is not yet in a position to explain how socially transmitted images of society relate to individual conceptions. Indeed, we know little enough even about the degree of consensus that exists in society about apparently simple constructs such as prestige orderings and social classes, despite a long tradition of social research in the area. To attempt to assess consensus involves one necessarily in what the positivist terms 'problems of aggregation' and what the ethnomethodologist calls 'the problem of glossing.' Our position on these problems should now be clear: aggregation should follow inspection of individual differences, not precede it, and should be focused upon averaging parameters derived from fitting explicit models to individual-level data (*Class and Hierarchy*, p. 187). By the same token sociological glossing of subjects' accounts, which is necessary in order to detect similarities and differences, is not a dubious pseudo-scientific practice; it is inherent to *any* sort of explanation. But once comparison is made, it becomes abundantly clear that there is *not* massive consensus over conceptions of the occupational (or any other social) structure. We have been at pains to point out that the consensus which exists does so at particular points or sections of the structure, and if one concentrates too heavily on the agreement, it is very easy to mask the significant areas of disagreement.

Moreover, as the task or construct becomes more subtle and complex, the areas of dissensus become more evident. There is no absolute answer to the question of consensus. If we wish to limit attention to the crudest data possible, then we may expect to find considerable consensus and stereotyping; there is not much, after all, to disagree about. So it is with the raw material of most occupational prestige measurement: the ubiquitous 5-point rating-scale. But when the shift is made to somewhat more complex data such as rank orderings, then systematic dissensus begins to become evident, and by the time we come to inspect more complex cognitive structure such as categorisations and hierarchies, the problem is, rather, to find systematic areas of *consensus*.

Have the representations and models we have chosen been subtle enough, or even suitable to this task? We have addressed this question in the final chapter in *Class and Hierarchy*, but some further methodological points can be made. We have made very extensive use of dimensional scaling models in these researches, and have put them to two main uses: both as a simple means of data reduction and also as explicit models of the processes which supposedly underlie occupational cognition. Perhaps the most significant example of the latter use occurred in the analysis of pairwise similarities in Chapter 3 of *Images*. In retrospect, it was the *departures* from the assumptions of the INDSCAL weighted distance model which proved to be more significant than anything else. It was the non-linear 'horse-shoe' sequence which contained the most important information, and the reason for this non-linearity seemed to lie in the non-continuous nature of the cognitive space and/or the unusual distance (composition) function underlying the subjects' judgements. Moreover, the meaning of the sequence was clearly not dimensional in any normally-accepted sense: rather, the content shifted from segment to segment, so that it came to resemble a series of overlapping properties, each with its own span of applicability. The only metaphor rich enough to capture this complexity is Wittgenstein's 'family theory of meaning', and it is an appropriate one. Of course, no single model — no matter how complex — can hope to capture all the subtleties and systematic differences involved in the cognition of complex social entities — a point we recognised at the outset of the Project. And as the 'tasks' became more demanding, and the data more complex, we found ourselves further removed from familiar dimensional (or even taxonomic) territory, and more aware of the subjects' 'natural reasoning and accounting processes', to which we have referred earlier. And this must be the direction of future research. Theories of stratification which ignore the purposive and instrumental nature of conceptions of the occupational world are doomed to sterility, and theorists who mistakenly interpret the undoubted technical *utility* of the prestige scale as having cognitive significance should be exceedingly cautious.

At the end of the second volume, we passed on some of the lessons we have learned from our research experience, and we have indicated how one might proceed from this point. To add any further methodological points would be otiose. That is not to say that recent innovative and exciting developments in methodology are not relevant to the development of research in social stratification. But as time goes on, today's innovation becomes tomorrow's common routine or a dated fad. Of course, we have some fairly distinct ideas about what new approaches and perspectives are likely to be fruitful in the analysis of occupational structures. But their utility will hinge neither upon their technical sophistication nor upon the ingenuity of their use, however important these features are. Rather, it will depend upon the extent to which such procedures help us find out how people come to understand occupational structures, and employ this understanding in their social life. In such an enquiry sociologists are in much the same position as Wittgenstein's philosopher:

> The philosopher is the man who has to cure himself of many sicknesses of the understanding before he can arrive at the notions of the sound human understanding. If in the midst of life we are in death, so in sanity we are surrounded by madness. (Wittgenstein 1956: IV-53, p. 157e)

Notes

Chapter 5

1. Our greatest initial concern was over the unsatisfactory way in which subjects had been selected from these two Quadrants. At a later stage the area-selection approach was also used to select subjects from Quadrants A and B as well.

2. These maps were produced using the GIMMS geographic plotting system (Waugh 1972), using 1966 Census data. The surface is viewed from the South West corner of Edinburgh, at an angle of elevation of 45 degrees.

3. We are grateful to Ms Francoise Rutherford, who was largely responsible for implementing these procedures, and who selected and trained the interviewers.

4. Information was obtained on the household composition, and on the age, sex, relation to head of household, level of economic activity and occupation of each member. In addition, the respondent was asked to make an estimate of the income of 20 occupations, and some were also asked to name the occupation of their four best friends. Full documentation of Household Listing, interviewer instructions and questionnaire schedules are lodged with the SSRC Survey Archive as supporting documentation to the Project data files.

5. A full description of these methods of data collection is contained in *Methods of data collection used in the Project on Occupational Cognition: a handbook for interviewers* (Lockhart and McPherson 1973) a copy of which is part of the supporting documentation to the Project files, and is available at cost from the SSRC Survey Archive. Each method is also discussed at greater length in the relevant chapters.

6. We are grateful to Garry Runciman for bringing this work to our attention.

Chapter 10

1. Labov and Waletzky (1967) discuss this problem very cogently in their analysis of the evolution of oral narratives. We are grateful to David Reason for bringing this paper to our attention.

288

List of Computer Program Abbreviations

1. *Acronyms of multidimensional scaling models* used in this volume and computer programs implementing them (Edinburgh-Cardiff MDS(X) Programs): documentation available from Program Library Unit, University of Edinburgh.

HICULUS (or HCS)   *Hierarchical Clustering Schemes:* analysis of a square symmetric data matrix using a non-metric inclusional clustering model (Johnson 1967)
Originator: S.C. Johnson, Bell Laboratories

INDSCAL   *Individual Differences Scaling:* by a weighted Euclidean distance model (Carroll and Chang 1970)
Originator: J.D. Carroll, Bell Laboratories

IDIOSCAL   *Individual Differences in Orientation Scaling:* analysis of sets of square symmetric (three-way) data matrices by a distance model, allowing idiosyncratic rotation and weighting of reference axes (Carroll and Wish 1975)
Originator: J.D. Carroll, Bell Laboratories

MINISSA   *Smallest Space Analysis,* of a square symmetric data matrix using a non-metric distance model (Roskam 1975)
Originator: E.E. Roskam, Nijmegen University

MDPREF   *Multidimensional Preference Analysis:* by analysis of a rectangular data matrix using a vector model (Carroll and Chang 1964)
Originator: J.D. Carroll, Bell Laboratories

MINIRSA   *Rectangular Similarity Analysis:* of a rectangular data matrix, using a non-metric distance model (Roskam 1975)
Originator: E.E. Roskam, Nijmegen University

PARAMAP   *Parametric Mapping:* analysis of a rectangular row conditional matrix, finding a configuration such that the data are related to the solution by a function which is as smooth and continuous as possible (Shepard and Carroll 1966)
Originators: R.N. Shepard, Stanford University and J.D. Carroll, Bell Laboratories

PREFMAP   *Preference Mapping:* (external) scaling of a rectangular
                 data matrix in a user-supplied *a priori* space, using a
                 hierarchy of distance and vector models, with metric
                 and quasi-non-metric options (Carroll 1972)
                 Originator: J.D. Carroll, Bell Laboratories

TRISOSCAL   *Triadic Scaling:* Edinburgh version of integral scaling
                 of triadic similarities data, using a non-metric
                 distance model (Roskam 1970 and Prentice 1973)
                 Originators: E.E. Roskam, Nijmegen University, and
                 M.J. Prentice, Edinburgh University

2. *Other Program Packages*

INQR   *The General Inquirer, III* (Edinburgh version).
(or Inquirer III) A series of linked programs for the content analysis of
                 natural language text, using the Harvard IV Psycho-
                 Sociological dictionary. The Edinburgh version is
                 documented in Coxon and Trappes-Lomax (1977),
                 Program Library Unit, Edinburgh.
                 Originators: Canonical version: P.J. Stone, Harvard
                 University; Australian version: D. Dunphy, University
                 of New South Wales; British version: A.P.M. Coxon,
                 University of Wales

COCOA (CONCOR) *Count and Concordance generation on Atlas.*
(Concordance)   A program to carry out a number of text processing
                 operations, centred chiefly upon the production of
                 concordances. (Berry-Rogghe and Crawford 1973)
                 Originators: G.L.M. Berry-Rogghe, Atlas Computer
                 Laboratory, and T.D. Crawford, University College,
                 Cardiff

WORDS   A system library of subroutines from which the user
                 selects a sequence of programs. Designed primarily for
                 the analysis of the associative structure in natural
                 text (Iker 1976)
                 Originator: H.P. Iker, University of Rochester, N.Y.

References

Alexander, C.N. (1972). 'Status perceptions'. *Am. Sociol. Rev.*, 37, 767-73.
Anderson, N.H. (1962). 'Application of an additive model to impression formation', *Science*, 138, 817-18.
Anderson, N.H. (1968). 'A simple model for information integration', in R.P. Abelson *et al.* (eds), *Theories of Cognitive Consistency.* Chicago: Rand McNally, pp. 731-43.
Andrews, D.F. (1972). 'Plots of high-dimensional data', *Biometrics,* vol. 28, 125-36.
Andrews, D.F. (1973). 'Graphical techniques for high dimensional data', in T. Cacoullos (ed.), *Discriminant Analysis and Applications.* London: Academic Press, 37-60.
Anglin, J.A. (1970). *The Growth of Word Meaning.* London: MIT Press.
Arabie, P., and S.A. Boorman (1973). 'Multidimensional scaling of measures of distance between partitions', *Journ.Math.Psychol.*, 10, 148-203.
Arnold, J.B. (1971). 'A multidimensional scaling study of semantic distance', *Journ.Exp.Psychol.*, 90, 349-72.
Attneave, F. (1950). 'Dimensions of similarity', *Am.Journ.Psychol.*, 18, 405-18.
Attneave, F. (1959). *Applications of Information Theory to Psychology.* New York: Holt, Rinehart.
Bannister, D., and J.M.M. Mair (1968). *The Evaluation of Personal Constructs.* London: Academic Press.
Barnes, B., and J. Law (1976). 'Whatever should be done with indexical expressions?', *Theory and Society*, 3, 223-37.
Barrett, M. (1914). 'A comparison of the order of merit method and the method of paired comparisons', *Psychol.Rev.*, 21, 278-94
Beals, R., D.H. Krantz and A. Tversky (1968). 'Foundations of multidimensional scaling', *Psychol.Rev.*, 75, 127-42.
Berlin, B., D.E. Breedlove and P.H. Raven (1968). 'Covert categories and folk taxonomies', *Am.Anthrop.*, 70, 290-9.
Bernstein, B. (1971). *Class, Codes and Control*, vol 1: *Theoretical Studies Towards a Sociology of Language.* London: Routledge and Kegan Paul.
Berry-Rogghe, S., and T. Crawford (1973). COCOA *Users Manual.* Rutherford and Cardiff: Science Research Council.
Black, M.B. (1963). 'On formal ethnographic procedures', *Am.Anthrop.*, 65, 1347-51.
Bloxom, B. (1974). 'An alternative method of fitting a model of individual differences in multidimensional scaling', *Psychometrika*, 39, 365-7.

Blum, Z.D. *et al.* (1969). 'A method for the collection and analysis of retrospective life histories', Baltimore: Center for the Study of Social Organization of Schools, Johns Hopkins University, Report No. 48 (July).

Blumenthal, L.M. (1953). *Theory and Applications of Distance Geometry.* Oxford University Press.

Blumenthal, L.M. (1961). *A Modern View of Geometry.* London: W. Freeman.

Boorman, S.A. (1970). 'Metric spaces of complex objects', unpubl. thesis, Cambridge, Mass: Harvard College.

Boorman, S.A., and P. Arabie (1972). Structural measures and the method of sorting, in R.N. Shepard *et al. Multidimensional Scaling: Theory and Applications in the Behavioural Sciences,* Vol. 1. London: Seminar Press.

Boorman, S.A., and D.C. Olivier (1973). 'Metrics on spaces of finite trees', *Journ.Math.Psychol.,* 10, 26-59.

Bousfield, W.A. *et al.* (1958). 'Associative clustering in the recall of words of different taxonomic frequencies of occurrence', *Psych. Reports,* 4, 39-44.

Brandt, S. (1976). *Statistical and Computational Methods in Data Analysis.* 2nd ed., Amsterdam: North-Holland.

Burton, M.L. (1972). 'Semantic dimensions of occupation names', in Shepard *et al.* (1972), Vol. 2, 55-71.

Burton, M.L. (1975). 'Dissimilarity measures for unconstrained sorting data', *Mult.Beh.Res.,* 10, 409-24.

Burton, M.L., and Sara Beth Nerlove (1971). 'Brevity with balance: an exploration of a judged similarity task', Working Paper No. 2, School of Social Sciences, University of California at Irvine, mimeo. Published (1976) as 'Balanced designs for triads tests: two examples from English', *Soc. Sci. Res.,* 5, 247-67.

Burton, M.L., and A.K. Romney (1975). 'A multidimensional representation of role terms', *Am. Ethnologist,* 2, 397-407.

Carroll, J.D. (1972). 'Individual differences and multidimensional scaling', in Shepard *et al.* (1972) Vol 1 105-55.

Carroll, J.D. (1976). 'Spatial, non-spatial and hybrid models for scaling', *Psychometrika,* 41, no. 4, 439-63.

Carroll, J.D., and J.J. Chang (1964). 'Non-parametric multidimensional analysis of paired comparisons data', Murray Hill, New Jersey: Bell Laboratories (mimeo).

Carroll, J.D., and J.J. Chang (1970). 'Analysis of individual differences in multidimensional scaling via a N-way generalisation of "Eckart-Young" decomposition', *Psychometrika,* 35, 283-319.

Carroll, J.D., and J.J. Chang (1974). 'Some methodological advances in INDSCAL, paper presented at the Spring meeting of the Psychometric Society, Bell Telephone Laboratories (mimeo).

Carroll, J.D., and M. Wish (1974a). 'Models and methods for three-way multidimensional scaling', in D.H. Krantz, R.C. Atkinson, R.D. Luce and P. Suppes (eds), *Contemporary Developments in Mathematical Psychology,*

Vol. II, San Francisco: W.H. Freeman, 57-105.

Carroll, J.D., and M. Wish (1974b). 'Multidimensional perceptual models and measurement methods', in E.C. Carterette and M.P. Friedman (eds), *Handbook of Perception*. New York: Academic Press, 391-447

Chang, J.J., and J.D. Carroll (1970). 'How to use PRO-FIT; a computer programme for property fitting', Murray Hill, New Jersey: Bell Laboratories (mimeo).

Cooley, W.W., and P.R. Lohnes (1971). *Multivariate Data Analysis*. New York: Wiley.

Coombs, C.H. (1964). *A Theory of Data*. New York: Wiley.

Coombs, C.H. (1975). 'A note on the relation between the vector model and the unfolding model for preferences', *Psychometrika*, 40, 115-16.

Cormack, R.M. (1971). 'A review of classification', *J.Roy.Stat.Soc.A.*, 134 (3), 321-67.

Coxon, A.P.M. (1974). 'The mapping of family-composition preferences', *Social Science Research*, 3, 191-210.

Coxon, A.P.M. (1975). *Multidimensional Scaling: ECPR Course Notes*. University of Essex: ECPR Monographs on Social Science Data Analysis.

Coxon, A.P.M., and C.L. Jones (1974a). 'Occupational similarities: some subjective aspects of social stratification', *Quality and Quantity*, 8, 139-57.

Coxon, A.P.M., and C.L. Jones (1974b), 'Problems in the selection of occupational titles', *Sociological Review*, 22, 369-84.

Coxon, A.P.M., and C.L. Jones (1974c). 'Occupational categorization and images of society', Edinburgh University: Project on Occupational Cognition Working Paper No. 4 (mimeo).

Coxon, A.P.M., and C.L. Jones, (eds) (1975). *Social Mobility*. Harmondsworth: Penguin Books.

Coxon, A.P.M., and C.L. Jones (1976). Final report: Occupational cognition: Representational aspects of occupational titles and sociological aspects of subjective occupational structures. (SSRC Grant 1883/2), (mimeo), Boston Spa: National Library.

Coxon, A.P.M., and C.L. Jones (1977). 'Multidimensional scaling', in C. O'Muircheartaigh and C. Payne (eds), *Exploring Data Structures* (Vol. 1 of *The Analysis of Survey Data*). London: Wiley, 159-82.

Coxon, A.P.M., and C.L. Jones (1978). *The Images of Occupational Prestige*. London: Macmillan.

Coxon, A.P.M., and C.L. Jones (1979). *Class and Hierarchy*. London: Macmillan.

Coxon, A.P.M., and H.R.N. Trappes-Lomax (1977). *Inquirer III (Edinburgh version) User's Guide*. Edinburgh: Program Library Unit, Report no. 29.

Cross, D.V. (1965). 'Metric properties of multidimensional stimulus generalization', in D.I. Mostofsky (ed.), *Stimulus Generalization*. Stanford: University Press.

David, H.A. (1963). *The Method of Pair Comparisons*. London: Griffin.

Dawes, R.M. (1972). *Fundamentals Of Attitude Measurement*. New York: Wiley.

De Leeuw, J. (1974). 'Some contributions to INDSCAL', Murray Hill, New Jersey: Bell Laboratories (mimeo).

Doeringer, P.B., and M.J. Piore (1971). *Internal Labor Markets and Manpower Analysis.* Lexington: Heath.

Erickson, B.H., and T.A. Nosanchuk (1977). *Understanding Data.* New York: McGraw Hill.

Fine, S.A., and C.A. Heinz (1958). 'The functional occupational classification structure'. *Personnel and Guidance J., 37,* 180-92.

Fisher, R.A. (1953). Dispersion on a sphere, *Proc. Roy.Soc.Lond.,* A217, 295-305.

Flament, C. (1963). *Applications of Graph Theory to Group Structure.* Englewood Cliffs: Prentice-Hall.

Goldthorpe, J.H., and K. Hope (1974). *The Social Grading of Occupations.* Oxford: Clarendon Press.

Goldthorpe, J.H., D. Lockwood, F. Bechhofer and J. Platt (1969). *The Affluent Worker in the Class Structure.* Cambridge: University Press.

Golledge, R.G., and G. Rushton (eds) (1976). *Spatial Choice and Spatial Behaviour: Geographic Essays on the Analysis of Preferences and Perceptions.* Columbus: Ohio State University Press.

Good, I.J., and T.N. Tideman (1976). 'From individual to collective ordering through multidimensional attribute space', *Proc.Roy.Soc.Lond.,* A347, 371-85.

Gordon, D.M. (1972). *Theories of Poverty and Underemployment.* Lexington: Heath.

Gould, P. (1976). 'Cultivating the garden: a commentary and critique on some multidimensional speculations', in Golledge and Rushton (1976), 83-91.

Green, P.E., and V.R. Rao (1972). *Applied Multidimensional Scaling.* New York: Holt, Rinehart & Winston.

Guildford, J.P. (1928). 'The method of paired comparisons as a psychometric method', *Psychol. Rev.* 35, 494-506.

Guildford, J.P. (1954). *Psychometric Methods.* New York: McGraw-Hill.

Gulliksen, H. (1946). 'Paired comparisons and the logic of measurement', *Psychol. Rev.,* 53, 199-213.

Hall, J., and D.C. Jones (1950). 'The social grading of occupations', *Brit.Journ.Sociol.,* 1, 31-55.

Harre, R. (ed.) (1976). *Life Sentences: Aspects of the Social Role of Language.* London: John Wiley.

Hartigan, J.A. (1967). 'Representation of Similarity Matrices by Trees', *J.Am.Stat.Assoc.,* 62, 1140-58.

Hodge, R.W. and P.M. Seigel (1966). 'The Classification of Occupations: some Sociological Considerations', *Proc.Amer.Stat.Assoc.: Soc. Section.*

Hodge, R.W. and P.M. Siegel (1968). 'Social Stratifications: III-The Measurement of Social Class. pp. 316-25 in Vol. 15 of D. Sills (ed.) *International Encyclopaedia of the Social Sciences.* New York: Free Press.

Hodge, P.W., P.M. Siegel and P.H. Rossi (1964). 'Occupational prestige in the United States, 1925-1963', *Am.J.Sociol.* 70, 286-302.

Hodson, F.R., D.G. Kendall and P. Tautu (eds.) (1971). *Mathematics in the Archaeological and Historical Sciences.* Edinburgh: University Press.

Holman, E.W. (1972). 'The relation between hierarchical and euclidean models for psychological distances', *Psychometrika,* 37, 417-23.

Horan, C.B. (1969). 'Multidimensional scaling: combining observations when individuals have different perceptual structures', *Psychometrika,* 34, 139-65.

Hubert, L. (1974). 'Some applications of graph theory and related non-metric techniques to problems of approximate seriation: the case of symmetric proximity measures', *Brit.Journ.Math.Stat.Psychol.* 27, 133-53.

Hyman, R., and A. Well (1967). 'Judgments of similarity and spatial models', *Percept. and Psychophysics,* 2, 233-48.

Iker, H.P. (1976). WORDS System Manual. Rochester: University Medical Center, (mimeo).

Imai, S., and W.R. Garner (1968). 'Structure in perceptual classification', *Psychonomic Monog. Suppl.,* 2.

Isaac, P.D., and D.D.S. Poor (1974). 'On the determination of appropriate dimensionality in data with error', *Psychometrika,* 39, 91-109.

Jackson, D.N., and S. Messick (1963). 'Individual differences in social perception', *Brit. Journ.Soc.Clin.Psychol.,* 2, 1-10.

Jardine, N., and R. Sibson (1971). *Mathematical Taxonomy.* London: Wiley.

Johnson, S.C. (1965). 'Hierarchical clustering schemes', *Psychometrika,* 32, 241-54.

Jones, R.A., and R.D. Ashmore (1973). 'The structure of intergroup perception: categories and dimensions in views of ethnic groups and adjectives used in stereotype research', *Journ.Pers. and Soc.Psychol.,* 25, 428-38.

Kelly, E., and P.J. Stone (1975). *Computer Recognition of English Word Senses.* Amsterdam: North-Holland.

Kendall, D.G. (1971a). 'Maps from marriages', in F.R. Hodson *et al.* (1971) 303-18.

Kendall, D.G. (1971b). 'Seriation from abundance matrices', in F.R. Hodson et al. (1971), 215-52.

Kiss, G.R. (1966). 'Networks as models of word storage' in N.L. Collins and D. Michie (eds), *Machine Intelligence I.* Edinburgh: The University Press.

Kiss, G.R. *et al.* (1972). *An Associative Thesaurus of English,* (Microfilm version). London: EP Group of Companies, Microform Division.

Klahr, D. (1969). 'Decision-making in a complex environment: the use of similarity judgements to predict preferences', *Management Science,* 15, 595-618.

Kraus, Vera, E.O. Schild and R.W. Hodge (1978). 'Occupational prestige in the collective conscience', *Social Forces,* 56, no. 3, 900-18.

Kruskal, J.B. (1964a). 'Multidimensional scaling by optimizing goodness of fit to a nonmetric hypothesis', *Psychometrika,* 29, 1-27.

Kruskal, J.B. (1964b). 'Nonmetric multidimensional scaling: a numerical method', *Psychometrika*, 29, 115-29.

Kruskal, J.B., and J.D. Carroll (1969). 'Geometrical models and badness of fit functions', in P.R. Krishnaiah (ed.), *Multivariate Analysis*, Vol. II. New York: Academic Press, 639-71.

Labov, W. and J. Waletzky (1967). 'narrative analysis: oral versions of personal experience', in J. Helm (ed.) *Essays on Verbal and Visual Arts*, Proc. Ann. Spring Meeting, Am. Ethological Soc.

Levine, J. (1972). 'The sphere of influence', *Amer.Sociol.Rev.*, 37, 14-27.

Lingoes, J., and E.E. Roskam (1973). 'A mathematical and empirical study of two multidimensional scaling algorithms', *Psychometrika*, 38, Monog. Suppl., 1-93.

Lockhart, R., and M. McPherson (eds.) (1973). 'Methods of data collection used in the Project on occupational cognition: a handbook for interviews', Edinburgh, Project on Occupational Cognition, Research Memorandum no. 2 (mimeo).

Lyons, J. (1968). *Introduction to Theoretical Linguistics*. Cambridge: University Press.

MacCallum, R. (1977). 'Effects of conditionality on INDSCAL and ALSCAL weights', *Psychometrika*, 42, no. 2, 297-305.

MacDonald, K.I. (1972). 'MDSCAL and distances between socio-economic groups', in K. Hope (ed.), *The Analysis of Social Mobility*. Oxford: The Clarendon Press, 211-34.

McFarland, D.D., and D. Brown (1973). 'Social distance as a metric: a systematic introduction to smallest space analysis', in E.O. Laumann, *Bonds of Pluralism*. New York, 213-53.

McNeil, D.R. (1977). *Interactive Data Analysis*. New York: Wiley Interscience.

Mardia, K.V. (1972). *Statistics of Directional Data*. London: Academic Press.

Messick, S.L., and R. Abelson (1956). 'The additive constant problem in multidimensional scaling', *Psychometrika*, 21, 365-75.

Miller, G.A. (1967). 'Psycholinguistic approaches to the study of communication', in D.L. Arm (ed.), *Journeys in Science*. Albuquerque: University of new Mexico Press, 22-73.

Miller, G.A. (1969). 'A psychological method to investigate verbal concepts', *J.Math.Psychol.*, 6, 169-91.

Mosteller, F. (1968). Data analysis, including statistics in G. Lindzey and E. Aronson (eds.) *Handbook of Social Psychology*, Vol. 2, 2nd ed. Reading, Mass.: Addison-Wesley.

Mosteller, F., and J.W. Tukey (1977). *Data Analysis and Regression*. London: Addison-Wesley.

Murray, H.A., W.G. Barratt and E. Homburger (1938). *Explorations in Personality*. Oxford: University Press.

Osgood, C.E. (1965). *The Measurement of Meaning*. Urbana: University of Illinois Press.

Osgood, C.E. (1970). 'Interpersonal verbs and interpersonal behavior', in, J.C. Cowan (ed.), *Studies in Thought and Language.* Tucson: University of Arizona Press, 133-228.

Osgood, C.E., and Z. Luria (1954). 'A blind analysis of a case of multiple personality using the semantic differential', *J.Abnorm.Soc.Psychol.,* 49, 579-91.

Pearson, E.S. and H.D. Hartley (eds). (1972). *Biometrika Tables for Statisticians,* vol. II. Cambridge: University Press, 123-33.

Prentice, M.J. (1973). 'On Roskam's nonmetric multidimensional scaling algorithm for triads'. Edinburgh, Project on Occupational Cognition (mimeo).

Ramsay, J.O. (1977). 'Maximum likelihood estimation in MDS'. *Psychometrika,* 42, 241-66.

Rapoport, A., and S. Fillenbaum (1971). *Structures in the Subjective Lexicon.* New York: Academic Press.

Reiss, A.J. (1961). *Occupations and Social Status.* Glencoe: Free Press.

Richardson, M.W. (1938). 'Multidimensional Psychophysics', *Psychol. Bull.,* 35, 659-60.

Richardson, M.W., and G.F. Kuder (1933). 'Making a rating scale that measures', *Person. Journ.,* 12, 33-60.

Robinson, J.P. *et. al.* (1969). *Measures of Occupational Attitudes and Occupational Characteristics.* Ann Arbor, Mich.: Survey Research Center.

Roskam, E.E. (1968). *Metric Analysis of Ordinal Data in Psychology.* Nijmegen: Voorschoten.

Roskam, E.E. (1969). 'Data theory and algorithms for nonmetric scaling', Catholic University of Nijmegen: Dept. of Mathematical Psychology (mimeo).

Roskam, E.E. (1970). 'The method of triads for nonmetric multidimensional scaling', *Nederlands tijdschrift voor de psychologie,* 25, 404-17.

Roskam, E.E. (1972). 'Multidimensional scaling by metric transformation of data', *Nederlands tijdschrift voor de psychologie,* 27, 486-508.

Roskam, E.E. (1975). 'A documentation of MINISSA – (N)', Catholic University of Nijmegen: Department of Psychology Report 75-MA-15.

Schonemann, P.H. (1972). 'An algebraic solution for a class of subjective metrics models', *Psychometrika,* 37, 441-51.

Seligson, M.A., (1977). 'Prestige among peasants: a multidimensional analysis of preference data', *Amer.Journ.Sociol.,* 83, 632-52.

Shepard, R.N. (1960). 'Similarity of stimuli and metric properties of behavioral data', in H. Gulliksen and S. Messick (eds.), *Psychological Scaling: Theory and Application.* New York: Wiley.

Shepard, R.N. (1962). 'The analysis of proximities: multidimensional scaling with an unknown distance function' (Parts 1 and 2), *Psychometrika,* 27, 125-40; 219-46.

Shepard, R.N. (1964). 'Attention and the metric structure of the stimulus space', *J.Math.Psychol.,* 1, 54-87.

Shepard, R.N. (1966). 'Metric structures in ordinal data', *J.Math.Psychol.*, 3, 287-315.

Shepard, R.N. (1969). 'Some principles and prospects for the spatial representation of behavioral science data', paper presented at the Advanced Research Seminar on Scaling and Measurement, Newport Beach, California.

Shepard, R.N. (1974). 'Representation of structure in similarity data: problems and prospects', *Psychometrika*, 39, 373-421.

Shepard, R.N., and J.C. Carroll (1966). 'Parametric representation of nonlinear data structures', in P.R. Krishnaiah (ed.), *Multivariate Analysis*, Vol. I. New York: Academic Press, pp. 561-92.

Shepard, R.N., A.K. Romney and S.B. Nerlove (eds) (1972). *Multidimensional Scaling: Theory and Applications in the Behavioral Sciences* (Volume 1: Theory; Volume 2: Applications). London: Seminar Press.

Siegel, P.M. (1971). 'Prestige in the American occupation structure'. Ph.D. thesis, University of Chicago.

Silverman, S.F. (1966). 'An ethnographic approach to social stratification: prestige in a central Italian community', *Am. Anthrop.*, 68, 899-921.

Slater, P. (ed.) (1976). *The measurement of Intrapersonal Space by Grid Technique* (2 vols). London: Wiley.

Smith, M. (1943). 'An empirical scale of prestige status of occupations', *Amer.Sociol.Rev.*, 8, 185-92.

Spence, I., and J.C. Ogilvie (1973). 'A table of expected stress values for random rankings', *Mult.Behav.Res.*, vol. 8. 511-517. *Mult.Behav.Res.*, vol. 8.

Spence, I., and J. Graef (1974). 'The determination of the underlying dimensionality of an empirically obtained matrix of proximities', *Mult.Behav.Res.*, vol 9, 331-341.

Stefflre, V., P. Reich and M. McClaran-Stefflre (1971). 'Some eliciting and computational procedures for descriptive semantics', in P. Kay (ed.), *Explorations in Mathematical Anthropology*. Cambridge, Mass.: MIT Press, 79-116.

Steinheiser, F.H. (1970). 'Individual preference scales within a multidimensional "similarities" space', *J.Exptl.Psychol.*, 86, 325-7.

Stenson, H.H., and R.L. Knoll (1969). 'Goodness of fit for random rankings in Kruskal's non-metric scaling procedure', *Psychol. Bull.*, 71, 122-6.

Stephens, M. (1962). 'The statistics of directions', Ph.D. thesis. University of Toronto.

Stephens, M. (1969). 'Multi-sample tests for the Fisher distribution for directions', *Biometrika*, 56, 169-181.

Sturtevant, W.C. (1964). 'Studies in ethnoscience', in *Romney and D'Andrade*. 1964.

Thurstone, L.L. (1927). 'The method of paired comparisons for social values', *J. Abnorm. and Soc. Psychol*, 21, 384-400.

Thurstone, L.L. (1931). 'Rank order as a psychophysical method', *J.Exp.Psychol.*, 14, 187-201.

Torgerson, W.S. (1958). *Theory and Methods of Scaling*. New York: Wiley.

Towler, R.C. and A.P.M. Coxon (1979). *The Fate of the Anglican Clergy*. London: Macmillan.

Treiman, D.J. (1977). *Occupational Prestige in Comparative Perspective*. London: Academic Press.

Tucker, L.R. (1960). 'Intra-individual and inter-individual multidimensionality', in H. Gulliksen and S. Messick (eds.), *Psychological Scaling: Theory and Application*. New York: Wiley.

Van de Geer, J.P. (1971). *Introduction to Multivariate Analysis for the Social Sciences*. San Francisco: Freeman.

Wagenaar, W.A., and P. Padmos (1971). 'Quantitative interpretation of stress in Kruskal's multidimensional scaling technique', *Brit.J.Math. Statist.Psychol.*, 24, 101-10.

Watson, G.S. (1956). 'Analysis of dispersion on a sphere', Monthly notices, *Roy.Astr.Soc., Geophys.Suppl.*, 7, 153-9 and 160-1.

Waugh, T.C. (1972). 'The choropleth mapping system', *Inter-University/ Research Councils Series, Report No. 7*. University of Edinburgh, Scientific and Social Science Program Library.

Williams, M. (1976). 'Presenting oneself in talk: the disclosure of occupation', in Harré (1976).

Wilson, B.R. (1966). *Religion in Secular Society*. London: Watts.

Wish, M., and J.D. Carroll (1974). 'Applications of individual differences scaling to studies of human perception and judgment', in E.C. Carterette and M.P. Friedman (eds), *Handbook of Perception*, Volume II. New York: Academic Press, 449-91.

Wittgenstein, L. (1956). *Remarks on the Foundations of Mathematics*. Oxford: Blackwell.

Yntema, D.B., and W.S. Torgerson (1961). 'Man-computer cooperation in in decisions requiring common-sense', *IRE Transactions in Electronics*, HFE-2, 20-6.

Young, F.W. (1972). 'A model for polynomial conjoint analysis algorithms,' in Shepard *et al.* (1972), 69-104.

Young, F.W. (1975). 'Scaling replicated conditional rank order data', in D.R. Heise (ed.), *Sociological Methodology, 1975*. London: Jossey-Bass, 129-70.

Name Index

Subject Index